Snowing in Chicago

THE STORY OF A FORTUNATE DETOUR AND THE
FOUNDING OF COOK INCORPORATED

"It's nice to come home at night knowing you produced 20 products, and 20 lives will be saved because of it."

Snowing in Chicago

THE STORY OF A FORTUNATE DETOUR AND THE
FOUNDING OF COOK INCORPORATED

by Jim H. Smith

GREENWICH PUBLISHING GROUP, INC.

© 2009 Cook Incorporated. All rights reserved.

Printed and bound in the United States of America. No part of this publication may be reproduced or transmitted in any form or by any means, electronic or mechanical, including photocopying, recording or any information storage and retrieval system now known or to be invented, without permission in writing from Cook Incorporated, P.O. Box 489, Bloomington, Indiana 47402-0489, except by a reviewer who wishes to quote brief passages in connection with a review written for inclusion in a magazine, newspaper or broadcast.

Produced and published by Greenwich Publishing Group, Inc.
Old Saybrook, Connecticut
www.greenwichpublishing.com

Designed by Clare Cunningham Graphic Design

Library of Congress Control Number: 2009920722

ISBN: 0-944641-75-X

First Printing: February 2009

10 9 8 7 6 5 4 3 2 1

Any trademarks in this book are property of their respective owners.

Photo Credits:
All photographs in the book are courtesy of Cook Incorporated, except the following:

Page 3, Getty Images/Panoramic Images
Page 8, © Bettmann/CORBIS
Page 9, Forssmann W., Experiments on Myself. New York; St. Martin's Press, 1972
Page 10, Courtesy of Archives & Special Collections, Columbia University Health Sciences Library
Page 29, © Time Incorporated
Page 66, © 2006 Indianapolis Business Journal
Page 103, Radiologic Clinics of North America (1968, Volume 6), © Elsevier/W.B. Saunders Co. Courtesy of Eileen Judkins
Page 104, © Dale Shank
Page 105, Courtesy of the Dotter Interventional Institute
Page 106, Courtesy of Maria Schlumpf
Page 130, © shawnspence.com
Page 150, Courtesy of Rose-Hulman Institute of Technology

Table of Contents

Chapter One
Revolutionaries — 8

Chapter Two
The First Team — 24

Chapter Three
Expansion — 36

Chapter Four
Growing Pains — 54

Chapter Five
Intervention — 76

Chapter Six
Adapting to Regulation — 102

Chapter Seven
The World's Largest — 120

Chapter Eight
Evolution — 138

Acknowledgments — 158

Timeline — 160

Cook Medical Company Officers — 164

Cook Group Affiliate Company Officers — 166

Index — 167

Chapter One: 1949–1963

Revolutionaries

In 1929 Dr. Werner Forssmann was only 25 years old and just beginning his surgical residency when he defied convention and his superiors, gambling his life to demonstrate the value that vascular catheters could bring to medicine. Threading a flexible catheter through an incision in his arm and pushing it through to his heart, he submitted to an X-ray, right, to prove it could be done.

By all appearances Werner Theodor Otto Forssmann seemed an unlikely revolutionary. He was a stocky young German man whose round, clean-shaven face and conservatively groomed hair, slicked back over his scalp in the style of the time, suggested a more conventional nature. His eyes, wide-set below a broad forehead, twinkled with curiosity and intelligence. Yet there was no clue in his appearance to suggest he was about to transform the world of medicine. In the autumn of 1929, however, he set medical technology on a path that would change it forever. He did it by committing an act so unorthodox that it might have ended not only his budding career but his life.

Forssmann was a 25-year-old graduate of the University of Berlin's School of Medicine. He was just commencing his surgical residency at the Auguste Viktoria Home, a hospital in the Berlin suburb of Eberswalde.

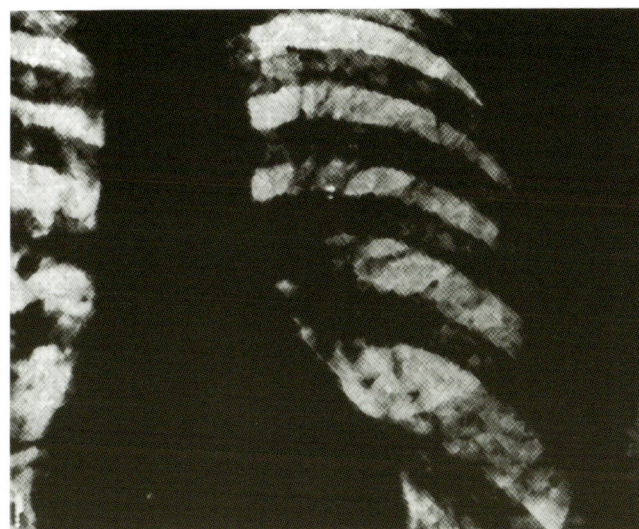

Were he a more compliant man or a less visionary one, Forssmann might simply have completed his training and gone on to a successful if not especially distinguished career in medicine. But he was obsessed with an idea he had harbored throughout medical school, and he was determined to put it to the test.

For more than two centuries scientists had been experimenting with a procedure known as vascular catheterization. The earliest of these experiments focused on blood transfusion, and by

1929 it had become an accepted form of medical treatment. Other investigators in the 18th and 19th centuries used catheters to measure blood pressure.

Forssmann wanted to go much further. He believed it was possible to introduce a thin catheter into one of the body's major blood vessels and thread it all the way to the heart. He believed that doing this would allow doctors to directly inject drugs in order to resuscitate a failing heart without the necessity of major surgery.

He was swimming against the current of prevailing medical wisdom. When young Forssmann submitted his idea to his supervisors, they derided his theory. Any attempt to catheterize the heart would surely prove fatal, the chief of surgery sneered, as though such dogma ought to be an article of faith for anyone qualified to practice medicine at the Auguste Viktoria Home.

Forssmann was undeterred. Taking matters into his own hands, he

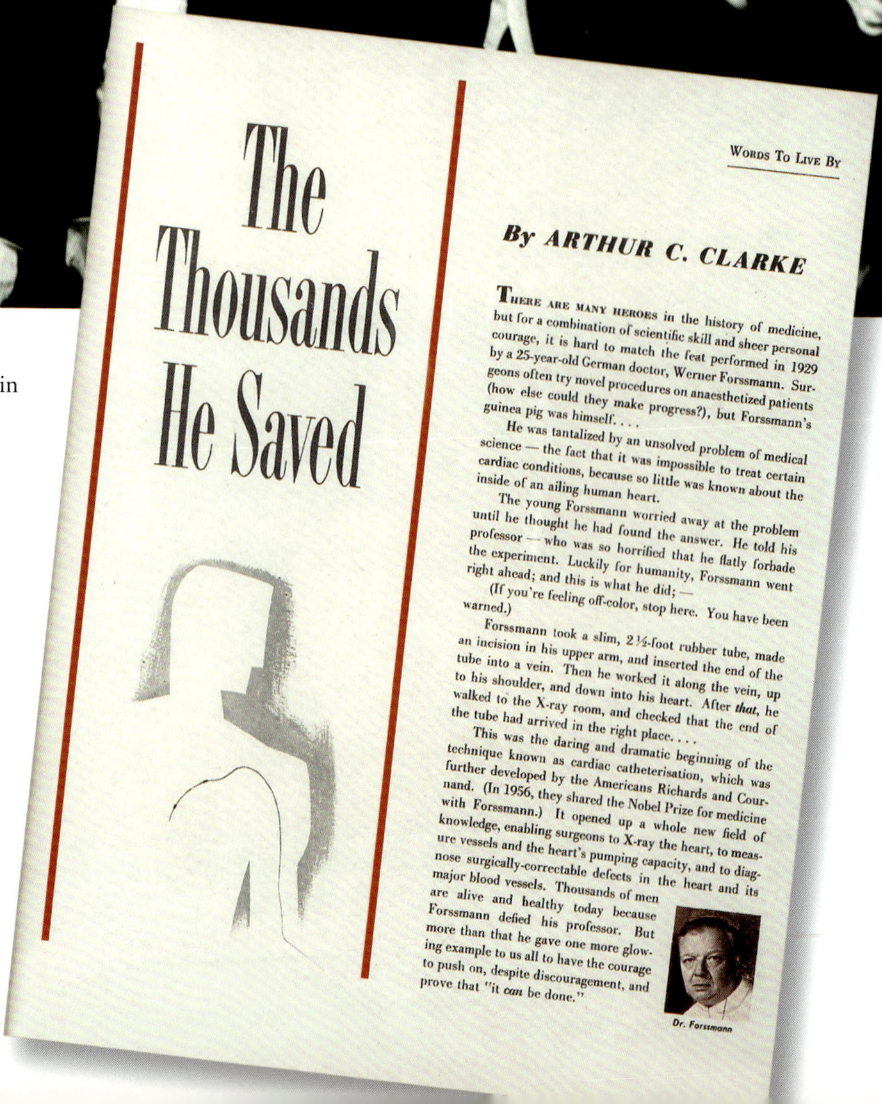

WORDS TO LIVE BY

The Thousands He Saved

By ARTHUR C. CLARKE

THERE ARE MANY HEROES in the history of medicine, but for a combination of scientific skill and sheer personal courage, it is hard to match the feat performed in 1929 by a 25-year-old German doctor, Werner Forssmann. Surgeons often try novel procedures on anaesthetized patients (how else could they make progress?), but Forssmann's guinea pig was himself. . . .

He was tantalized by an unsolved problem of medical science — the fact that it was impossible to treat certain cardiac conditions, because so little was known about the inside of an ailing human heart.

The young Forssmann worried away at the problem until he thought he had found the answer. He told his professor — who was so horrified that he flatly forbade the experiment. Luckily for humanity, Forssmann went right ahead; and this is what he did; —

(If you're feeling off-color, stop here. You have been warned.)

Forssmann took a slim, 2½-foot rubber tube, made an incision in his upper arm, and inserted the end of the tube into a vein. Then he worked it along the vein, up to his shoulder, and down into his heart. After *that*, he walked to the X-ray room, and checked that the end of the tube had arrived in the right place. . . .

This was the daring and dramatic beginning of the technique known as cardiac catheterisation, which was further developed by the Americans Richards and Cournand. (In 1956, they shared the Nobel Prize for medicine with Forssmann.) It opened up a whole new field of knowledge, enabling surgeons to X-ray the heart, to measure vessels and the heart's pumping capacity, and to diagnose surgically-correctable defects in the heart and its major blood vessels. Thousands of men are alive and healthy today because Forssmann defied his professor. But more than that he gave one more glowing example to us all to have the courage to push on, despite discouragement, and prove that "it *can* be done."

Dr. Forssmann

Northwestern University graduate Bill Cook, below, enlisted as a surgical technician in the army during the Korean War. Stationed at Fort Sam Houston in Texas, he got his first glimpse of the future of medical technology and foresaw exceptional "growth opportunities in medicine." He had joined Nelson Instrument, a Chicago medical technology company, by 1957, the year after Dr. Werner Forssmann, opposite, standing right of center in the front row, received the Nobel Prize. Famed author Arthur C. Clarke profiled Forssmann in the January 26, 1964, issue of the *National Sunday Magazine*.

enlisted a sympathetic nurse and took a leap of faith. In a quiet room at the hospital, he anesthetized his elbow, made an incision, inserted a Deschamps aneurysm needle into his antecubital vein, opened it and inserted a catheter designed for use in the bladder. Ever so cautiously, centimeter by centimeter, he threaded the slender rubber cannula into his arm.

He knew exactly where the path of the vein would take it, and, though he was acting without the aid of radiological equipment to guide him, he calculated he would need to insert about two feet of the catheter to reach the heart. When he had inserted the catheter, he stood up and, with the tube dangling from his arm, walked to the hospital's radiology department, where he allowed himself to be X-rayed in order to show the tube in place, safely penetrating his beating heart.

Forssmann's seemingly impulsive act was, in fact, grounded in rock-solid conviction based on years of study. He believed—one might say, with all his heart—that catheters had enormous untapped potential, that they could dramatically change the way medicine was practiced and improve outcomes for patients. Though he was dismissed from the Auguste Viktoria Home for defying his superiors, he never wavered in his belief.

When, in 1931, he published a paper describing how he had catheterized himself, many prominent physicians dismissed him as a crackpot. Still, he carried on with his catheterization experiments, honing his technique on laboratory animals and on himself.

It would be a quarter of a century before he was awarded the Nobel Prize in Physiology or Medicine, in 1956, finally getting the recognition and the vindication he deserved for his courageous experiments. By then the medical establishment had significantly modified its view of vascular catheterization, largely due to the work of a Swedish radiologist named Sven-Ivar Seldinger. In 1953 Seldinger developed a new technique to introduce angiographic catheters into blood vessels directly through the skin without having to make an incision. Seldinger's technique, wrote Leslie and LaNelle Geddes in their book *The Catheter Introducers,* was "a historic breakthrough of mammoth proportions," the vanguard of innovation in both diagnostic and interventional catheterization that would thoroughly alter medicine over the next half century.

A HARD WORKER WILLING TO TAKE RISK

In Chicago, the year after Forssmann won the Nobel, a young Midwesterner named Bill Cook was trying his hand at sales with a small company called Nelson Instrument Company, which manufactured stress treadmills and psychological testing equipment. He was a 25-year-old graduate of Northwestern University and an army veteran. He had already done a stint with a large medical equipment supply company, which might have turned into a career except for the fact that it just wasn't right for him.

He was fixed upon the notion of carving out his own destiny, but he wasn't making much progress. In fact, he appeared to be going in the wrong direction. He had surrendered the security of a good job with an

Bill Cook, above and right, sprang from solid Midwestern values. Bright and gregarious, he was an exceptional student and an All-State high-school football standout. A natural leader, he inherited an aptitude for business and a flair for risk taking while growing up in the family business.

established company to go to work for Nelson, but it was hardly a step up. He was—literally—living in the Nelson factory, trying to make ends meet and driving a beat-up 1946 Packard that often failed to start. Nothing about him or his situation suggested that in just a few years he would pioneer a way for doctors to easily utilize Seldinger's innovation or that doing so would make him successful beyond his wildest dreams. All things, as he would soon discover, happen for a reason.

Cook was a lanky youngster from Canton, Illinois, when he enrolled at Northwestern in the autumn of 1949 as a pre-med student. Moonlighting as a cab driver to earn his way through college, he soon learned his way around the Windy City. Cook had grown up in a family that prospered in the grain elevator business and later owned several ice cream stores. From that formative experience he had acquired two seemingly contrary characteristics: a capacity for nose-to-the-grindstone work and an audacious willingness to take risks.

"He was a very personable guy," remembers Brian Baldwin, another Illinois native, who met Cook that first year at Northwestern, where they were roommates. "He was very intuitive and bright. He got good grades. He had this knack for learning a lot about people in a very short time. He had no compunctions about asking people questions, even personal questions. He was also a good athlete—big, but fast. He was All-State in football. He was very competitive, and he was determined to win."

Cook and Baldwin, who was a mechanical engineering major, hit it off right away. They shared an interest in technology, and by the end of their freshman year they had become fast friends. That summer, Cook came to visit Baldwin in his home town of Moline, Illinois. "He called one day from the airport in Davenport, Iowa, and asked me to come pick him up," Baldwin remembers.

Cook had just arrived in a Taylorcraft airplane that he bought for $450 from a farmer in Canton, and he learned to fly with that plane. The trip to Davenport was his first solo flight, but it would hardly be his last. Aviation soon became much more than a hobby for Cook. When he launched his own business, his piloting eventually helped distinguish him from competitors.

By their junior year in college Cook and Baldwin were discussing the possibility of going into business together. Only 21 years old, Baldwin had already learned an important lesson that would shape his career decisions for the rest of his life. He had signed up for a Northwestern

co-op program with International Harvester, the big Chicago–based agricultural equipment company, where he was enrolled in management training. "I hated it," he recalls. "I told Bill that was the last time I ever wanted to work for a big company."

Cook could certainly relate to his friend's position. "I always wanted to be in business for myself," he says today. "Even in college, I didn't like working for someone else. I always felt I knew enough that I could get the job done."

Before the two friends could act upon their business ideas the Korean War intervened. Cook enlisted in the army. Stationed at Fort Sam Houston in San Antonio, he first served as a surgical technician until his commanding officer asked him if he would like to teach the physics of anesthesia to physicians who were about to become army anesthesiologists. Cook later recalled, "I accepted the teaching job, and it gave me a great perspective on the power of medical science. Even in 1953 there were tremendous new products being developed, and I realized that there were many growth opportunities in medicine."

He was especially impressed whenever he encountered a new device that was uncomplicated—a tool whose elegance lay in its capacity to simplify complex procedures. That there was a growing market for such tools and that they could be readily produced were realizations that shaped Bill Cook's view of medical technology for the rest of his career.

APRIL FOOL'S DAY

When he was discharged from the army in 1954, Cook returned to Chicago and, despite his aversion to working for someone else, took a position with Martin Aircraft as an engineering recruiter. It was not the job he was looking for. It wasn't even the right field, so when a more interesting opportunity opened up, Cook didn't hesitate to move.

His new employer was the nation's largest medical products distributor, American Hospital Supply. The company was doing some $30 million in sales annually, and Cook, who brought a considerable amount of medical equipment knowledge with him, was installed in the advertising department, editing catalogs for the company's Scientific Products division.

Working for a medical products supplier, Bill Cook had taken a big step toward the career that he was destined to pursue—but already he was imagining a life beyond American Hospital Supply. When he was interviewed by Angelo Pizzo for *Bloom* magazine more than half a century later, he recalled that, "During that time I started coming up with ideas for possible products. One was … disposable hypodermic needles."

Cook's old pal Brian Baldwin, meanwhile, was by then employed by Shure Brothers, a large Chicago–area audio electronics company, where he was not much happier than he had been at International Harvester.

Bill Cook developed his values and cut his business teeth growing up in several family businesses, including this grain elevator in the country outside his hometown of Canton, Illinois.

14 SNOWING IN CHICAGO

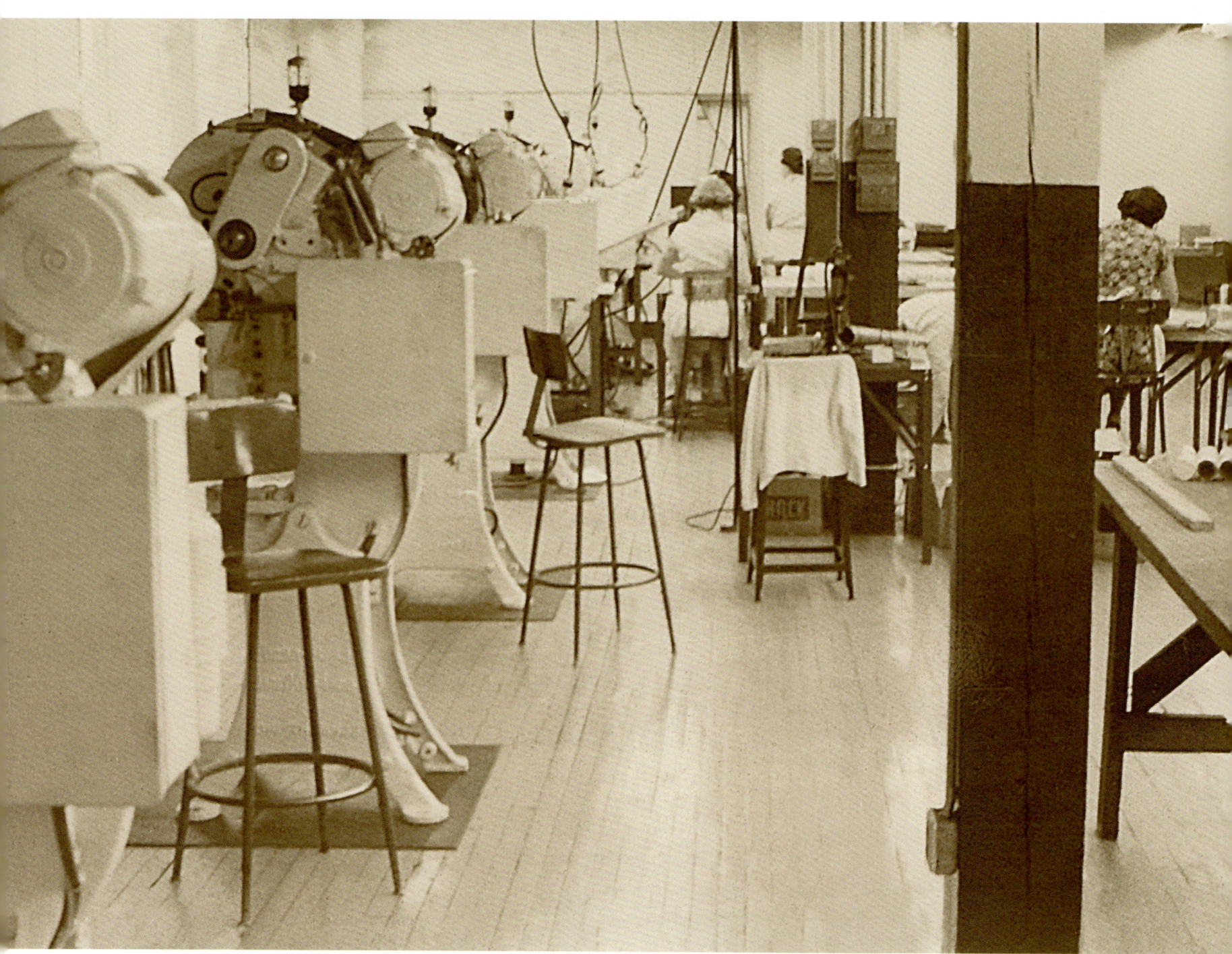

He and Cook soon renewed their friendship, and one day in 1955 Cook called to let him know about a job opportunity with American Hospital Supply. The company was looking for an engineer to help screen new products and uncover growth opportunities. Baldwin interviewed for the slot, and soon he and Cook were working for the same company.

Little more than a year later, the company's vice president of sales, Harry DeWitt, presented Baldwin with a problem. Disposable needles, which hospitals used by the thousands, were an important part of American Hospital Supply's product line, and the company was having difficulty ensuring a consistent supply. In an effort to address the problem, they had acquired a small start-up operation. DeWitt wanted Baldwin to travel to Connecticut and evaluate another possible acquisition.

Baldwin came back from New England with a positive report, but American Hospital Supply rejected his recommendation. That, he recalls, is when he got serious about starting his own company. "I was enamored with manufacturing," he says, "and I saw a need for disposable needles."

He didn't have to convince Bill Cook. When he offered Cook a 10 percent share of the business for sweat equity, Cook leaped at the opportunity, and Baldwin set about raising the money to get started. By that time Cook had already tendered his resignation to American Hospital Supply and taken the job with Nelson Instrument. The few months he stayed with that company further convinced him that he had the stuff to succeed in business on his own.

The company Cook and Baldwin launched was called Manufacturing Process Laboratories (MPL). Among the first companies in the United States to manufacture disposable hypodermic and dental needles, MPL eventually became the nation's third largest. For Bill Cook, it was the place where he would truly cut his teeth in the medical technology manufacturing field.

While still working for American Hospital Supply, Baldwin began rounding up investors, eventually corralling $200,000. Cook, meanwhile, quickly located suitable industrial space and set about cleaning it up. He'd been at it for a few months when, in the spring of 1958, Baldwin joined him full-time, severing his ties with American Hospital Supply and plunging into the management of his own business.

"I'll never forget the date," Baldwin recalls. "It was the first of April, 1958. It was April Fool's Day."

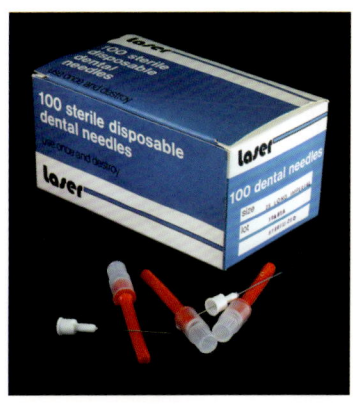

In 1958, with $200,000, Brian Baldwin and Bill Cook, below, with their wives, followed their entrepreneurial urges and launched Manufacturing Process Laboratories (MPL), opposite, in Chicago. In time it would become the third largest manufacturer of medical and dental needles in the United States.

"WHAT WOULD YOU THINK ABOUT STARTING A COMPANY?"

Bill, with his dog, was still living at the little Nelson Instrument Company factory in the spring of 1957 when Lloyd Nelson, the company's owner, introduced him to his cousin, a comely young woman named Gayle Karch. They met at Nelson's home when both were invited to participate in a Saturday night card game. A few weeks later, Cook called Gayle and asked her out.

Despite Bill's peculiar living situation, the two hit it off right away. Gayle had been raised in Evansville, Indiana, on the same Midwestern values as Cook, and like him, she had an inquiring mind. She was an alumna of Indiana University, a Phi Beta Kappa fine arts major who had landed an advertising job in Chicago soon after graduation. By the time they discovered that they wanted many of the same things in life, they were already smitten with each other. By autumn of that year, they had become—but for the breadth of Chicago—nearly inseparable. They were residents of the same city, but Gayle had an apartment on the city's south side, while Bill's Spartan quarters at the Nelson plant were miles away on the north side.

In September, when Cook's unreliable car broke down for the umpteenth time, he made a spontaneous decision. With colder weather only a few weeks away, he decided he knew Gayle Karch well enough to want to spend the rest of his life with her. If there was one thing Gayle would learn about the man who was about to become her husband, it was that once he made up his mind, he didn't hesitate to take decisive action. They had been dating only three and a half months the night he popped the question. "He asked me, 'What would you think about starting a company?'" Gayle remembers. "I told him it sounded like fun. Then he proposed to me."

It was a whirlwind engagement. The following weekend, the couple flew down to Evansville—in a plane not much more reliable than Cook's car—to announce their engagement to Gayle's family. Then, on September 21, 1957, less than a month after Bill's proposal, they tied the knot.

GOOD-BYE, MPL

Nobody could say Bill Cook didn't give MPL his best shot. He may have been only a minority shareholder, but he threw himself into the work 100 percent. But by 1960 a host of problems threatened to bury the young company. MPL was deeply in debt

Gayle Karch was working for a Chicago advertising agency when she met Bill Cook in the spring of 1957. Five months later they flew to Evansville, Indiana, in Bill's airplane to tell her family of their engagement. Bill moonlighted as a cab driver to help pay for college; right, his taxi driver's union card, which he kept updated—just in case.

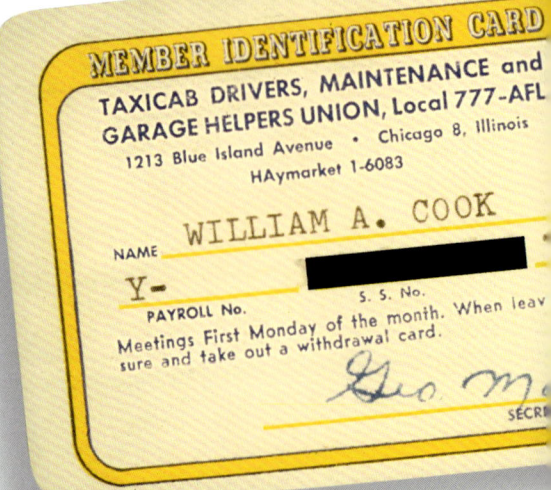

and having trouble collecting receivables through its network of distributors. Obligations to the investors who had helped Baldwin get the company off the ground made it difficult to manage with a free hand.

Production problems further compounded things. A significant number of the needles it produced were defective and had to be recalled. More often than not, it fell upon Cook to retrieve those needles and try to reassure dissatisfied customers. The problems weighed on Cook, and he chafed at the fact that he wasn't building a business of his own and watching it blossom. "No question, we had problems," says Baldwin. "But aside from them, Bill wasn't cut out to work for anyone. He was by nature an autocrat. He really wanted to start his own business."

Cook was also increasingly dissatisfied with life in Chicago. He yearned for a more pastoral setting, away from the congestion of the city and the brutal Chicago winters. On trips to Indiana Gayle introduced him to Bloomington and her alma mater, and he felt right at home. Whenever he and his bride visited the Hoosier State, he found it harder and harder to return to the Windy City. Like any young couple, the Cooks talked about their dreams for the future. They talked about what kind of company to start and they talked about where they wanted to live—a small place, they agreed, close to the towns where they grew up and away from the snow.

As Bill Cook's frustrations with MPL and with life in Chicago mounted, he knew he was going to have to make a change. It was just a matter of when. The man who showed him the way out was his cousin, Dr. Ivan "Van" Fucilla. He was a young radiologist living with his wife, Judy, in Chicago. The Cooks often got together with them on weekends to play bridge. One night in 1960 Fucilla took Cook into his kitchen after the card game and, over coffee, showed him some odd-looking medical instruments. They were catheters, guide wires and needles, the equipment required to perform the percutaneous catheterization procedure that Seldinger had introduced seven years earlier. "I told him this was the way the specialty was moving," Fucilla remembers. "Of course, I didn't foresee the way it would develop or the role Bill would play."

The Seldinger procedure was still very new, Fucilla told Cook. Not many doctors in the United States were using it yet, and some thought it was nothing more than a novelty, well outside mainstream clinical practice. But, Fucilla said, more physicians were getting on the bandwagon every year. Then he got to the point. The doctors who were performing the Seldinger procedure often had to produce their own equipment, and they were using a variety of catheters. Some were using piano wire for guides. There was no single source in the United States from which to order standardized catheters, guide wires and needles to perform the procedure.

That got Cook's attention. He went home that night and thought for two days about what Fucilla had shown him. He talked with Fucilla about it some more. Then, with

In the 1960s, Bill Cook's cousin, Dr. Van Fucilla, center, and his wife Judy often hosted Bill and Gayle Cook for weekend card games. One night, Fucilla showed Cook some tools for performing percutaneous catheterization. It was, Cook would later remember, a moment that changed his life.

thoughts of starting his own business producing the kind of equipment he had seen on his cousin's kitchen table, he began to learn everything he might need to know about percutaneous catheterization.

"IT'S SNOWING IN CHICAGO"

In 1961 Van and Judy Fucilla moved to California, where Fucilla spent the rest of his distinguished career in a practice affiliated with El Camino Hospital in Mountain View. Back in Chicago Bill Cook continued to study percutaneous catheterization and bided his time. He would remain with MPL for another year, hoping things might improve. They didn't.

Then two events convinced Cook to make the move he'd been contemplating ever since that night in Fucilla's kitchen. The first was the birth of the Cooks' son, Carl, on August 19, 1962. The new father was 31 years old, and he knew he could no longer put off staking his own claim. At MPL he was simply spinning his wheels. He needed to start his own business, and he needed to get out of Chicago. He made up his mind that he would take action before another year passed.

That winter turned out to be one of the coldest on record. Savage winds howled down off the Canadian plains and raked the Midwest. In Chicago, where the Cooks were renting

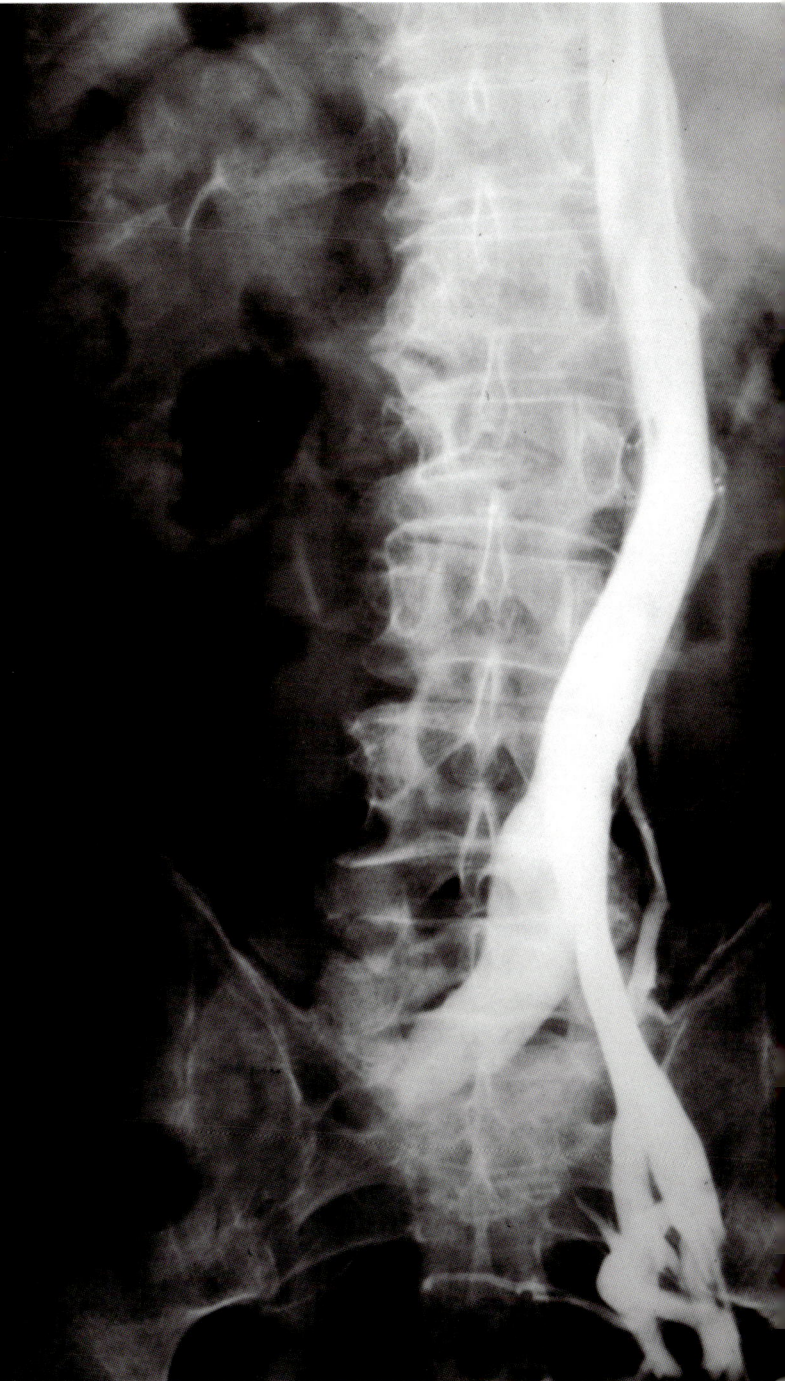

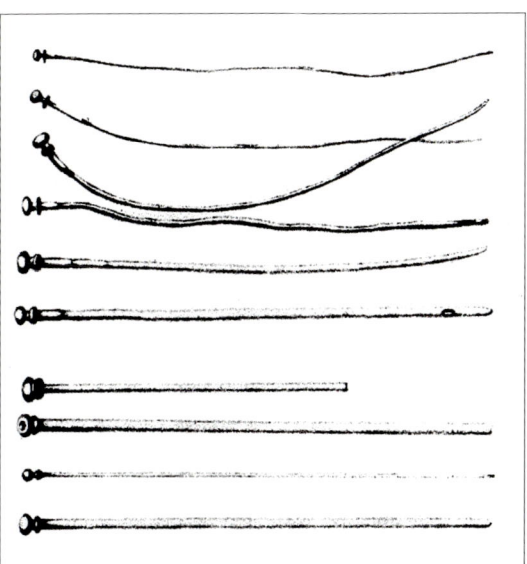

Cook's new tools significantly improved the capacity to produce radiographs of the body's blood vessels, like this one, far right, of the occluded right common iliac artery. This artery could be treated using the Dotter technique to open the occlusion. Near right, early 19th-century urologists made tools, such as these whalebone catheters—smooth, pliable and resistant to urine—to widen urethral strictures.

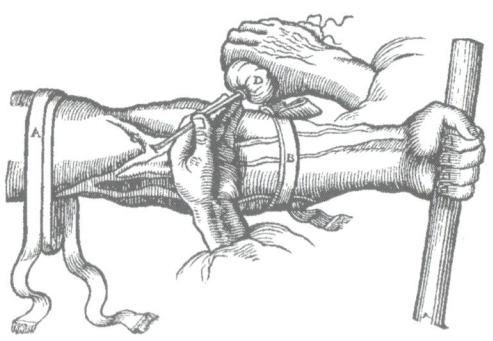

As early as the 17th century, physicians experimented with vascular catheters for blood transfusion. By the time Dr. Sven-Ivar Seldinger pioneered his groundbreaking technique in the early 1950s, doctors had been paving the way for three centuries.

a drafty fourth-floor walk-up apartment for $135 a month, the average outdoor temperature was 15.9° F. "It was cold as hell!" Cook remembers.

Sometime early in 1963 Cook traveled to Michigan to pick up another batch of dull needles from a medical distributor, and for the second time in less than a year fate seemed to give him a push toward his own business. It is 175 miles from Chicago to Grand Rapids, a long enough drive in the winter. But Cook had to journey from there on to Cadillac, Michigan, another 90 miles due north.

It was snowing when he reached his destination that afternoon, and it snowed for the next two days. He was obliged to hunker down at a hotel for three nights before the roads were clear enough for travel. On his way back to Chicago he was stuck in the wake of a snowplow. It was slow going until he reached the Michigan/Indiana border. That's where he made one of those spur-of-the-moment decisions that, in the years to come, would earn him a reputation as a maverick. When he got to Fort Wayne, Indiana, instead of turning west toward Chicago, he kept driving south toward Indianapolis and Bloomington.

There was snow on the ground in Fort Wayne, and Cook vividly recalls his mind-set: "I decided that if it wasn't snowing in Bloomington we were going to move there," he says. There was nary a flake flying when he arrived several hours later. That night he called Gayle and asked her if she would like to move to Bloomington. She asked him why. His response: "It's snowing in Chicago."

When Cook got back to Chicago, he told Brian Baldwin that he was resigning. Baldwin wasn't surprised; he had expected it. By 1963 MPL had become a $2 million operation, manufacturing not only hypodermic needles but also its own needle points and needle hubs. In addition, it had a sterilization operation. None of that made a difference to Bill Cook. His mind was made up. He was moving on.

Baldwin bought back Bill's shares of the company for $10,000, and they parted as friends. By spring Bill and Gayle and their young son had moved to Bloomington, where they set up their home in the Bart Villa Apartments complex at 2305 East Second Street. It was in that unpretentious setting that Cook Incorporated was founded on July 1, 1963.

COOK'S FIRST "FACTORY"

Although Bill had been thinking about cardiovascular catheters since the night Van Fucilla told him about them, they did not represent the first business opportunity that he considered. Instead he contemplated something that was an extension of both his MPL experience and his father's grain milling business.

What he envisioned was the manufacture of disintegrators—devices that grind up disposable needles for safe disposal. In Minneapolis there were some milling machines that could do the trick. Built for the U.S. Navy during World War II, the machines had been declared surplus after the war. Bill intended to buy them, but fate took a hand once more, and the building in which they were stored burned down before he could move on his plan.

SAILING OVER THE EDGE

The tools needed to perform Sven-Ivar Seldinger's technique for percutaneous insertion of catheters into blood vessels were deceptively simple. All that was required was an introducer needle, a thin, coiled wire guide and a tapered angiographic catheter. With only a simple puncture through the skin, radiologists could easily use the cardiovascular system to access any part of the body, using X-rays as a guide.

Leslie and LaNelle Geddes wrote in the book *The Catheter Introducers*, "By sailing over the edge of established medical practice with [those simple tools], Sven Seldinger discovered a whole new world of possibilities for angiographers, a world that quickened the medical profession and inspired many other members of the radiology community to embark on exploratory missions of their own."

Seldinger was born in Mora, Sweden, in 1921 and earned his medical degree from the Karolinska Institute in 1948. He began training in radiology in 1950, and he was just 32 years old when, in 1953, he published the groundbreaking description of his percutaneous entry technique. "This technique is simpler than it appears on paper and after a little practice should present no difficulties," he wrote.

In fact, many of the pioneer radiologists who developed the extraordinary range of diagnostic and therapeutic procedures that have evolved from Seldinger's technique never trained in it at all. They "simply learned how to perform by watching someone else do it," noted the Geddeses.

Like many technological advances, Seldinger's technique was the consequence of a desire to find a simpler way to do things. Before percutaneous catheter insertion, doctors who wished to insert a catheter into a blood vessel were compelled to first perform a surgical incision through an arm or leg, providing access to the vessel. Seldinger stumbled upon a better way. With his technique, a hypodermic needle was simply inserted into an artery or vein. Then a wire guide was threaded through the needle. Once the needle was withdrawn, a catheter could be inserted easily over the wire guide. No surgery was needed.

The simplicity of Seldinger's technique revolutionized the medical world, proving to be the catalyst for a host of innovative applications in interventional radiology, urology, anesthesiology, cardiology, critical care and many other areas of medicine. Oddly, Dr. Seldinger, who lived to be 78, never practiced the procedure much. But it was quickly adopted by his colleagues in Sweden, making that country a mecca for angiographers who traveled from all over the world in the 1950s and 1960s to train there.

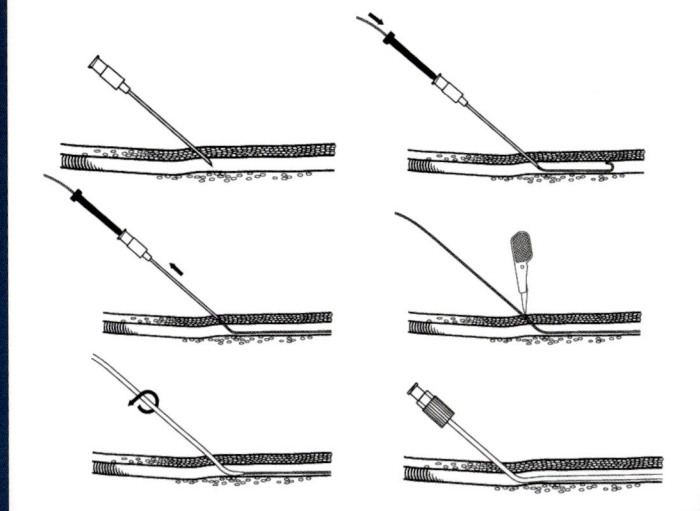

The tools required to perform Seldinger's percutaneous catheterization technique—an introducer needle, a thin wire guide and a tapered angiographic catheter—were so simple that Seldinger could illustrate the technique with six line drawings.

> *"Working in the medical products business is very satisfying," Cook says. "I was drawn to it for two reasons. One is ego. I felt I could make these things better. And it's nice to come home at night knowing you produced 20 products, and 20 lives will be saved because of it."*

Cardiovascular catheters were his "fallback" concept. "It was very important for us to find a product that would quickly generate income so we could retain ownership of the company," Gayle Cook remembers. But neither Gayle nor Bill had any idea just how quickly the company might generate income. Their first "factory" was the spare bedroom of the Cooks' apartment. And the first products manufactured and sold were percutaneous entry needles, wire guides and catheters, the equipment needed to practice the Seldinger technique.

"I once asked Bill how he came to succeed with his company," Baldwin remembers. "He told me that he thought a lot about the mistakes we made at MPL. He decided never to have any shareholders, never to borrow a dime and never to sell through a distributor."

It also helped that Cook had found something he truly enjoyed. "Working in the medical products business is very satisfying," he says. "I was drawn to it for two reasons. One is ego. I felt I could make these things better. And it's nice to come home at night knowing you produced 20 products, and 20 lives will be saved because of it."

From the moment the Cooks decided to invest their savings in a business of their own, Bill was determined that it would not fail. He got up every morning, dressed in a suit and tie and went to work in the spare bedroom, dividing his time between making sales calls, building his network and creating small batches of catheters, guide wires and needles by hand. Every night, after young Carl had gone to sleep, Gayle took care of the company's financial records and performed quality-control inspections on Bill's products, typically wrapping up around 1 a.m. Reflecting on that time, Gayle says, "It was very intense. We had to do the work. There was no one else to do it, so we could never get away from it."

The company's first catalog, produced that year, was just four pages long. It offered three kinds of radiopaque Teflon catheters, four kinds of radiopaque Teflon tubing, three kinds of modified thinwall percutaneous needles, a stainless steel wire guide, three kinds of Teflon-coated wire guides and three kinds of percutaneous catheterization sets. All of the products were sold unsterilized. Accessories the company offered included a catheter-tip-forming wire set and an aluminum cleaner and brightener to clean needle hubs and catheter adapters.

It took most of the first summer for the Cooks to obtain product liability insurance—coverage that would grow increasingly expensive but without which they were afraid to sell any products. When they finally acquired the insurance for an annual premium of $1,000, their first sale followed almost immediately.

In late August 1963 Illinois Masonic Hospital bought a shipment of catheters and wire guides. "We were so excited, we typed up the order and rushed to the post office," Gayle Cook remembers. Then the young couple celebrated by going out to dinner at McDonald's.

After two months in business, they were convinced that there was a real market for their products, that the market would grow and that they could do modestly well. But they didn't foresee the mysterious man who would come into their lives when Bill went to Chicago on business a few weeks later. Nor could they have guessed how quickly or how dramatically their company would grow because of this stranger.

Cook Incorporated's first catalog, produced in 1963, was just four pages long. By 2008 the company required four catalogs, some more than 200 pages long, to itemize all its products.

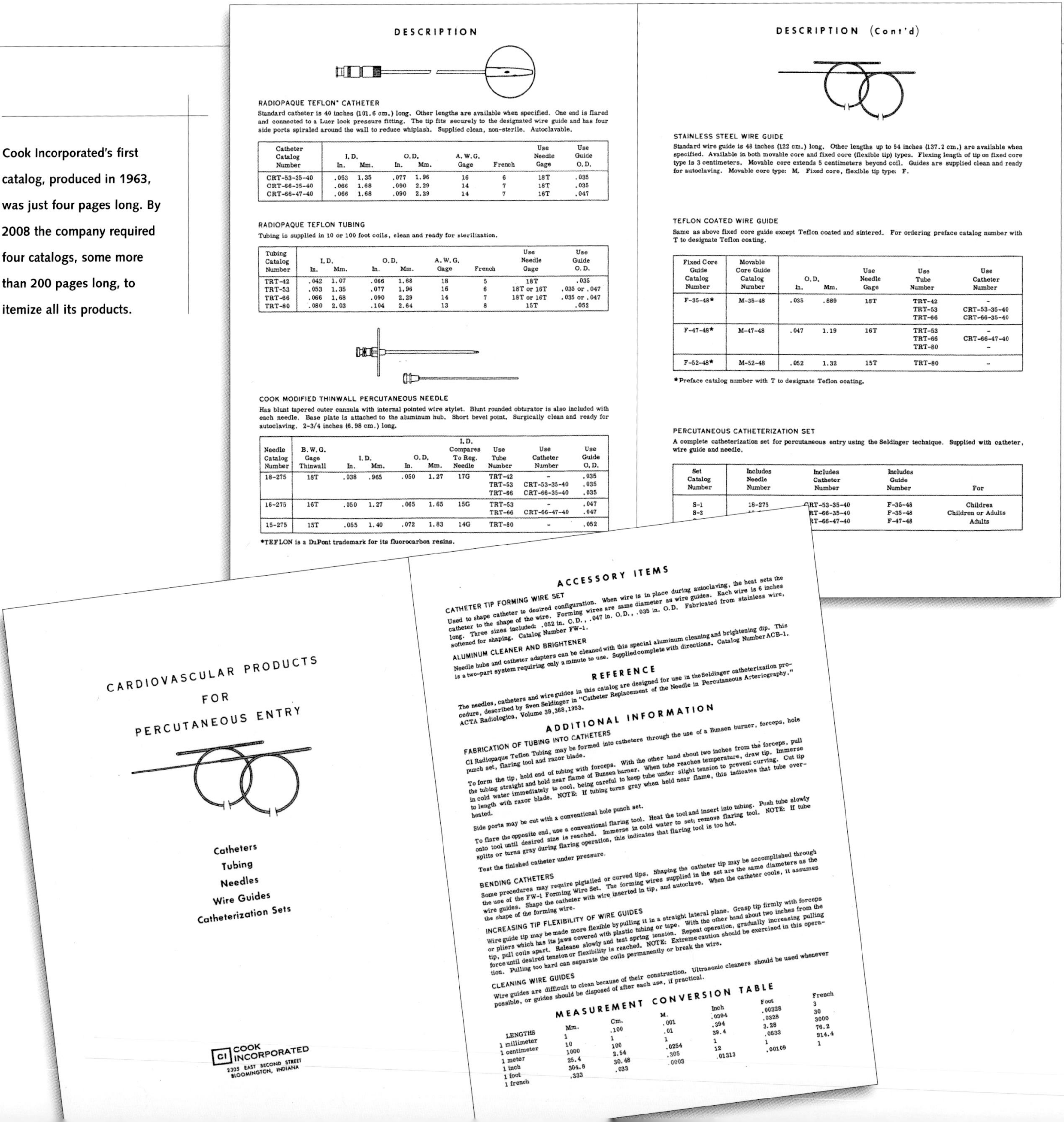

DESCRIPTION

RADIOPAQUE TEFLON* CATHETER

Standard catheter is 40 inches (101.6 cm.) long. Other lengths are available when specified. One end is flared and connected to a Luer lock pressure fitting. The tip fits securely to the designated wire guide and has four side ports spiraled around the wall to reduce whiplash. Supplied clean, non-sterile. Autoclavable.

Catheter Catalog Number	I.D. In.	I.D. Mm.	O.D. In.	O.D. Mm.	A.W.G. Gage	French	Use Needle Gage	Use Guide O.D.
CRT-53-35-40	.053	1.35	.077	1.96	16	6	18T	.035
CRT-66-35-40	.066	1.68	.090	2.29	14	7	18T	.035
CRT-66-47-40	.066	1.68	.090	2.29	14	7	16T	.047

RADIOPAQUE TEFLON TUBING

Tubing is supplied in 10 or 100 foot coils, clean and ready for sterilization.

Tubing Catalog Number	I.D. In.	I.D. Mm.	O.D. In.	O.D. Mm.	A.W.G. Gage	French	Use Needle Gage	Use Guide O.D.
TRT-42	.042	1.07	.066	1.68	18	5	18T	.035
TRT-53	.053	1.35	.077	1.96	16	6	18T or 16T	.035 or .047
TRT-66	.066	1.68	.090	2.29	14	7	18T or 16T	.035 or .047
TRT-80	.080	2.03	.104	2.64	13	8	15T	.052

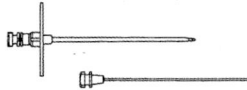

COOK MODIFIED THINWALL PERCUTANEOUS NEEDLE

Has blunt tapered outer cannula with internal pointed wire stylet. Blunt rounded obturator is also included with each needle. Base plate is attached to the aluminum hub. Short bevel point. Surgically clean and ready for autoclaving. 2-3/4 inches (6.98 cm.) long.

Needle Catalog Number	B.W.G. Gage Thinwall	I.D. In.	I.D. Mm.	O.D. In.	O.D. Mm.	I.D. Compares To Reg. Needle	Use Tube Number	Use Catheter Number	Use Guide O.D.
18-275	18T	.038	.965	.050	1.27	17G	TRT-42	-	.035
							TRT-53	CRT-53-35-40	.035
							TRT-66	CRT-66-35-40	.035
16-275	16T	.050	1.27	.065	1.65	15G	TRT-53	-	.047
							TRT-66	CRT-66-47-40	.047
15-275	15T	.055	1.40	.072	1.83	14G	TRT-80	-	.052

*TEFLON is a DuPont trademark for its fluorocarbon resins.

DESCRIPTION (Cont'd)

STAINLESS STEEL WIRE GUIDE

Standard wire guide is 48 inches (122 cm.) long. Other lengths up to 54 inches (137.2 cm.) are available when specified. Available in both movable core and fixed core (flexible tip) types. Flexing length of tip on fixed core type is 3 centimeters. Movable core extends 5 centimeters beyond coil. Guides are supplied clean and ready for autoclaving. Movable core type: M. Fixed core, flexible tip type: F.

TEFLON COATED WIRE GUIDE

Same as above fixed core guide except Teflon coated and sintered. For ordering preface catalog number with T to designate Teflon coating.

Fixed Core Guide Catalog Number	Movable Core Guide Catalog Number	O.D. In.	O.D. Mm.	Use Needle Gage	Use Tube Number	Use Catheter Number
F-35-48*	M-35-48	.035	.889	18T	TRT-42	-
					TRT-53	CRT-53-35-40
					TRT-66	CRT-66-35-40
F-47-48*	M-47-48	.047	1.19	16T	TRT-53	-
					TRT-66	CRT-66-47-40
					TRT-80	-
F-52-48*	M-52-48	.052	1.32	15T	TRT-80	-

*Preface catalog number with T to designate Teflon coating.

PERCUTANEOUS CATHETERIZATION SET

A complete catheterization set for percutaneous entry using the Seldinger technique. Supplied with catheter, wire guide and needle.

Set Catalog Number	Includes Needle Number	Includes Catheter Number	Includes Guide Number	For
S-1	18-275	CRT-53-35-40	F-35-48	Children
S-2	18-275	CRT-66-35-40	F-35-48	Children or Adults
		CRT-66-47-40	F-47-48	Adults

ACCESSORY ITEMS

CATHETER TIP FORMING WIRE SET

Used to shape catheter to desired configuration. When wire is in place during autoclaving, the heat sets the catheter to the shape of the wire. Forming wires are same diameter as wire guides. Each wire is 6 inches long. Three sizes included: .052 in. O.D., .047 in. O.D., .035 in. O.D. Fabricated from stainless wire, softened for shaping. Catalog Number FW-1.

ALUMINUM CLEANER AND BRIGHTENER

Needle hubs and catheter adapters can be cleaned with this special aluminum cleaning and brightening dip. This is a two-part system requiring only a minute to use. Supplied complete with directions. Catalog Number ACB-1.

REFERENCE

The needles, catheters and wire guides in this catalog are designed for use in the Seldinger catheterization procedure, described by Sven Seldinger in "Catheter Replacement of the Needle in Percutaneous Arteriography," ACTA Radiologica, Volume 39, 368, 1953.

ADDITIONAL INFORMATION

FABRICATION OF TUBING INTO CATHETERS

CI Radiopaque Teflon Tubing may be formed into catheters through the use of a Bunsen burner, forceps, hole punch set, flaring tool and razor blade.

To form the tip, hold end of tubing with forceps. With the other hand about two inches from the forceps, pull the tubing straight and hold near flame of Bunsen burner. When tube reaches temperature, draw tip. Immerse in cold water immediately to cool, being careful to keep tube under slight tension to prevent curving. Cut tip to length with razor blade. NOTE: If tubing turns gray when held near flame, this indicates that tube overheated.

Side ports may be cut with a conventional hole punch set.

To flare the opposite end, use a conventional flaring tool. Heat the tool and insert into tubing. Push tube slowly onto tool until desired size is reached. Immerse in cold water to set; remove flaring tool. NOTE: If tube splits or turns gray during flaring operation, this indicates that flaring tool is too hot.

Test the finished catheter under pressure.

BENDING CATHETERS

Some procedures may require pigtailed or curved tips. Shaping the catheter tip may be accomplished through the use of the FW-1 Forming Wire Set. The forming wires supplied in the set are the same diameters as the wire guides. Shape the catheter with wire inserted in tip, and autoclave. When the catheter cools, it assumes the shape of the forming wire.

INCREASING TIP FLEXIBILITY OF WIRE GUIDES

Wire guide tip may be made more flexible by pulling it in a straight lateral plane. Grasp tip firmly with forceps or pliers which has its jaws covered with plastic tubing or tape. With the other hand about two inches from the tip, pull coils apart. Release slowly and test spring tension. Repeat operation, gradually increasing pulling force until desired tension or flexibility is reached. NOTE: Extreme caution should be exercised in this operation. Pulling too hard can separate the coils permanently or break the wire.

CLEANING WIRE GUIDES

Wire guides are difficult to clean because of their construction. Ultrasonic cleaners should be used whenever possible, or guides should be disposed of after each use, if practical.

MEASUREMENT CONVERSION TABLE

LENGTHS	Mm.	Cm.	M.	Inch	Foot	French
1 millimeter	1	.100	.001	.0394	.00328	3
1 centimeter	10	1	.01	.394	.0328	30
1 meter	1000	100	1	39.4	3.28	3000
1 inch	25.4	2.54	.0254	1	.0833	76.2
1 foot	304.8	30.48	.305	12	1	914.4
1 french	.333	.033	.0003	.01313	.00109	1

CARDIOVASCULAR PRODUCTS FOR PERCUTANEOUS ENTRY

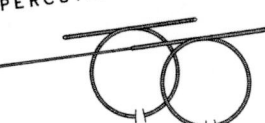

- Catheters
- Tubing
- Needles
- Wire Guides
- Catheterization Sets

COOK INCORPORATED
2305 EAST SECOND STREET
BLOOMINGTON, INDIANA

Chapter Two: 1963-1964

The First Team

When Bill Cook attended his first trade show in 1963, he couldn't afford a booth. He set up a small table in a corner, and there, with a blowtorch, he manufactured the future of health care from Teflon tubing. Advances in radiographics that made possible images like the one below set the stage for Cook's entry into the medical technology field.

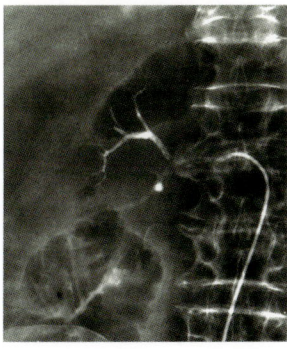

Just 27 years old, Frank Longson was already a veteran of the medical technology field when he walked into Chicago's historic Palmer House Hotel for the autumn 1963 meeting of the Radiological Society of North America (RSNA). A tall, thin entrepreneur who wore his enthusiasm like a new suit, he manned an 8-by-12-foot booth at the convention, showing off the evolving line of devices made by his company, Ensco.

The booth next door belonged to Cordis, a competitor based in Florida. Longson's counterpart at the Cordis booth was Miles Kanne, an electrical engineer and Minnesota native who had worked for ten years as a Westinghouse power equipment sales engineer before joining Cordis. The two men were by now friends; they had met three years earlier at an RSNA conference, and their paths crossed often on the road.

This was Longson's fourth RSNA conference, and it augured to be little different from the others he and Kanne had attended over the years—with the curious exception of the man down the row from their booths. He seemed strangely out of place. He didn't have an actual booth in which to display the few wares he'd brought; he simply set up a table in a corner near the Coca-Cola booth. And there he stood—with a blowtorch, manufacturing devices for which there was no clearly defined market: Teflon catheters.

By 1963, five years after Longson launched Ensco because he couldn't find a job after college in his native Salt Lake City, he had repeatedly crisscrossed the United States and Canada, building his customer base. Ensco was still very small, but Longson felt optimistic about where it was headed. As Longson watched the wiry man alone and intense at his bare table, he reflected on the dues he'd paid to survive his first five years in business. "Look at that poor guy trying to get started," Longson thought. Never for a moment could he have guessed the impact the man with the blowtorch would have on his life—and Kanne's, for that matter—in the years to come.

Kanne, on the other hand, knew that "poor guy" as Bill Cook. They had met a couple months earlier and

Cook Incorporated had been in existence three days short of two months when Illinois Masonic Hospital became the company's first customer on August 29, 1963. The order was modest, but Bill and Gayle Cook took it as a good omen and celebrated by dining out, at McDonald's.

were engaged in an ongoing correspondence. Kanne was familiar with Cook's start-up business venture, and he had reason to be more optimistic about Cook's chances for success than did Longson, who saw only a man who seemed inadequately prepared for this major event.

Longson's instinctive appraisal of Cook was not entirely wrong, however. After all, diagnostic angiography was still largely a novelty in 1963, and Cook was trying to serve a very small market. But Cook was utterly convinced the market would grow. Moreover, his company, though tiny, was the only one in the nation manufacturing all of the equipment radiologists needed to perform the percutaneous catheterizations pioneered by Dr. Seldinger just a decade earlier.

The potential market was huge. Most radiologists weren't even performing percutaneous catheterizations yet. Those who were generally cobbled together their own equipment, using available hypodermic needles, steel piano strings for wire guides and catheters they fabricated from a host of materials. Cook believed they would welcome a company like his that could produce all the equipment they needed—especially since he was willing to customize his products to meet the unique needs of radiologists, who were essentially improvising catheterization on the job.

MEETING WITH THE "SPACE CADET"

Cook's reasoning seemed borne out as a crowd of conventioneers, initially drawn to the nearby Coke booth, gathered around his table on the first afternoon of the Chicago conference, sipping their beverages and watching him demonstrate how to pull tips on Teflon catheters. He was well into his presentation when he noticed a "short, muscular, bald man with darting eyes" sitting behind him on a box. Cook had no idea who the stranger was, but having someone in back of him while he demonstrated his trade made him nervous. So when the crowd thinned out a bit, Cook asked the man if he could help him. The stranger simply answered, "No," and left.

Later that afternoon the mystery man returned and asked if he could borrow Cook's blowtorch and some Teflon tubing. "He said he wanted to practice making catheters in his hotel room," Cook remembered later. "Thinking I had a real space cadet on my hands, I said, 'Sure. May I have your name?'"

The stranger introduced himself as Dr. Charles Dotter. Cook wasn't sure he'd ever see his blowtorch again, so he went out that evening and purchased another one. The next morning, Dotter was waiting for Cook when he arrived at his table. Overnight the doctor had fabricated "ten beautifully made Teflon catheters," Cook recalled, and by the end of the day Cook had sold them. Charles Dotter, Cook would later joke, "was my first production employee."

For the balance of that week, Dotter visited Cook daily. Once the topic turned to angiography, about which Dotter's interest and imagination were apparently boundless, he was remarkably loquacious. Kindred spirits, the two men shared ideas about wire guides and catheters and how to manufacture them.

Bill Cook had spent $300 to buy the space for his table at the show, and Gayle Cook had decorated it for $14. The money they made on the catheters Charles Dotter produced on the first night of the convention covered about half of the cost of the show.

Cook had come to Chicago hoping to find a few new customers, which he did. But he also left having embarked upon a collaboration with a man destined to be one of the giants of medicine, who was about to usher in the age of percutaneous intervention. On the last day of the conference, as Cook was packing up his supplies and getting ready to go home, Dotter returned to his table in the exhibition hall and invited him to Portland, Oregon, so they could work together in his laboratory. "You probably can't afford it," he told Cook, "so I'll pay your expenses."

Conventioneers at the Radiological Society of North America's 1963 fall meeting flocked around Bill Cook's table, fascinated by his technique for creating Teflon catheters.

THE FATHER OF INTERVENTIONAL RADIOLOGY

Born in 1920 in Boston, Massachusetts, Charles T. Dotter studied medicine and radiology at Cornell University, where he served in a staff position from 1950 to 1952. He was only 32 years old when he became professor and chairman of radiology at the University of Oregon Medical School, a position he would hold until his death in 1985.

Dr. Dotter altered medical treatment of cardiovascular disease. Modifying the Seldinger technique for therapeutic purposes, he initiated a medical revolution that reduced the number of surgical beds needed in hospitals, minimized patient risk and trimmed the length of time many patients were required to stay in hospitals. Thanks to Dotter's groundbreaking work, many expensive and traumatic surgical procedures were eliminated. The benefits of his research proliferated as, one by one, other areas of medicine adopted his technique.

Dotter was much more than a brilliant clinician. He was a genius with a boundlessly curious intellect. His contributions to the advancement of medicine extended well beyond the techniques that earned him a reputation as "the father of interventional radiology." He created a prototype for grid-controlled X-ray tubes. He developed a double-lumen balloon catheter. His safety guide wire and J-tipped guide wire dramatically improved wire guide technology. He introduced arterial stenting and stent-grafting. The winner of four gold medals in radiology, he was nominated for the Nobel Prize for medicine in 1978.

Like most geniuses, he was also a bundle of contradictions. A warm, gracious and witty host and a friend whose loyalty was unflagging, he also had a reputation for raining withering rage upon colleagues and subordinates whose work failed to meet his standards. An inveterate bird watcher, a seasoned mountain climber who scaled the Matterhorn and every continental United States peak over 14,000 feet, and an avid outdoorsman, he was also a chain smoker. An unabashed showman, a talented artist and a knowledgeable aficionado of classical music, he liked to compare himself to a plumber and often quipped, "Dilation is my bag."

He was, perhaps, most comfortable behind the wheel of fast cars, the only machines that seemed to be able to approximate the breakneck pace of his intellect. As Dr. Fred Keller said in his lecture at the Dotter Institute's celebration of Dr. Dotter's life and work, in 2000:

Charles' mind always operated at full throttle, often working in several diverse directions simultaneously. Frequently, in the middle of a conversation on a completely different topic, he would pull some sort of gizmo from his pocket to explain that with certain modifications it could be a useful tool for interventional radiology. Yet, despite this apparent "shotgun" approach, Charles had the uncanny ability to clarify and crystallize his thoughts. Those having the privilege of hearing him speak or reading his manuscripts marvel at the clarity and conciseness of his expression.

Almost from the beginning Dotter had a profound impact on the development of Cook Incorporated. In Bill Cook he found a great collaborator—someone who could assimilate the ideas that seemed to spill out of his mind, as though it were a constantly overflowing spring, and mold those ideas into useful products. Although he died in 1985, his contributions to Cook Incorporated are enduring and beyond measure.

With balloon-tipped catheters manufactured by Cook, Charles Dotter set the stage for uses of percutaneous catheterization that revolutionized medicine in the second half of the 20th century.

CRASH COURSE IN CATHETERIZATION

Cook spent several days in Portland. Dotter's laboratory, he remembers, "was state-of-the-art, the finest in the United States. When I arrived, I saw how his technicians made their own wire guides. Also, they were producing their own Teflon catheters using a recently purchased blowtorch and our Teflon tubing. Charles, by the way, was making the catheters."

For Cook, the time with Dotter was like a crash course in radiological catheterization. "We talked about wire guide and catheter manufacture and what he thought the future would be for angiography," Cook recalls.

One of the things Dotter discussed with Cook was angioplasty—the notion of using a coronary catheter not merely for radiological procedures but also as a tool to actually clear blocked blood vessels. For all his skills as a physician, Dotter hewed to the notion that he was really more like a tradesman. To reinforce that message, he showed Cook a picture of a plumber's wrench and a length of pipe with a threaded elbow joint at the end. Cook was so taken with the image that, years later, he had it carved in stone for display at the entrance to the Cook Incorporated factory.

Dotter insisted that he could do much more than simply use catheters to examine human plumbing. He could fix problems with less patient discomfort, less chance of infection and a speedier recovery than surgeons could. Soon enough, he would prove his point.

"Charles became very excited when he talked about his work," Cook remembers. Dotter had intense eyes, and his face was a palate of expressions, animated and constantly shifting as he held court. "Once his mind was started, it went nonstop," says Cook.

Meeting Dotter was precisely the spark that Cook's young business needed. Cook returned home, brimming with concepts for more new products and product enhancements than he might have thought up on his own in weeks or months.

> The irrepressible Charles Dotter was a brilliant radiologist and Bill Cook's great friend. His impact upon Cook Incorporated was incalculable.

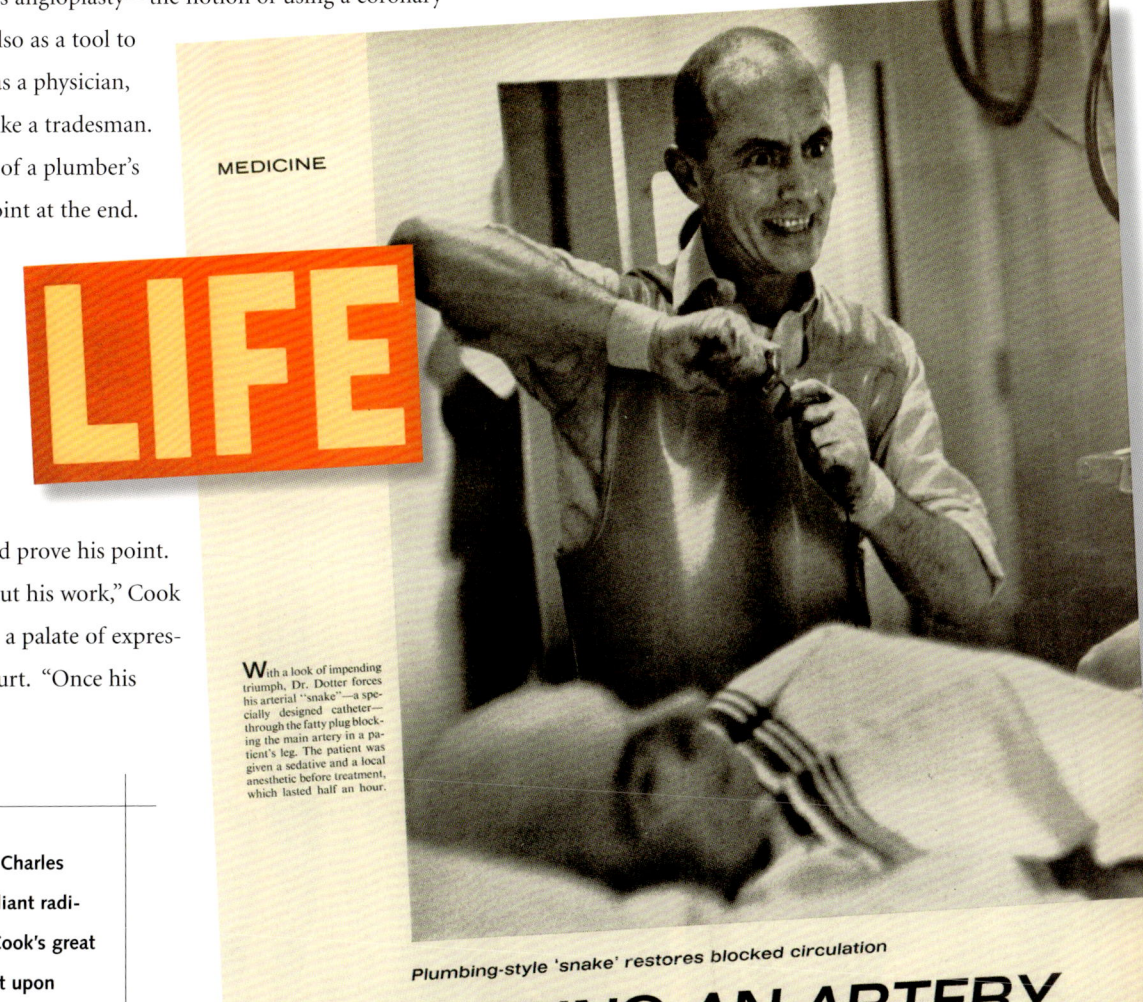

Naturally conservative, electrical engineer Miles Kanne was at first reluctant to join Bill Cook's start-up company. By the spring of 1964, however—convinced there was a big market for Cook's products—he took the plunge and helped Bill Cook turn that potential into success.

Among the first technological innovations to result from his collaboration with Dotter were Safe-T-J Wire Guides and the telescopic Dotter Dilatation Set, designed from sketches Dotter had given him just before he left Portland. Though the two men had discussed intervention in Oregon, Bill Cook had no way of knowing how soon Dotter would put those products to use or to what groundbreaking effect.

SEARCHING FOR OUTSIDE HELP

While Cook's sense of what radiologists needed was generally on the money, and his willingness and capacity to meet their needs paid off in dividends, he also realized that he needed to have his products professionally evaluated if his company was going to achieve its potential. For several months before the Chicago convention, Cook had been regularly visiting Dr. Walter Judson's cardiac catheter lab at the Indiana University Medical Center in Indianapolis—the nearest place where his devices could be tested.

There Cook met Ross Jennings, a technician who managed Judson's lab. Cook took a shine to Jennings and talked with him about the possibility of joining his nascent company. Jennings declined, saying that, at least for the time being, he was satisfied working at the medical center. He said he knew a sales representative Cook should meet, though. It was Miles Kanne, and one day that summer, when Kanne visited Judson's lab, Jennings told him, "There's a guy down in Bloomington who's working on catheters. We're doing some testing for him, and I think you should call him."

Jennings showed Kanne some of Cook's catheters, and Kanne, an electrical engineer, could see right away the potential of what Bill Cook was creating. He was intrigued by the possibility of working for Cook, especially since he was becoming disenchanted trying to sell Cordis dye injectors that cost upwards of $2,000—about the price of a new Ford sedan in the early 1960s.

Still, he hesitated to take the plunge into a start-up venture, especially because some of the doctors he knew predicted that cardiac catheterization would never catch on and told him he would be in "a dead-end business." In the end, though, Kanne decided it couldn't hurt to introduce himself to Cook. In August 1963, a couple of months before the RSNA conference in Chicago, he wrote Cook a letter inquiring about employment opportunities and proposing to represent Cook's products to his own customers, believing that this could help him move more Cordis injectors.

Three weeks passed before Cook responded, proposing that they get together. At that meeting Cook said Kanne was precisely the sort of person his company needed, but he couldn't afford him yet. Leaving the meeting, Kanne took some of Cook's sales literature with him and promised to talk up Cook's products with his customers. He remained with Cordis, but in an ongoing exchange of letters the two men advanced the dialogue that had begun in September. Then Bill Cook began to notice something: Kanne's promotional efforts were bringing him new orders.

THE MECHANICAL WUNDERKIND

By the spring of 1964 Cook's year-old business had outstripped his capacity to both manufacture products and market them. More doctors were coming to him for supplies, and they wanted more and more variations. If his company was going to continue growing, Cook realized, he needed someone to help him manufacture his products so he could devote the bulk of his time to selling them.

One afternoon, determined to improve his skill at making wire guides, Cook called upon a jeweler named Dick Osborne, who had a small shop in downtown Bloomington. A meticulous craftsman and artisan, Osborne repaired watches and jewelry and practiced the venerable art of hand engraving. Cook asked him for help.

Osborne had never had such a request, but he enjoyed challenges and quickly grasped what Cook wanted to accomplish. He showed Cook how to use several different kinds of solders. He taught him about new types of fluxes. He also introduced him to the tools a jeweler uses for soldering, grinding, buffing, polishing and cleaning—in short, everything Cook needed to produce wire guides. Cook told Osborne he'd like to find someone with skills like Osborne's to help him manufacture wire guides. Osborne said he had a son, Tom, who was a bright young man with a technological bent. He was about to graduate from high school, and he was looking for a job.

A week later, on a sunny morning in June 1964, Tom Osborne rode his motorcycle out to Bill and Gayle Cook's Bart Villa apartment. He was a gangling Indiana youth, a bit short on social skills, but he grasped Bill Cook's needs almost as soon as Bill showed him the workbench in the spare bedroom. "I could see how to make the wires right away," Osborne recalls. "It was easy."

It didn't take Bill Cook, an astute judge of talent, long to realize he had an authentic mechanical wunderkind on his hands. For a kid who had blown through three semesters of high-school drafting in just six weeks, it was a simple matter for Tom to create whatever Cook's customers needed. The capacity to customize products that Tom provided through his handiwork gave Cook Incorporated an engineering advantage. It also turned out to be one of the young company's first and greatest marketing strengths.

THE CUSTOM TOUCH

As soon as physicians discovered that a little company in Indiana could make high-quality catheters, wire guides and needles according to their unique specifications (and better than they could make

The son of a Bloomington jeweler, Tom Osborne was still in high school when he met Bill Cook. Osborne was a technical whiz, and when he became Cook's first production employee, Bill never had to worry about meeting the capacity for innovation that soon became his company's hallmark.

them themselves), they were delighted. More often than not, their orders specified a stock Cook item but requested some sort of modification. "They'd want a slightly different diameter," Osborne recalls, "or a different length or stiffness. They'd want some catheters straight and some with curves. Sometimes it was just a matter of modifying what we were already making, but often it required finding new materials or some new technique." In this way a vast array of specialized tools for catheterization soon began to emerge from Cook Incorporated's workshop.

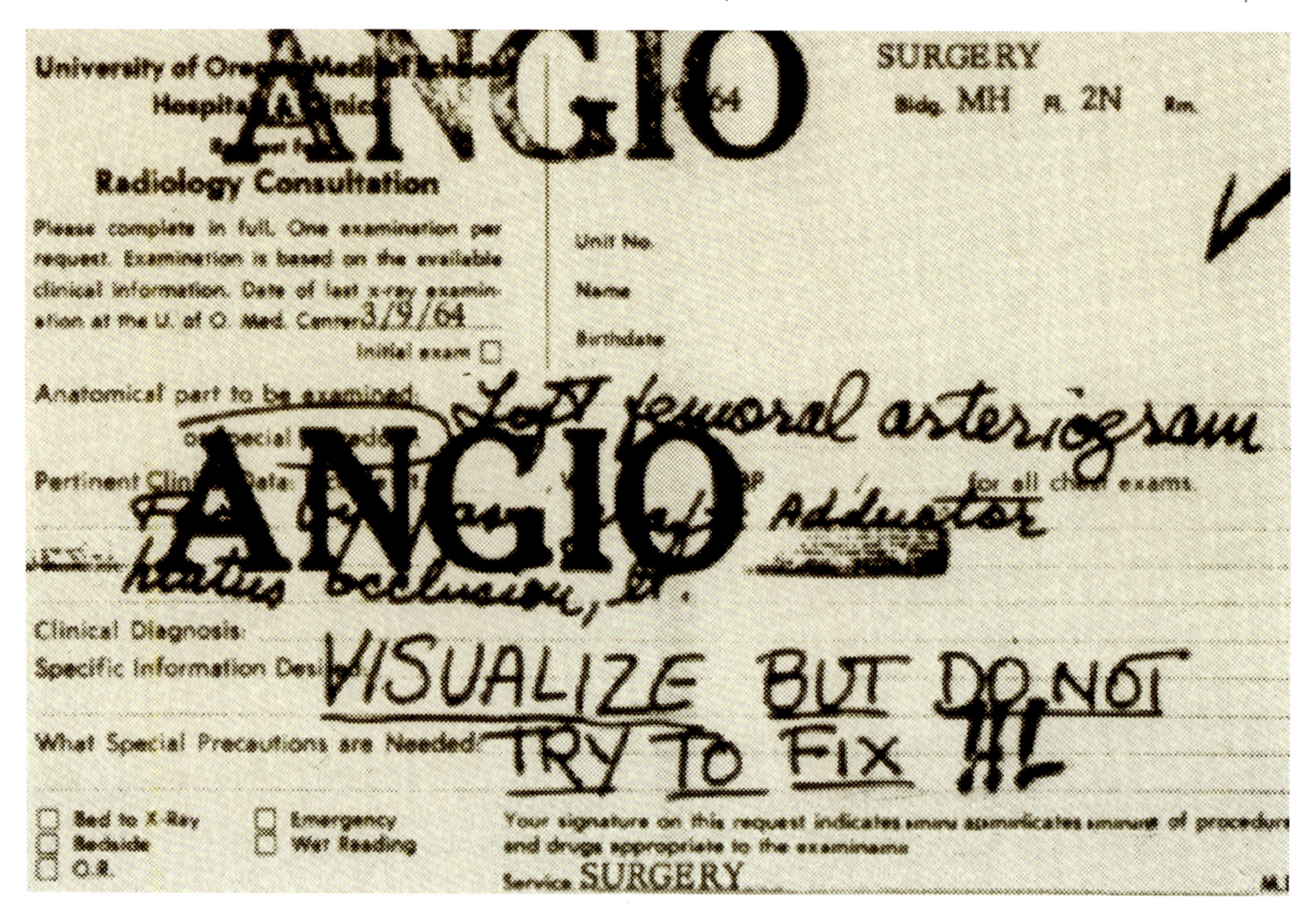

Osborne started work the same day he came to Bart Villa, and he never looked back. He arrived every morning and tackled a stack of orders Bill Cook had just picked up at the post office. With Cook conducting business by telephone in the background, the youth would sidle up to the workbench and prepare the orders in batches throughout the day. At the end of the afternoon, on his way out, he would drop off his day's production in the kitchen. Then Gayle Cook—ever vigilant for quality—subjected every catheter or wire to intense scrutiny during the evening and prepared them to be shipped the next day.

This was hardly the job Osborne had envisioned back in high school, when he expected to find employment at one of the area's many industrial plants, such as RCA, Westinghouse or General Electric. As time went on, however, he began to see the advantages of working with the Cooks. He enjoyed significantly more autonomy than he ever could have expected at any of the bigger companies. It was in many ways the ideal job for a talented young man who thrived on challenges and hoped for an exciting future.

The job was not stress-free, however. Doctors tended to pre-engineer their ideas. They'd show up to hand Cook's 18-year-old production whiz the schematics for a new tool, but regardless of how carefully the plans were drawn, they'd often have unforeseen design flaws. "Then," Osborne recalls, "I'd have to spend some sleepless nights making something that would work. I learned right away to try to get to that matter in initial conversations with the doctors—to try to find out exactly what they wanted to achieve."

For Tom Osborne, who felt he'd taken no particular risk coming to work for the Cooks, the question was whether he was willing to endure such stress for the prospect of long-term returns. It was a question he would defer answering—until, eventually, it answered itself.

Surgeons bristled at Dr. Charles Dotter's conviction that advanced atherosclerosis could be successfully treated with percutaneous transluminal angioplasty. The request for an angiogram, opposite, was one of many sent to Dotter that demanded he not "try to fix" the patient. Right, Irene Edwards was one of Cook's first employees.

"WE CAN MAKE A FAIRLY DECENT LIVING"

One day in that spring of 1964, not long after Osborne started working for Cook, Miles Kanne reached the end of his rope with Cordis. He realized that selling the company's expensive injectors wasn't worth the effort. He was 37 years old, and he knew it was time to make a change. That night he sat down and composed a letter to Bill Cook. "I don't know if you can afford to hire me," he wrote, "but I'm ready to make a move."

A few days later, while Kanne was on a business trip to Detroit, Bill Cook received his letter. Cook called, spoke to Kanne's wife, found out where Kanne was staying and tracked him down by telephone to make him an offer. Cook said he was supporting his family on the strength of business Kanne had already driven his way, and he reasoned that if Kanne came to work for him full time the company's financial picture would only get better.

Cook told Kanne that he was doing a consulting job for a needle manufacturer in Biloxi, Mississippi, that was paying him $800 per month, and he wanted to know: would Kanne be willing to work for Cook and take over the consulting job? Kanne could have the $800, plus traveling expenses and opportunities to earn commissions selling catheters to customers who were already purchasing needles.

"Bill didn't sell me on the idea that we were going to make millions," Kanne remembers. "He said, 'You know, Miles, I think that if everything goes right, we can make a fairly decent living here.'"

Kanne accepted the offer and borrowed against his life insurance policies to cover his living expenses until things got going. For the rest of that year, he worked out of his home in Chicago but often found himself in Bloomington, sleeping on a davenport in the Cooks' living room.

He reckoned that with the borrowed money and the $800 monthly income, he would be able to make a go of it for upwards of two years. It didn't take anywhere near that long. Barely three months after joining Cook, he was generating enough business to more than cover his expenses. "It was just a matter of finding who was doing the technique or talking with people who were considering doing the technique," he says. "I didn't make a sale every time, but typically, if they were interested, I'd get an order for $300 to $400. That would buy them enough catheters, wire guides and percutaneous needles to last three to six months. So I was starting to generate repeat business, as well."

With Osborne and Kanne on board, Bill Cook now had the first key pieces in place upon which his business would grow. He had a first-rate production employee, capable of both creating the company's primary products and working with physicians to customize those tools for ever-evolving needs. And he had a top-notch, experienced sales representative who, on the cusp of middle age, was finally working for a company about which he felt genuinely passionate.

To round out the package, Cook contracted the services of Dan Sterner, a corporate attorney with a firm in Indianapolis. Sterner was a fraternity brother who first met Cook in 1952 and remained in touch through the 1950s. His professional relationship with Cook commenced with a small legal matter; but in years to come, as Cook Incorporated grew by acquiring other companies and expanding both domestically and abroad, he would provide legal services that were essential to the company's success.

Cook and Kanne generated so much business working together that, before 1964 was over, Cook called Kanne and told him he could no longer manage the enterprise alone. He wanted Kanne to move to Bloomington and help him run the company. By then the little catheter operation Bill and Gayle Cook had launched scarcely two years earlier with just $1,500 had outgrown the spare bedroom in their Bart Villa apartment. Soon they would need to move the company outside Bill and Gayle's home.

"I didn't make a sale every time, but typically, if they were interested, I'd get an order for $300 to $400. That would buy them enough catheters, wire guides and percutaneous needles to last three to six months."

THE FIRST TEAM   35

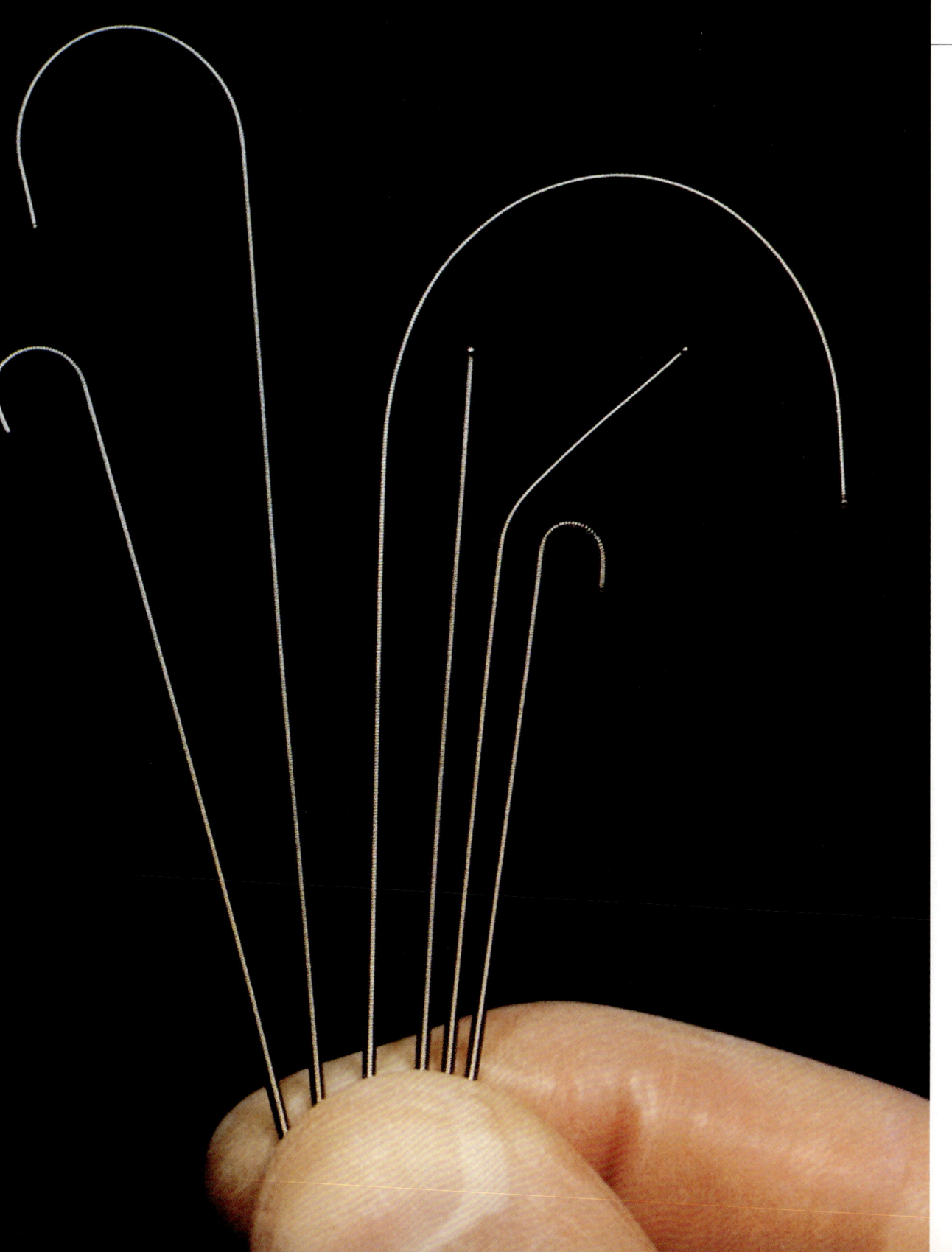

As more and more doctors began to perform percutaneous catheterizations, Cook's early success was founded on the company's capacity to swiftly customize specialized products, such as this array of wire guides for various catheterization procedures. Many Cook products were named for the doctors who first requested them.

Chapter Three: 1964-1973

Expansion

Ross Jennings, right, was a technician, managing Dr. Walter Judson's cardiac catheter lab at Indiana University Medical Center when Bill Cook first met him in 1963. In 1968 Jennings joined Cook Incorporated and became an "area manager" based in San Francisco and covering everything west of the Mississippi River.

The vascular surgeon told the patient there was nothing he could do for her. Peripheral vascular disease was destroying her foot, robbing it of blood. He took a look at the swollen, purple appendage and shook his head. The foot was badly infected, and several of the toes were gangrenous. To make matters worse, her cardiac health was poor.

The woman was 83 years old, and she had spent the last six months in bed, suffering from excruciating pain. But when the doctor recommended amputation—the sooner the better—she demurred and sought a second opinion, unwittingly opening the door for a milestone moment in the advancement of 20th-century medicine.

Charles Dotter had been waiting for that moment. When the surgeons ran out of options, and the woman refused amputation, they deigned to let Dotter take a look at the patient.

"It bothered Charles Dotter that many conditions could be diagnosed by radiology but could not be treated," Leslie and LaNelle Geddes wrote in *The Catheter Introducers*. "As was often the case, diagnosis was running ahead of therapy."

The woman with the infected foot gave Dotter the opportunity he had been looking for. On January 16, 1964, some three months after he had met Bill Cook in Chicago, Dotter went into an operating room and performed a groundbreaking interventional procedure. He inserted a Cook catheter through the skin of the woman's leg into her femoral artery and gradually guided it to the place where cholesterol deposits were inhibiting the flow of blood. There he used the tip of the catheter to push through the fatty buildup, reopening the artery.

As Dotter performed the world's first percutaneous transluminal angioplasty (PTA), it was easy to grasp why he sometimes compared himself to a plumber. When *Life* magazine published a quirky photo essay about Dotter's breakthrough later that year, the magazine used the plumbing analogy, describing the catheter as "similar to the 'snake' with which plumbers ream out clogged drains."

He certainly did a fine job cleaning the elderly woman's clogged artery. Almost immediately after the

Though his adaptation of the Seldinger technique for intervention rather than for diagnosis was revolutionary, Dr. Charles Dotter regarded it as a technically simple process. Comparing himself to a plumber, cleaning out clogged drains with a "snake," he adopted a crossed pipe and monkey wrench as a sort of renegade symbol of his work. Opposite, the catheter Dotter used for his first percutaneous transluminal angioplasty, in 1964.

procedure, her foot began to heal as blood flow was restored. The agonizing pain subsided. She was in the recovery room for about six hours, after which she was able to stand and walk for the first time in months. She continued to walk on the foot that had been sentenced to amputation until she died three years later. By August 1964 Dotter had performed nine similar procedures. He wrote:

Despite the frequency and importance of arteriosclerotic obstruction, current methods of therapy leave much to be desired. Nonsurgical measures, however helpful they may be, provide the patient little more than an opportunity to live with his disease.

With these facts in mind, pursuit of a previously proposed approach has led to the development of a safe, simple and effective technique for directly overcoming arteriosclerotic narrowing and occlusion in the arteries of the leg. Impressive salvages already achieved in otherwise doomed legs amply justify this preliminary report, even though long-term follow-up observations are not yet possible.

Dotter's first PTA lasted just minutes. But the procedure launched a wave that rolled across the field of medicine for the balance of the 20th century—an eventual tsunami that irrevocably changed everything it touched. In Europe, where it caught on almost immediately after Dotter introduced it, doctors appropriated his name to avoid the cumbersome technical name. They called the procedure "dottering," and it was soon being performed in hospitals all across the continent.

American doctors, meanwhile, debated the legitimacy of Dotter's procedure and wrangled over whether it was best performed by surgeons or radiologists. Most of a decade passed, during which many Americans who could have benefited from the procedure were deprived, before Dotter's wave finally swept back across the Atlantic. When it did, Cook Incorporated rose upon its mighty crest.

FROM HOME OFFICE TO DENTIST'S OFFICE

By 1965 Cook Incorporated had spilled out of Bill and Gayle's spare bedroom and into the rest of the Cooks' increasingly cramped apartment. Tom Osborne was making wire guides in the bedroom. Gayle balanced the company's books at the kitchen table. Bill used the oven to dry wire guides and set curves in catheters, and he appropriated the bathtub for a pot of nitric acid solution, in which he submerged wire guides to give them a light coating of oxide before shipping so they wouldn't rust.

"It was absolutely incredible," he says, looking back on that time, "but we did survive and managed not to blow ourselves up." Nevertheless, it was clear they could not continue running the business that way.

Things reached a head when Bill's mother came for a visit. While showering on her first morning in Bloomington, she dropped a bar of soap in the acid solution, and it foamed over the tub. The same day, baby Carl was frightened when he saw an oxygen tank fall over.

Dotter's first PTA lasted just minutes. But the procedure launched a wave that rolled across the field of medicine for the balance of the 20th century—an eventual tsunami that irrevocably changed everything it touched. In Europe, where it caught on almost immediately after Dotter introduced it, doctors appropriated his name to avoid the cumbersome technical name. They called the procedure "dottering," and it was soon being performed in hospitals all across the continent.

Gayle put her foot down. It was time for the company to find new quarters. So in September 1964 Cook Incorporated moved into a former dentist's office at 300 South Swain Avenue in Bloomington, near Indiana University. For Bill Cook, who had grown accustomed to getting dressed and going to work across the hall, it meant a slight change of routine. Now he would get dressed, without a coat and tie, grab the cardboard box that contained all of the company's business and financial records, and drive to the new office. At the end of the day he'd bring the box home with him so Gayle could balance the company's books every night, as she had since the beginning.

During his first two years in business, Bill Cook had successfully made the difficult transition from an unknown entity to an increasingly credible force in medical technology. Thanks to his friendship with Charles Dotter, he was becoming well known in radiological circles. More and more physicians recognized him when he attended major conventions. And being an airplane pilot proved to be an enormous advantage, since he was able to fly and meet with potential customers almost at the drop of a hat.

"Bill had lots of friends in radiology by then," Brian Baldwin recalls. "He got around so fast with his plane that many radiologists thought he was a big company."

A former dentist's office at 300 South Swain Avenue in Bloomington became the company's home in 1964 when Cook Incorporated outgrew Bill and Gayle Cook's apartment. Opposite, Bill's capacity to fly planes and reach customers quickly gave him a competitive edge.

A NEW WAY OF SELLING

It wasn't just his capacity to get places quickly that set Bill Cook apart. Working with Charles Dotter and other radiologists, Cook had instinctively forged a new model for sales. It was an approach that Miles Kanne, already a seasoned sales representative when he joined Cook, embraced immediately.

Rather than create a product line and then try to sell it to doctors, the two strove to operate as consultants, winning the confidence of

EXPANSION 41

Miles Kanne, left, conferring here with Bill Cook, borrowed money when he joined Cook Incorporated in 1964 so his family would be taken care of if sales were slow to develop. He need not have worried; by the end of his first three months, he was more than covering his expenses with the new business he was generating.

doctors by talking their language, listening to their problems and working hard to help them develop whatever tools they required. If a doctor told them that Cook catheters were good but that he now needed a shorter one, a longer one or one of a different diameter, Cook and Kanne came home to Bloomington and handed the assignment to Osborne. Every problem became an opportunity.

Word soon spread within the radiological community that Cook Incorporated could be counted on to deliver the goods. As the company created new devices to meet the unique needs of more and more doctors, the catalog of products grew. To the product line in 1964 Cook added a moveable core wire guide equipped with a mandril that allowed doctors to vary the stiffness of the guide during a procedure, and the first Dotter Angioplasty Catheter Set, which enabled doctors to perform Dotter's breakthrough procedure. New products introduced in 1965 included the Desilets-Hoffman Catheter Introducer Sheath Set, which made possible nonsurgical placement of closed-end catheters, temporary pacemaker leads and cardiac output catheters; safety wire guides; wire guides with tip-to-tip core wire to prevent elongation and breakage; and the J-Tipped Wire Guide, an enhancement that made it easier for wire guides to navigate the body's sometimes tortuous anatomy.

By the mid-1960s the company's financial affairs had become so complex that Gayle Cook could no longer manage the bookkeeping on a part-time basis at home. The company contracted the services of a Bloomington accountant named Phil Hathaway, who would later come to work for the company full time.

In 1966 Bill Cook also began working with Steve Ferguson, a young lawyer he'd met when he and Gayle first moved to Bloomington. A recent graduate of the Indiana University Law School, Ferguson handled legal matters not covered by Dan Sterner, including real estate issues related to the company's growth in and around Bloomington. Though Ferguson's entrée to the company was low-key, the role he would play in years to come was anything but.

With Bill barnstorming America, Miles Kanne on board full time in sales, and space to breathe in its new facility, the company began to hit its stride. "During the mid-1960s we were doubling our business every year," Kanne recalls. But an unexpected problem loomed on the horizon, and it threatened to bring the young company to its knees.

OSBORNE TO THE RESCUE

Wire guides—the devices that stiffen catheters and allow them to be introduced into blood vessels—are actually attenuated coils (very long springs similar to those on screen doors but with small diameters). Soon after arriving in Bloomington, Bill Cook contracted the Myers Spring Company in Logansport, about 70 miles north of Indianapolis, to produce his wire guides. It quickly became clear to Myers, however, that meeting Cook's needs would tax its production and liability insurance capabilities.

"They were set up to make large springs for heavy equipment," says Tom Osborne. "Making the kind of small spring used in a ballpoint pen was a challenge for them. And the springs we needed for wire guides are smaller than a hypodermic needle lumen, and much longer."

Myers was initially able to meet Cook's modest needs, laboriously producing batches of 200 to 300 coils that would sustain Cook for a while. But "as the business grew, it wasn't long before we needed lots of coils," says Osborne, "and we needed them in even smaller sizes."

Cook's needs soon outstripped the spring company's capacity. By 1966 Myers had to decline Cook's business. This put Cook Incorporated in a potentially disastrous position. The company was growing fast, and now Bill Cook was suddenly without a vendor to provide one of the components he needed most.

Myers offered some relief. The company sold Bill one of its coiling machines so he could produce his own coils. But it was a poor solution to the problem. "The machine simply wasn't designed to produce the kinds of coils we needed," says Osborne. "We spent a lot of time tinkering with it, trying to modify it, but nothing worked."

Bill Cook was getting desperate. Unless the problem could be solved, there was real risk that the company would have to relinquish orders. Considering the increasingly competitive arena in which the young company was operating, the coil problem could have been disastrous.

Then one morning Osborne showed up with some sketches. Unwilling to waste more time on the machine Bill had bought from Myers, Tom had spent long nights burning the candle as he pondered the problem, eventually coming up with a design for a completely different kind of machine.

He showed Bill Cook his drawings and asked for $50 to buy the parts he needed to assemble it. Bill couldn't grasp Osborne's concept, but he was getting desperate, and Osborne had a track record of success by now. If Tom was confident the new machine could work, Cook was willing to give him the money.

When Osborne unveiled his invention a few days later and put it to the test, it performed perfectly. It could produce the coils the company needed—and quickly—but it did much more than that. It significantly expanded the scope of wire coil lengths and diameters that Cook was capable of manufacturing, instantly positioning the company to take advantage of the demand for specialty wires as more doctors discovered more procedures they could perform with catheters.

Donna Hendrickson, here with Miles Kanne, right, and Bill Cook at South Swain Avenue, was Cook's first production manager. She oversaw a factory staff that grew to nearly 20 by 1966.

The Osborne coiler performed so well that it is still in use to this day and, never patented, remains a closely guarded trade secret. Only a handful of company employees have ever actually seen it in operation. Even fewer know how the coils are made.

The kid Bill Cook had hired right out of high school three years earlier had saved the day, and Bill will never forget his relief and his gratitude. "Tom's a mechanical genius," he tells people when he recounts that tale. "It's as simple as that."

MOVING AGAIN

It took the company two years to outgrow the Cooks' apartment; the South Swain Avenue office sufficed for barely a year. In 1966 Cook Incorporated moved to its third location, a five-room house on South Curry Pike in Bloomington, which was remodeled as a small office and factory. By then the four-year-old company was employing nearly 20 people, and though it would soon outgrow this facility, initially there was room to expand—and that's just what Cook Incorporated did.

When architect Richard Hartung announced in September 1967 that the company would soon be breaking ground for a new 5,000-square-foot addition to house manufacturing operations, Bloomington residents and civic leaders began to take notice of the fledgling business that had flown under the city's radar for four years. The expansion, said the architect, would allow the company to double its workforce.

It was the first step in a projected four-phase project that over the next decade transformed Cook Incorporated's physical plant into a sprawling complex occupying several city blocks. Bill Cook, who had moved his business three times in four years, was tired of being a nomad. Cook Incorporated would remain at 925 South Curry Pike for 35 years.

Surprisingly, though he had a plan to expand the physical plant, Bill remembers, "I never really had a plan for growth. I had a company that was profitable from the outset. It acquired wealth rather easily. The profit margins were quite high. And that was a problem: what to do with the money. I could invest in the stock market, but my personal preference was to reinvest in something. Cook Incorporated would not grow rapidly enough to utilize the cash as it was generated. So one of the things I investigated was the possibility of manufacturing my own plastic parts and tubing."

Ross Jennings, left, and Miles Kanne assume a low profile in front of the Cook workforce circa 1968. Jennings and Kanne were, in fact, anything but low profile. Together with Bill Cook, they formed the company's first executive team; thanks to their efforts, the workforce would grow exponentially during the 1970s.

SOLVING PROBLEMS—FOR CUSTOMERS AND PATIENTS

In 1968, after Bill Cook designated him to be the company's West Coast representative, Ross Jennings visited the neuroradiology department at the University of California in San Francisco. One of the leaders of that facility was Dr. Hans Newton, and he had a problem that immediately afforded Jennings an opportunity to employ Bill Cook's advice: "I don't want you to go out there and sell things. I want you to consult with the customer."

"This was in the days before CT scans," Jennings recalls, "At that time, to diagnose a problem in the head, you inserted a catheter and made injections."

But Newton was having difficulty inserting a catheter. Off the aortic arch, the point where the aorta makes an abrupt U-turn just above the heart, are the branches of the carotid and subclavian arteries—major vessels that carry blood to the head. Newton told Jennings that when he attempted to insert a catheter into the turn where those vessels left the aorta, the catheter would pull the guide wire out. "He'd lost access to the artery," Jennings remembers. "He asked me if Cook could make the tip of the catheter longer and more flexible so that he wouldn't have that problem."

It was a classic example of the kind of clinical problem Cook Incorporated was able to solve in its formative years, building solid relationships with customers and propelling the young company forward at the same time. Jennings hastened to a pay phone and called Bill Cook. It turned out Cook had anticipated Dr. Newton's problem, and Tom Osborne was already at work on a solution.

Catheter wire guides are tightly wound coils, like very fine springs. Within them, however, is a separate supporting wire called a mandril. Mandrils at the time were simply chopped off and left blunt when they were cut to fit the length of a guide wire. Cook was working on a new kind of mandril, tapered at the tip to give it more flexibility.

It turned out to be the solution to Dr. Newton's problem. Within a couple days of Jennings' call, a batch of the new wires with long, tapered mandrils was shipped to San Francisco. For Jennings it was the perfect way to get off on the right foot in his new assignment. But he is quick to say that his mindset—indeed the defining perspective of Cook—was about patients and doing what is right for them.

"Without a flexible, long-taper guide wire, Dr. Newton was unable to do what he needed to do to help his patients," Jennings says. "We had an obligation to help him.

"We always tried to do the right thing for the patient, and we strove to transfer that attitude to our employees who make our products. The equipment we make saves lives."

Most of Cook's products have been designed to solve specific problems brought to the company by leading physicians. Wire guides such as these were custom developed for dozens of different applications and conditions.

PLASTICS AND MORE

Since the newest generation of catheters was made of plastic, a high-cost commodity at the time, Bill Cook decided to launch his own plastics manufacturing operation. To head it up, he recruited Joseph Witkiewicz, who had more than 25 years of experience in mechanical engineering, business, education and plastics.

Witkiewicz had been working for a company in New York, developing products for Cook. When that company was bought out by a larger electronics firm that no longer had an interest in manufacturing medical supplies, Cook seized the opportunity to bring Witkiewicz to Bloomington and establish a new plastics company. The new business, called Sabin Corporation, opened in November 1968 with Witkiewicz at its helm.

Sabin was the first of numerous satellite companies that Bill Cook would establish in the years to come to meet the growing needs of his core business. "Percutaneous entry for catheter placement was so easy," he says, "that physicians in several disciplines were soon asking us to help develop their products."

Just as Sabin was getting started, Dr. Cesare Gianturco was winding down his long career at the Carle Clinic in Champaign, Illinois, where he was chief of radiology. He was 62 and a founding member of that clinic, having come to Champaign in 1934 after three years of practice in Europe and a four-year fellowship at the Mayo Clinic.

For many doctors a career that spanned more than 40 years would have been enough. But Gianturco was just getting started. When Dr. Sidney Wallace invited him to come to the University of Texas M. D. Anderson Cancer Center, he readily agreed. As a professor of radiology and a consultant in diagnostic radiology, he spent part of each of the next 20 years working at the Houston cancer center. With support from Cook Incorporated, in the experimental radiology laboratory that Wallace created for him, Gianturco developed some of the most remarkable medical devices created during the 20th century.

An early innovator in percutaneous catheterization, Dr. Sidney Wallace, left, created an experimental radiology lab for Dr. Cesare Gianturco at the University of Texas in 1968. There, with support from Cook Incorporated, Gianturco produced a range of extraordinary medical tools in the autumn of his life.

JENNINGS COMES ON BOARD

Back in Indiana, Ross Jennings was also deciding it was time to make a career move. At the Indiana University Medical Center where he had met Bill Cook several years earlier, the technician had been supported principally by research grants. But those began to dry up as the tumultuous 1960s wound down. Seeing the writing on the wall, Jennings approached Bill Cook about joining the company.

Cook was delighted. The rapidly expanding business was already exceeding his and Miles Kanne's capacity to handle all of the sales and marketing needs. He'd been trying to recruit Jennings for several years, so when Jennings called, Cook offered him a sales job right away.

"When I came to Cook I had never been involved in sales," Jennings recalls. "But that really wasn't important. Bill told me, 'I don't want you to go out there and sell things. I want you to consult with the customers.' I took that very seriously, and during all my years with Cook I never asked anyone to buy anything from us."

His first job title was "area manager," and it was quite a geographic area that Cook asked him to cover. Stationed in San Francisco, an important market for the catheter industry and a city noted for its enlightened medical community, Jennings was responsible for everything west of the Mississippi River. It was a huge territory, but "diagnostic angiography was very new," Jennings says. "Not many medical centers were doing it." This enabled him to focus initially on a few key areas in his territory.

He spent much of his time meeting and consulting with doctors at the University of California San Francisco, Stanford, UCLA and Los Angeles County Hospital, and with Dr. Dotter's team in Oregon. Otherwise, Jennings says, "There wasn't much, but enough to keep me busy. I traveled periodically to Denver, Phoenix and Seattle.

"I spent most of my time on product development. Wherever I went, the same question would eventually come up: 'Can you make something that will do this?' And, of course, the answer was 'Yes.' I would call Bill on the phone and tell him what was needed. He'd take the assignment to Tom Osborne."

Products developed specifically to meet the needs of Cook customers were among a host of additions to Cook Incorporated's 1968 catalog, including:

- The Desilets-Hoffman Mylar Sheath Set, used to introduce closed-end catheters;
- High delivery rate Aortogram Catheters, which enhanced the capacity to produce radiologic images of the aorta;
- The Lymphangiographic Catheter Set, used for radiologic procedures for the lymphatic system and lymph nodes;
- The Gianturco Duodenal Intubation Set, which made it easier to perform hypotonic duodenographies, or X-rays of the duodenum (a part of the small intestine);
- Wire guides of different diameters with variable-length flexible tips, which doctors could use when they encountered tortuously twisted blood vessels.

Those and many other tools, including instruments developed for Jennings' customers, reflected the company's growing confidence in its ability

Ross Jennings, left, with Bill Cook, joined the company two years after it moved to South Curry Pike, opposite. Deployed to California, he was Cook's link to leading medical centers west of the Mississippi River.

4 8 SNOWING IN CHICAGO

In collaboration with Dr. Sidney Wallace at the University of Texas, Dr. Cesare Gianturco developed many kinds of embolizing devices that could be percutaneously inserted to treat disorders ranging from gastrointestinal bleeding and blood vessel malformations to nosebleeds. Sprouting cotton fibers in various configurations, they were nicknamed "cotton tails" and "wooly tails."

to serve multiple medical disciplines. But they had an even greater significance: they were among the earliest signs in the United States of a move toward interventional products for therapeutic applications—the tidal wave that Dotter had unleashed upon medicine four years earlier.

COOK INVADES EUROPE

Given that Dr. Dotter's PTA procedure had immediately caught on in Europe, it made sense for Cook Incorporated to have a European presence. The market for innovative interventional equipment was growing much more rapidly there than in the United States, and Bill Cook was anxious to take advantage of it. His conduit to Europe was a Canadian named Don Wilson, about whom Bill once declared, "Don loved to sell! He was always there to make that first sale in the morning, always had a smile on his face."

Wilson owned a business called Cardiovascular Specialties, a medical supplies distributor based in Toronto. Wilson knew Bill Cook because he had been importing Cook products for distribution in Canada. He was also importing heart-lung oxygenation equipment from a Danish firm called Polystan. Both Wilson and Polystan's owner, Erik Kyvsgaard, knew Bill Cook wanted to move into the European market, so it was only natural for them to get together and discuss their mutual interests.

As Bill Cook explained in a 1980 interview, he zeroed in on Denmark because he found the Danes to be like Americans in a number of important respects. "Their sense of humor is very similar to ours," he noted. "They speak English very well. Unlike Americans, they speak many languages. They have a fine work ethic. And surprisingly, even though you hear that it's an expensive place to do business, corporations do very well in Denmark."

In 1968 Cook and Wilson met with Kyvsgaard in Denmark. The three reached an agreement, and a year later William Cook Europe was launched to develop, manufacture and distribute Cook devices to meet the demand for quality medical products in Europe and other foreign markets. A manufacturing facility in Polystan's plant in Denmark ensured that the new subsidiary always had a handy supply of the products it needed for the European market. Chris Simonsgaard, Cook's first employee with Polystan, later became William Cook Europe's managing director, guiding its growth.

Once Cook Incorporated had established a beachhead in Europe, it quickly invaded the rest of the continent. Over the next few years lawyer Dan Sterner played an essential role in the expansion, helping Cook set up and incorporate sales offices all over Europe. Much later he helped Cook establish manufacturing facilities in Ireland and England.

Remembering the company's initial foray into Europe, Sterner recalls that, "The U.S. wasn't welcomed with open arms. Not that foreign countries were

In 1968 Don Wilson, below left, who had been distributing Cook's products in Canada for several years, introduced Bill Cook to Erik Kyvsgaard, head of the Danish company Polystan, setting the stage for Cook's advance into Europe. Below, the first headquarters of William Cook Europe, located in Søborg, Denmark.

Productive collaborations with medical giants such as Dr. Sidney Wallace, left, and Dr. Charles Dotter, right, below with Ross Jennings, fueled Cook's growth in the 1970s. By 1972 the company, not yet a decade old, was employing 160 people —eight times the 1966 workforce.

hostile to us, but every nation had different legal and regulatory requirements that had to be carefully researched and addressed. We had to be extremely cautious about dotting our *i*'s and crossing our *t*'s."

Creation of the European Union some 20 years hence eventually helped resolve the problem of local issues immensely. But for the time being, the company's presence in Denmark was essential, says Sterner. "In Europe it was much easier to sell products manufactured in Denmark than in Bloomington, mostly because there was no 30 percent duty levied on products made in Europe."

EXPLOSIVE GROWTH BEGINS

Back in the United States great medical minds were developing more tools of the future—devices that continued to both revolutionize medicine and create more markets for Cook Incorporated. Dr. Dotter was experimentally demonstrating the possibility of successful intraluminal stenting—placing in an artery a tiny metal mesh scaffold called a stent that could be expanded to counter stenosis or restenosis, the narrowing of the vessel or its collapse once it had been opened. Dr. Gianturco, four years into his relationship with M. D. Anderson in Texas, was about to perform the world's first balloon angioplasty—inflating a tiny balloon on the tip of a catheter within a clogged artery to open it.

Like many of the changes that were occurring at Cook, the company's European presence represented the vanguard of sweeping change. In this case it was the first outpost beyond the borders of the United States in what would soon become a global network.

Though Cook Incorporated would migrate far from its humble roots in Indiana over the next decade and a half, Bill Cook insists there was no strategic plan behind those developments. Rather, "as market opportunities abroad presented themselves, the company would move quickly to take advantage of them," he says. That has been characteristic of his sometimes swashbuckling approach to business throughout his career.

By early 1972, when the South Curry Pike plant was being expanded for the third time since 1967, Cook Incorporated had 112 workers. Only six years earlier the company had employed just 20 people. Bill had once speculated that he might have a workforce of 100 by 1978—and it was, he thought at the time, a remarkably optimistic projection. He had started the company in 1963, envisioning it supporting himself and maybe two or three other people. The company had grown at such an unexpectedly robust pace that he now told *Bloomington Courier Tribune* reporter Mike Hinant that he believed he'd have 150 employees by midsummer 1972. In fact, by the end of 1972 there were 160 employees, and the company's catalog had become a 98-page book featuring 24 different categories of equipment. Cook was shipping products that allowed doctors to perform 2,000 cardiovascular catheterizations per day.

When Cook told the *Courier Tribune*, "We have a backlog [of orders] of about six to eight weeks," he wasn't exaggerating. That statistic served momentarily as a symbol of the company's success—but the company's increasingly inefficient production soon emerged as a greater threat than the coiling machine dilemma in 1966.

For the time being, however, things couldn't have been much better or busier. Cook and Kanne had their hands full, and Bill realized it was time to recall Ross Jennings from California. Jennings' new responsibilities in Bloomington covered both sales and product development—a role that overlapped those of Kanne and of Cook, who was devoting most of his time now to collaborating with Tom Osborne on new products.

Announcing the 1972 facilities expansion, Bill Cook also let it be known that the company had purchased more than nine acres of land just north of the South Curry Pike complex. Sabin, like its parent company, needed to grow to meet demand, and the plastic extrusion operation moved to that new parcel of land.

Things were not rosy in Europe, however. The joint venture in Denmark between William Cook Europe and Polystan, just four years old, had soured. Bill and Gayle and their son briefly moved to Europe to address the problem. They remained there for two months while Bill expedited the separation of the partners and found new facilities where Cook's European operation could grow without constraint.

THE NEW RECEPTIONIST

Almost incidental to all of the changes was a moment of historic significance that must have seemed rather prosaic at the time. With Miles Kanne's office responsibilities demanding more of his time and taking him away from sales (the job he did best), he advertised for a secretary and receptionist to help lighten his workload.

The company already employed a front-office secretary who handled accounting and payroll and also typed Bill Cook's correspondence, which he drafted in longhand on legal pads. The new secretary would type letters for Kanne and Jennings, both of whom preferred to use a Dictaphone rather than pen and paper. She would also provide important sales support—answering phones, interfacing with customers, recording orders and issuing and tracking invoices.

Launched to serve the needs of radiologists performing percutaneous catheterizations, Cook Incorporated had diversified significantly by its tenth anniversary.

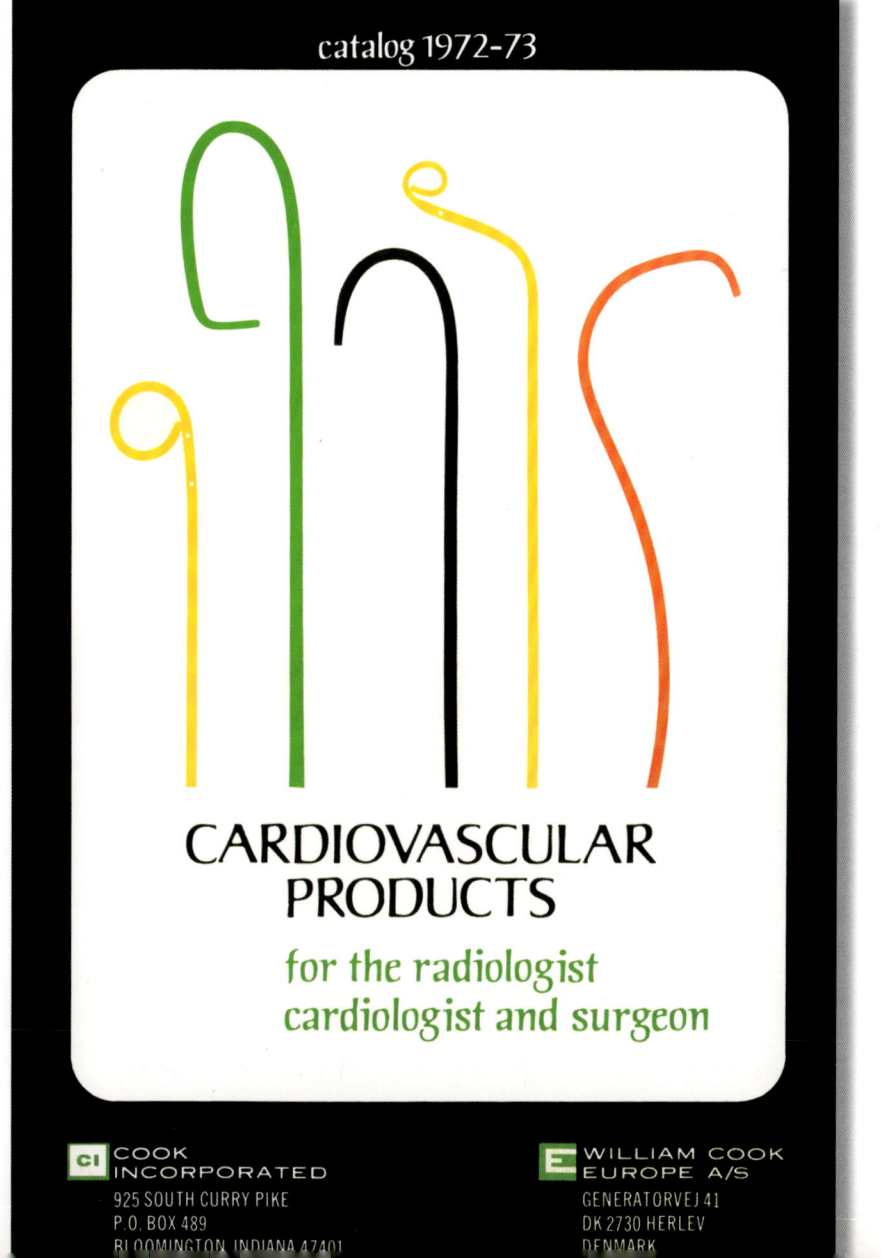

The job called for someone who was personable, organized and capable of juggling a lot of balls at once. On a Monday in late June 1972 a petite brunette came to Cook Incorporated to be interviewed. The interview went well, and she was given a tour of the plant. By the time she returned to the front office, where she met Jennings and Cook, it was clear they had found Kanne's secretary. She was offered the job, and she accepted it instantly.

The new employee was Phyllis McCullough, and her first day on the job was Wednesday, June 29, 1972, two days after her interview. She made an impression right from the start. It quickly became clear that she would not remain a secretary and receptionist for long. She was ambitious and smart and, as everyone soon found out, she had a lot to offer Cook Incorporated.

Phyllis McCullough, right, joined Cook Incorporated in 1972 as an executive secretary but soon demonstrated that she had the right stuff for a great role in the company. Above, an array of Cook products was displayed in the production department circa 1970.

"THE GOODNESS OF HIS HEART"

When the Greater Bloomington Chamber of Commerce held its annual meeting at the Poplars Research and Conference Center on April 16, 1973, Cook Incorporated was less than three months from celebrating its tenth anniversary. The business that Bill and Gayle Cook had founded with $1,500 was by then a $4 million operation and had awarded over $150,000 to researchers in the field of cardiovascular disease.

As if to address any lingering doubts that Cook Incorporated was no longer Bloomington's best kept secret, the chamber was honoring the company at the event. "Bloomington is fortunate to have a firm like Cook Incorporated located here," Bloomington's *Daily Herald-Telephone* opined the next morning, "not only because of the economic contribution it makes to the community but because of its willingness to play the role of good corporate citizen as well."

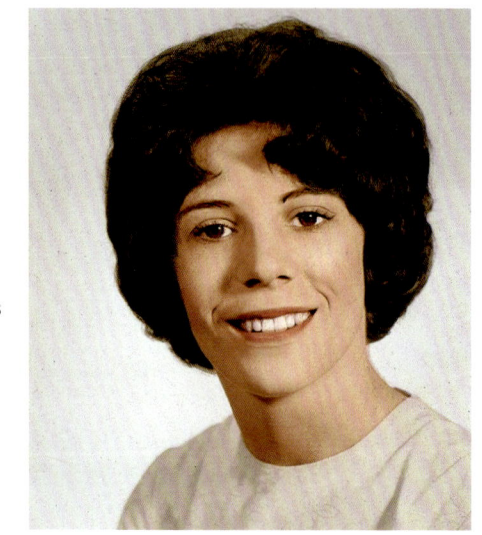

Indiana Lieutenant Governor Robert Orr and Dr. Charles Dotter were in town to offer their congratulations. Dotter, who had by then acquired a reputation for his bloodless surgery, was a featured speaker at the event, and he told the 300 guests that cardiovascular disease was one of "the prime problems for medicine to tackle" and "a major cause of aging." Half of the people attending the dinner that evening, he warned, would die of strokes, heart attacks, arteriosclerosis and related diseases.

Then he said he had never met a manufacturer who had done so much for American medicine "out of the goodness of his heart" as Bill Cook. The cardiovascular disease problem "is as much under assault by Cook Incorporated as by any doctor I know," he added. Thanks to Cook, "There is now no need for surgery in many cases that ten years ago would have [required] major abdominal surgery. Surgery should never be used to find out something. It should be used to fix something."

Hans Timmermans, Connie Boruff, Beth Ann Kirts, Patty Arnett and Frank Parrish, left to right, made up Cook's research and development staff in the late 1970s.

Chapter Four: 1973-1977

Growing Pains

Many eminent physicians contributed to the design and introduction into modern medicine of balloon-tipped catheters such as these. Among them were Cesare Gianturco, Charles Dotter and Andreas Grüentzig, all of whom collaborated with Cook Incorporated.

Gene DeVane might have been a bird in a former life. Built wiry, he moves with easy grace, as though he might be able to defy gravity through the sheer lightness of his spirit. Though he served in the Air Force, he learned to fly as a civilian. Once he got his pilot's license he bought an airplane as soon as he could. After that he flew whenever he got the opportunity. He didn't need an excuse to get up among the clouds, though Cook Incorporated gave him the best excuse he could ask for: a job in sales.

Gene had a special rapport with other pilots. That's how he met Bill Cook. Long before their professional relationship, they were, as DeVane puts it, "flying buddies." Cook and DeVane were alike in many other ways, also. They had a knack for sizing people up quickly, they didn't like to waste anyone's time or have their own wasted and they shared an interest in science and technology.

After completing his military service, DeVane worked for many years as a laboratory technician. By the time he met Bill Cook, though, he thought his medical technology career was behind him. He worked as an air traffic controller in Bloomington and Terre Haute. He also had opened a record store in Bloomington, and he liked his new life.

Cook, on the other hand, saw DeVane as a sales representative. He liked DeVane's personality and work ethic. The two men met at one of those moments when life trajectories intersect to mutual advantage. Cook needed to grow his sales team, and DeVane was precisely the kind of man Bill wanted representing his company.

DeVane wasn't so sure. "Before I got into sales at Cook, I always thought of sales representatives as guys who went door-to-door selling vacuum cleaners," he remembers. "I really didn't think I'd be interested in that. When I came to Cook, though, it was entirely different. What we did, I didn't call it selling. I thought of it as going out and doing something for the patient. We knew patients would be best served if we came up with a good product."

It didn't take him long to fall in love with his work. As he came to understand the company's product line, DeVane also made a point of teaching himself about human anatomy, learning the subject so well, he says, that he probably knew it better than some of the doctors he met with regularly. He met with a lot of them. "I set a personal goal to call on no fewer than four people every day," he remembers. That kind of work ethic became the standard for every successful Cook sales representative.

In 1971, when Ross Jennings returned to Indiana, Brian Bates, right, was hired to serve the vast western territory Jennings had served since 1968. Above, Tom Bowen, Staffan Grigholm, Gene DeVane, Jerry Williams, Wayne Vaughan, Frank Longson and Rick Grenfell, left to right, were among the young hotshots recruited around the same time to boost sales.

THE NEW LIONS

DeVane was the first of a new generation of sales representatives who joined the company at the dawn of the 1970s. He came to work for Cook Incorporated just after Ross Jennings returned to Indiana.

Jennings' replacement in California was a transplanted Midwesterner named Brian Bates. Bates had been working in a Stanford cardiovascular research lab for four years when he met Jennings at a dinner on the first night of the annual American Heart Association meeting in Anaheim in the autumn of 1971.

Bates knew about Cook Incorporated, and he told Jennings that he was looking for a job. Jennings was so impressed with the young man that he invited him to breakfast the next morning, where Miles Kanne joined them. Bates was working for Cook three weeks later.

Based in Palo Alto, Bates was supported by Stanco Medical, a distribution company that represented Cook products in California. Stanco did a good job, but it was the last such company Cook Incorporated would work with in the United States. Bill Cook had terminated relationships with similar distributors in 1972. He realized that to be able to control the destiny of his growing company he needed a team of sales representatives who worked directly with doctors—just as he, Kanne and Jennings had done, building durable relationships and cutting out the middlemen.

DeVane took over a big chunk of Kanne's old territory, covering Indiana, Ohio, Michigan, Wisconsin and part of Missouri. Unlike Kanne, he used his plane to get to most of his meetings, which considerably increased his productivity. "It was a lot of fun," he recalls. "I loved flying."

The sales force of which DeVane found himself a member was a growing pride of hungry young lions that included Wayne Vaughan covering the southern states, Tom Bowen in the mid-Atlantic region, Henry Kahn in the Northeast and Dale Chamness in the Midwest. In January 1973 that group was augmented by two more.

One was Staffan Grigholm, a young Swede who had migrated to the United States at the age of 25 to work for O'Neill International, a large New York marketing firm that represented U.S. medical and dental companies in Europe. It was in this role that he had become acquainted with Cook Incorporated, an O'Neill client. When Bill Cook became increasingly interested in establishing a presence in Europe, Grigholm traveled as an O'Neill representative to Bloomington to meet with Cook, Kanne and Jennings.

Impressed with Grigholm's work, Bill took him aside in 1972 and told him that his goal was to make Cook Incorporated a $100 million-a-year company. Achieving that goal would require success in Europe.

Cook asked Grigholm if he would ever consider returning to Sweden or other parts of Europe to work. It was not something Grigholm had been actively considering, but just after Labor Day Kanne called him and offered him a sales management job in Europe. Coincidentally, Grigholm's boss, Oscar O'Neill, had offered him a position just half an hour earlier as manager of O'Neill International's office in Brussels. O'Neill's offer was attractive, but after six years at the firm Grigholm was ready for a change. "I was interested in the clinical aspects of Cook's business," he says.

The following week, he flew to Denmark to start training for his new post in Düsseldorf from which he would guide Cook's move into Germany, Austria and Switzerland. Bill Cook, already in Denmark, met him at the airport. The day Grigholm returned to Scandinavia was a happy one for him—it was his mother's birthday.

The second sales representative to join the Cook team early in 1973 was Frank Longson, the man who had first laid skeptical eyes on Bill Cook a decade earlier at the Radiological Society conference. In the ten years since that historic meeting, Longson's company, Ensco, had grown to the point where it had catheter laboratory monitors in many hospitals around the United States—but

The women in one of Cook's production departments gather for a group photo. They are, left to right, Cleo McGruder, Linda Kelly, Edna Costello Clark, Patty Fisher, Jean Prince, Marylou Garrison Boger and Carol Ellett. Cook Incorporated was expanding at a brisk pace and had become a job-creation machine in central Indiana.

THE GRAND OLD MAN

A scientist and inventor of protean intellect, Dr. Cesare Gianturco joined the Carle Clinic in Champaign, Illinois, in 1934 and remained there until 1968, when he "retired" at the age of 63—only he didn't retire. He simply moved to the University of Texas' M. D. Anderson Hospital and Tumor Institute in Houston, and there, with support from Cook Incorporated, he spent the next two decades imagining entirely new medical technologies and turning his ideas into products.

As Bill Cook recalls, the first time he met Dr. Cesare Gianturco was when he was invited to Gianturco's house. Cook and his son, Carl, arrived to an astounding sight. The doctor was mowing his lawn, seated on a small riding mower, impeccably attired in a suit and tie and a hat. Where Charles Dotter had a flair for the outrageous, Gianturco was the soul of decorum—but when it came to innovation, the two men were cut from the same fabric.

Gianturco was one of those rare souls whose greatest achievements occurred during the last years of his life. Retirement from the Carle Clinic in 1968 seemed to liberate him to express his genius in a protean burst of creativity.

Born in Naples, Italy, in 1905, Gianturco was 25 years old when he arrived in the United States, having completed medical school at the University of Naples and residencies in radiology, at the University of Rome, and pathology, at the University of Berlin. After completing postgraduate work in radiology and physiology at the University of Minnesota and a radiology fellowship at the Mayo Clinic, he became a founding member and chief of radiology at the Carle Clinic, where he remained until 1968.

After he retired from the Carle Clinic and joined the M. D. Anderson Hospital and Tumor Institute in Houston, he began to devise a startling array of simple, easy-to-use solutions to profoundly complex medical challenges—solutions that would garner him the gold medal of the Radiological Society of North America in 1970.

Dr. Gianturco's collaboration with Cook Incorporated was one of the most profitable and mutually gratifying relationships in the company's history. With Cook support, Gianturco spent his last 27 years doing what he loved most: solving complex problems. In the bargain, he birthed such revolutionary devices as:

- the Gianturco-Wallace Chemotherapy Pulser, a pump to more efficiently deliver chemotherapy drugs and simultaneously reduce patient discomfort (regulatory demands were so onerous that Cook never marketed and sold the product);
- the Cook-Z Stent, whose patented, novel zigzag construction could be tightly compressed for easy insertion into an artery but immediately expanded once the catheter was removed (this basic design is the design used for all intravascular stents and stent grafts manufactured today);
- the Gianturco-Roehm Bird's Nest Vena Cava Filter, a percutaneously inserted device short enough to accommodate the challenging physiological configuration of the vena cava, a large vein that carries deoxygenated blood to the heart, and capable of filtering clots without impeding blood flow;
- Occluding Spring Emboli, a safe and permanent new material that was easily introduced percutaneously through a catheter to treat arteriovenous malformations, gastrointestinal bleeding, neoplasms of the uterus and kidney, epistaxis (nosebleed) and other conditions;
- the Gianturco-Roubin Flex-Stent Coronary Stent, the world's first intravascular coronary stent.

Up until the age of 87 Gianturco was still tinkering with percutaneous instruments for a variety of applications, sending prototypes to Tom Osborne at Cook and testing the new devices in his laboratory at M. D. Anderson. He passed away in 1995 at the age of 90.

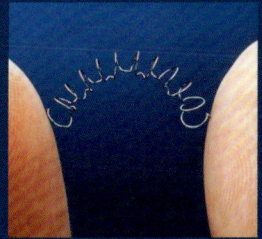

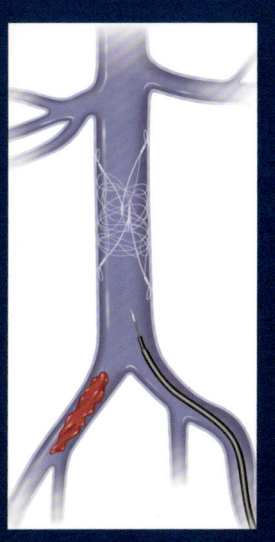

Among the many inventions to spring from the fertile imagination of Dr. Cesare Gianturco were, clockwise from top left, the Chemotherapy Pulser, the Flex-Stent, the Bird's Nest Vena Cava Filter and embolization coils.

Wayne Vaughan, Frank Longson, Kem Hawkins, Dexter Elkins and Miles Kanne, left to right, pause for a moment to have their photo snapped at one of the many national professional association meetings that Cook people have always made it a practice to attend.

around 1970 the business took a turn for the worse, and Longson sold out.

Bill Cook's company, on the other hand, had prospered beyond anyone's dreams. In December 1972 Longson, looking for work, flew to Indiana to meet with his old friend, Miles Kanne. Like Gene DeVane, Longson was a Cook Incorporated kind of guy. He had the right personality and the right work ethic. He knew medical technology, and he was well known and highly regarded in the industry.

"Bill wanted me to move," Longson recalls, "but I told him I was committed to staying in Salt Lake City." He had a big family—five kids—and he was firmly rooted in his hometown. So Cook accommodated his needs. Like Jennings, Longson joined Cook Incorporated with responsibility for virtually the entire American West, though he would manage that vast territory from Utah. Bates handled California and the rest of the West Coast, a big market on its own.

"Bill Cook's philosophy was family first, job second," Longson says. "I remember being with him years later at another convention in Chicago. We had a big convention booth by then. We were talking about how I came to work for the company, and I thanked him for being so considerate about my family. He attributed his loyal workforce to that philosophy."

HAS THE COMPANY PEAKED?

Phyllis McCullough's job title may have been secretary and receptionist, but what she really became passionate about was sales and sales service. "I knew nothing about Cook or about the products when I came to work," she says, but she learned very quickly as she interacted with customers, took their orders and helped them when they had complaints. Soon those customer complaints would occupy her attention to a degree she could never have imagined.

"We were concentrating our sales greatly on teaching hospitals," she remembers, "so that when residents left to go into practice they went with the Cook catalog. They took into their practice the tools they were used to working with."

McCullough found the product line interesting and the work gratifying. She liked being back in the bustle of business again. So the last thing she expected little more than a month after starting her new job was to learn that she was pregnant. She had no choice but to apprise Cook, Jennings and Kanne of her condition. "They wanted to know if I planned to come back to work," she remembers, "and I assured them I did."

Kanne asked her again just before the winter holidays. "When I told him I was sure I was going to come back to work after my baby was born, he said that when I did he wanted me to take over as office manager," she remembers. Her child was born in February 1973, and, true to her word, she returned to work a month later. In her new role she went on to reorganize the growing front office and manage personnel issues. Even in the short span of her maternity leave, the company seemed to have grown.

Bill Cook didn't share that perspective. He was convinced that the business had reached a plateau. Years later he would recall, "I existed in Bloomington, Indiana, from 1963 until about 1973 without a physician in our town knowing what Cook Incorporated did. That's how little was known about angiographic techniques and dilation and intervention procedures. Between 1963 and 1973 only about 400 to 500 people in the United States and maybe another 500 in the world were doing these procedures routinely."

Even in Europe, where doctors had now been "dottering" for several years, it seemed to Bill that the novelty of the procedure was wearing off. "He returned from Denmark and told me there were approximately 1,200 physicians trained in angiography," McCullough says. "He thought everybody who was going to be doing angiography was doing it already. There were only so many who could perform the procedure, he said. He thought the company had probably peaked in size."

Bill could not have been more wrong. Had the utility of catheters remained exclusively in the realm of diagnostics, his assessment might have been accurate. The company he and Gayle founded a decade earlier had earned the respect of physicians around the world—and even if Cook Incorporated stopped growing, the business might have remained stable for years to come. But everything was about to change, and, as though to prove Bill wrong, his workforce kept getting bigger. If the market was stagnating, it certainly wasn't evident in the company's meteoric growth.

SELF-INSURANCE AND MORE GROWTH

Obtaining product liability insurance had always been a challenge for Cook Incorporated. By 1971 the cost of insurance had become astronomical, and Cook was having difficulty finding a company that would offer coverage.

Phyllis McCullough, below with Dr. Charles Dotter, joined Cook on the cusp of a phenomenal, decade-long expansion and moved quickly beyond her original position as a secretary and receptionist. In 1973 she became office manager, displaying a skill at management that set the stage for greater responsibility to come.

Bloomington's Cochran House became the home of Monroe Guaranty Insurance Company in 1979. It was the first of many historic Indiana buildings that Bill and Gayle Cook restored. Their philosophy: don't merely preserve old buildings as antiquities; put them back into productive use.

So that year, Cook founded Northern Financial & Guaranty Company, Ltd. It was an insurance company based in Bermuda to take advantage of that country's laws on self-insurance. For the next three years Northern Financial & Guaranty would satisfy Cook's product liability needs. However, the IRS contested the premiums the company was sending to the Bermuda operation.

The issue became moot when, in 1974, the insurance company had grown sufficiently large to be moved back to Indiana and operate as an entity distinct from Cook Incorporated, even though it continued to insure Cook. Under Phil Hathaway's leadership, it became Monroe Guaranty Insurance Company. In the mid-1970s the IRS ruled that insurance agencies had to take at least 50 percent of their risk from non-affiliated firms. Monroe Guaranty then partnered with a general insurance agency in Indianapolis to share the risk and take on more property and casualty lines; it quickly established a network of more than 100 agents throughout Indiana.

In 1979 the general agency partnership was no longer required, and Monroe Guaranty moved into the historic James Cochran House in Bloomington, which had been purchased and restored by Bill and Gayle Cook. There it remained until the mid-1990s, when it moved its offices to Carmel, Indiana, and was led by former Indiana State Insurance Director Pete Hudson. Sold to its employees in 1991, by which time it had annual sales of nearly $50 million, Monroe Guaranty continued to insure Cook Group until 1995.

In the face of the dramatic explosion of business in the early 1970s, Cook needed to bolster the executive management team yet again. So in 1973 Cook transferred Brian Bates from California to Bloomington, where he assumed responsibility for sales—overseeing the team that now included Kahn, Bowen, Vaughn, Longson and DeVane—as well as new-product development. Staffan Grigholm, who had been back in Europe for less than a year, returned to the United States to take Bates' place in California.

Bates' first order of business was to create marketing materials. The company's trade-show booth was by then somewhat more sophisticated than the simple table Bill Cook manned at his first show, back in 1963. It still fit entirely in a suitcase—convenient but hardly impressive. "The company had no product literature,"

Bates recalls. "When the sales representatives went out to meet new customers, all they had to take with them was the catalog." So he started creating sheets on a per-need basis for each product. It was the first new marketing communications literature in a decade.

At about the same time, Cook launched two more companies. The first was Cook Canada Inc. Its president was Don Wilson, the man who had hooked Bill up with Polystan, the Danish firm. Wilson's company, Cardiovascular Specialties, had been promoting and distributing Cook products in Canada for several years, but Cook Incorporated's growing sales force reflected Bill's determination to sell his products directly wherever possible. With a warehouse and distribution center, Cook Canada now gave him that capacity north of the border.

The other company Cook created in 1973 was a new needle manufacturing operation with his old partner Brian Baldwin, who had remained at the helm of MPL. The new venture was soon saddled with legal problems, however, when Affiliated Hospital Products sued Cook and Baldwin, claiming they had stolen trade secrets. The subsequent litigation was protracted, stretching into 1983. Though it taxed the energies of the litigants, it also resulted in Cook's acquiring exciting new subsidiary companies—Baxa Corporation and K-Tube Corporation—that further extended the company's reach. Moreover, it would compel the creation of a new umbrella entity, Cook Group, to oversee the company's growing portfolio of businesses.

THE SUGAR BOWL SCARE

For Cook Incorporated 1973 was a momentous year, and, as it wound down, Bill Cook looked forward to a special opportunity to celebrate. Steve Ferguson had tickets to the Sugar Bowl football game at Tulane Stadium in New Orleans, and it could not have shaped up as a better entertainment package.

For starters, the contestants were Alabama and Notre Dame, coached by two legends, Bear Bryant and Ara Parseghian. Both clubs had completed their regular seasons undefeated, and top-ranked Alabama was favored to win the national title. To make things even more exciting, the game was being played on New Year's Eve. Postgame festivities couldn't help but be spectacular. Cook, Ferguson and their wives looked forward to a great experience.

The trip turned out not quite as planned. The flight was smooth, and they arrived on time. The game lived up to advance billing—a nip-and-tuck affair that found Notre Dame leading by a score of 21 to 17 at the start of the fourth quarter, before a touchdown followed by a muffed kick put Alabama up, 23–21. Then, with 4:26 remaining, Notre Dame kicked a field goal to edge 'Bama by one point—a thrilling performance that ended up clinching the national title for the Fighting Irish.

By that time, however, Bill wasn't really focused on the game. He had begun to experience pain in his chest and shortness of breath. He guessed it was his heart, and the next day, after a restless night in New Orleans,

Determined to control the destiny of his company, Bill Cook began establishing Cook operations all over the world in the 1970s. One of the first such entities was Cook Canada, above, which he created in 1973 with Don Wilson.

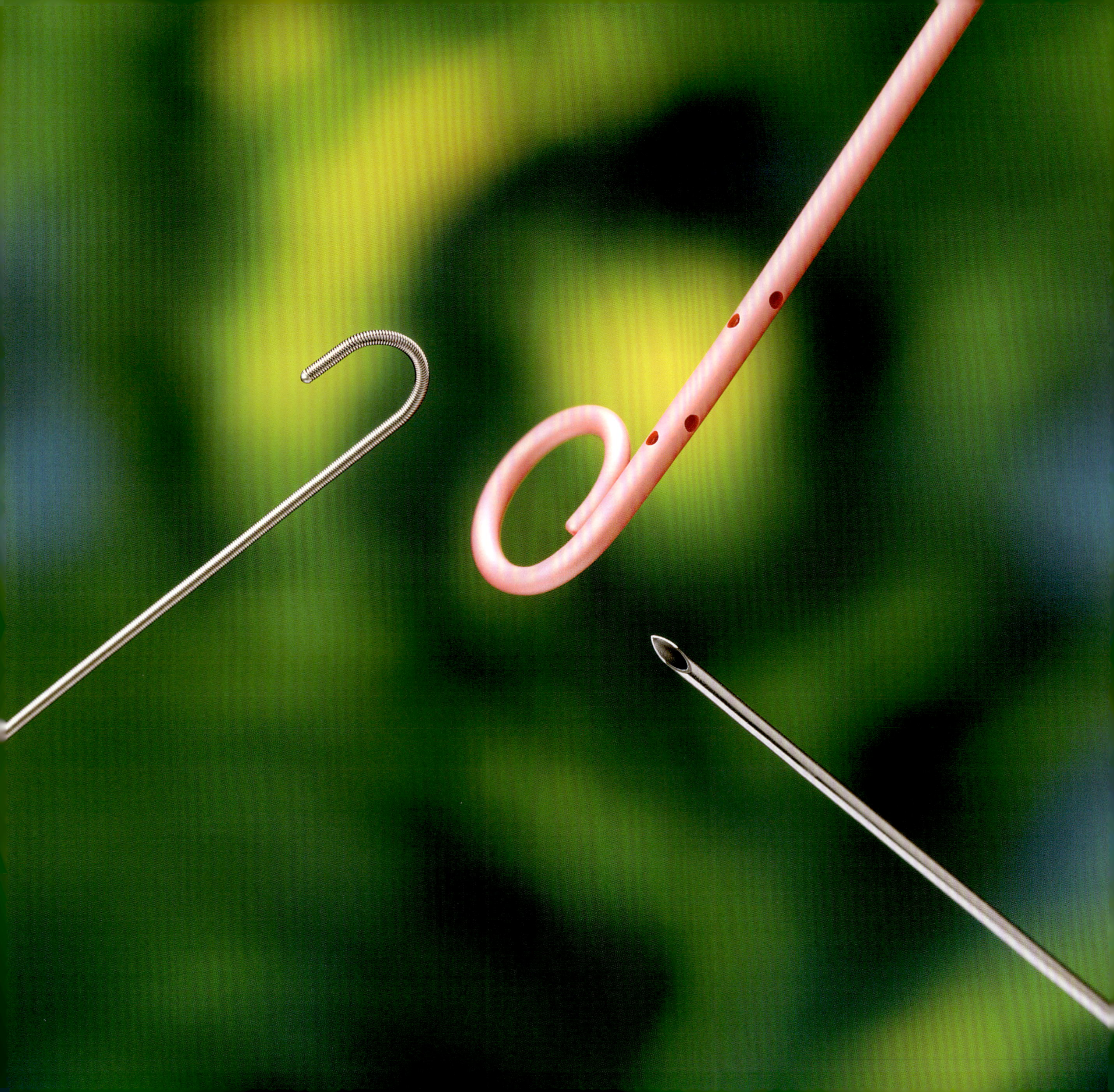

"IF IT'S HELPFUL, IT'S GOING TO SELL ITSELF"

Today if a company like Cook Incorporated wants to introduce a new medical tool—especially a product that falls in the FDA's Class III category, such as an implant or a heart valve for a procedure that is potentially life-threatening—the product development process can take the better part of a decade, from concept and design through testing to meet regulatory muster. Class I products, which have little potential to harm consumers, are often simply designed and are marketed under "General Control," the FDA's least restrictive category. Class II products are somewhat more complex and require additional regulatory controls. The FDA demands pre-market approval for Class III, including a thorough medical and scientific review of the device's safety and effectiveness.

But in the wild and wooly, pre-regulatory era of the 1960s and early 1970s, Cook was churning out new products at the breakneck clip of one every couple of weeks. Here's how it happened: A Cook sales representative consulted with a doctor who would tell him about some gadget he needed. The sales representative took notes and called the idea in to Bloomington, where a member of the executive team—sometimes Bill Cook, sometimes Miles Kanne, later Brian Bates—would take notes and then hand the idea off to one of the workers in the production area.

"An hour or two later you could expect to have an actual device on your desk," Bates remembers. "Pretty much, whether we proceeded with development of a product depended on whether we were technologically capable of producing it," says Bates.

To illustrate the point, Bates tells a story about an event that happened in the fall of 1973, when he and sales representative Frank Longson made a reconnaissance foray into the world of anesthesiology, attending an American Society of Anesthesiology convention in San Francisco. "We wanted to show anesthesiologists our wire guides and needles and see what they thought," Bates says.

At the time, anesthesiologists were using catheters attached to needles. If the anesthesiologists wanted to introduce a large catheter with their conventional approach, they had to use a large needle. Cook's tools offered significant advantages. With the Seldinger technique, using a wire guide, a large catheter could be introduced through an opening made by a small needle.

"We put our stuff out on the table, and the anesthesiologists would come and take a look at it and, predictably, they would try to put the catheter on the needle," Bates says. "We'd correct them and show them how to insert the catheter using a small needle, and you could see the light go on."

A year later, in Chicago, Bates and Longson went back to the anesthesiology conference. By that time they had made such inroads with this community of physicians that they brought with them a brand-new device developed specifically for their use: the world's first subcutaneous pressure monitoring sets—catheters that could be introduced using the Seldinger technique and used to monitor blood pressure during surgical procedures.

"I had an absolute ball helping to develop products outside our general field of interest," Bates says of those creatively unbridled years before the FDA threw a lasso around the medical technology industry. "Our view was: if it's helpful to the patient, it's going to sell itself. We didn't worry about marketing or sales much. If the product filled a niche, we knew that doctors would talk among themselves, and it would sell."

Opposite, a wire guide, catheter and needle—Cook Incorporated reduced to its least common denominators—seemed to many like equipment from the future when Frank Longson, above, and Brian Bates displayed them at the American Society of Anesthesiology convention in 1973.

the two couples flew back to Indiana. Bill contacted his cousin Dr. Van Fucilla, and they agreed that Cook should come to California right away.

Once he got there, an examination using Cook catheters revealed that Bill had serious blockage of the coronary arteries. Bypass surgery, a life-saving procedure that had been developed at the Cleveland Clinic only a few years earlier, was essential. Cook was 43 years old that year, and for nearly two decades he had been engaged in the business of making products to help people with health problems, particularly those of the heart. Now he had become the patient.

PARTNERING WITH PURDUE

While Bill Cook was recovering from his heart surgery, a major development unfolded at Purdue University that was to have a significant impact upon the fortunes of Cook Incorporated in the years to come. It began when Purdue recruited Dr. Leslie Geddes from Baylor University to establish a biomedical engineering program and develop new technologies in that pioneering field.

Geddes had served as director of Baylor's biomedical engineering department for more than 20 years. A renowned expert on the electrical properties of the cardiovascular system, he conducted groundbreaking research into such subjects as electromyography, cardiac output, cardiac pacing, ventricular defibrillation and blood pressure.

Attracting such a luminary to Purdue was a major coup for the engineering school. Not only did Geddes come to the campus in West Lafayette, Indiana, he brought his entire research team with him. Overnight Purdue had a world-class biomedical engineering program. In the years to come the facility they created (often with financial help from Cook) would more than live up to the promise to develop important new technologies.

Geddes' lab produced dazzling devices. Among them was Bill Cook's idea for a pacemaker to automatically increase a person's heart rate during exercise. The pacemaker technology was licensed by Cook Incorporated in 1981 and received regulatory approval in 1987. Other devices to emerge from Geddes' lab were an automated miniature defibrillator so small it could be implanted within a person's body and a remarkably versatile regenerative tissue extracted from the small intestines of pigs—a bio-wonder that would have seemed like science fiction if anyone had proposed it in 1974. Cook received a license for the tissue, called SIS, from Purdue in 1995 and received the FDA's first regulatory permission to sell it in 1998. By 2006 Geddes and his program had earned 30 patents for their work and generated millions of dollars in royalties for Purdue.

The day Geddes arrived, a graduate student named Neal Fearnot met him at the door and helped his team move into their new facility. It was an auspicious meeting. Fearnot and Geddes would soon become

Recruited to Purdue in 1974, Dr. Leslie A. Geddes—receiving the 2006 Health Care Hero Award from the *Indianapolis Business Journal*, above—collaborated with Cook Incorporated on many medical inventions, including pacemakers, defibrillators and SIS, a natural tissue scaffold for organ repair.

close collaborators. By the time Bill Cook met Geddes in 1976, the scientist was engaged in research on the measurement of blood pressure using catheters—research that so piqued Bill's interest that he underwrote Geddes' work, ensuring a future that boded well for everyone involved.

A PROBLEM WITH PRODUCTIVITY

In 1972 the company had a six- to eight-week backlog of orders, thanks to strong sales and a robust customer base. But by 1976 orders were sometimes delayed for up to three months, indicative of a problem with productivity that became a source of increasing frustration for customers. During 1975 and 1976 Bill Cook doubled the number of employees at Cook in a deliberate effort to improve the situation. But simply increasing the number of workers was not enough, as Cook soon found out. The problem proved to be so complex that solving it took nearly three years, and the culture of the company would be forever altered in the process.

Looking back on that period years later, Miles Kanne observed, "There came a time when it became apparent that the entrepreneurial spirit of the company had to give way to something more controlled."

No one was more intimately involved in that difficult period of transition than Phyllis McCullough, who in 1976 was named customer service manager and charged with fixing problems in production. In a memoir produced for the company's 40th anniversary in 2003, she wrote:

> By 1976 Cook Incorporated was beginning to experience production problems, some internal and some externally caused. Our polyethylene catheters had used lead oxide as the opacifier [a substance mixed into the plastic catheters to make them opaque when they were subjected to X-rays], and the EPA required that lead oxide no longer be used in any products that could potentially cause lead poisoning (Cook catheters did not cause lead poisoning). It was first thought that changing opacifiers would not cause any changes in catheter performance, but this proved to be a wrong assumption. Our catheters, particularly the torque control variety, no longer functioned the same in the user's hands, and that created a customer service nightmare.

The company had no choice but to redesign the product, which was called the Torcon Blue. Since no one was sure what was wrong with the new product, McCullough began a series of interviews in the field to find out what happened. Between June 1976 and the following summer, she traveled all over the United States

Don Wilson, staffing a Cook display in the 1970s, was a salesman par excellence. "Don loved to sell!" Bill Cook once observed. "He was always there to make that first sale in the morning, always had a smile on his face."

"Changes were made in attendance, wage, leave of absence, vacation, holiday, absenteeism—literally every policy we had," McCullough later recalled when she was interviewed for an article on Cook's "innovative employee relations" for Business in Bloomington magazine. *"We wrote them to be easily understood [and] consistently implemented and [to] allow the employee the opportunity for productivity …"*

with Cook pilot Russ East, meeting the company's customers, talking with them about the catheters, watching them use the catheters and bringing her observations back to the team working on the redesign. As often as not she took along a load of products so that, as she retrieved defective catheters, she could instantly replace them with new ones. "It made a big impression with the customers that we cared enough to send someone from Bloomington to meet them face-to-face," she says.

Eventually McCullough's field research led to the development of a more workable tool. However, she says, "The polyethylene catheters were never as satisfactory as before. Only years later, when nylon material was developed for the Australian market, did the torque control catheters regain a healthy worldwide position in that product line."

GETTING TO THE HEART OF THE PROBLEM

As McCullough sought to expeditiously address customers' requests for speedier delivery of their orders, she quickly discerned that Cook Incorporated actually had a much bigger problem on its hands. "I promised our customers that I would address the product delivery problem, but then I'd be unable to get products back to them when I had promised I would," she remembers. "It was very frustrating."

The production department at that time "ruled the plant," she says, but every department—production, quality control, machine shop and front office—had its own manager, "and none of them communicated with each other," she adds. "They operated as independent fiefdoms. It was almost impossible to get anything done quickly." The departments' autonomy was a vestige of the company's entrepreneurial heritage. Once that had given them flexibility; now it was dragging them down. McCullough also discovered that the expanded workforce had developed serious morale problems. A union organization was attempted in the production department, and union leaders were meeting with Cook employees. Something had to be done and quickly.

The first step was to give employees an opportunity to be heard, so in the summer of 1976 McCullough organized a companywide meeting. Employees submitted written questions and concerns, and—in a gathering of all 175 in the courtyard—Bill Cook patiently addressed them one by one and promised changes.

The company then followed up by creating a new position, personnel advisor, whose job would be to listen to employees' concerns and then, with the employees' permission, take their concerns to McCullough to be addressed. The first personnel advisor was Kay Watts, a vivacious individual who had previously managed Cook's production payroll. Recognizing that special skills would be needed to make some of the required changes, McCullough enrolled in a class in Theory Z management, the so-called "Japanese" management style based on the work of W. Edwards Deming, a scholar of management and motivation.

In 1977 McCullough was named executive assistant to Bill Cook and Miles Kanne. She identified the roles of group leader, supervisor and manager and held weekly meetings with the people who were named to those

GROWING PAINS 69

Just as 13 years of hard work were beginning to pay off and Cook Incorporated was experiencing unprecedented growth, the company faced production problems. In 1976 Bill Cook held an "all-hands" meeting with the workforce to give ear to their questions and concerns.

positions. The intent was to bring problems to the surface and teach managers how to function under their responsibilities to employees and to the company. The new leadership group received management training; meanwhile, the personnel advisor worked with employees. Over time, management practices and policies at Cook changed dramatically, and a participatory style of management began to emerge.

"Changes were made in attendance, wage, leave of absence, vacation, holiday, absenteeism—literally every policy we had," McCullough later recalled when she was interviewed for an article on Cook's "innovative employee relations" for *Business in Bloomington* magazine. "We wrote them to be easily understood [and] consistently implemented and [to] allow the employee the opportunity for productivity …" Additionally, she noted, the revised policies enhanced the company's ability to predict costs and plan for growth.

It took time to change the corporate culture, and Phyllis McCullough's refinements did not happen without some fireworks. Some managers left the company, as did some employees. Those who remained came to understand the new policies and, moreover, found them fair. As morale improved, executives were able to establish much more fluid methods for managing and tracking workflow, which dramatically increased the

At Cook Incorporated there has always been room for employees who show up on time, work hard and abide by the Midwestern values that are at the foundation of the company's success.

THE COOK COMPANY PHILOSOPHY

Our company philosophy emphasizes beliefs and attitudes which encourage individual contribution toward the success of the group. To be successful, we must always…

- Produce quality products in a timely manner.
- Maintain a close relationship with customers in order to better serve them.
- Grow through innovation while being aware of what we make and whom we serve.
- Remunerate by sharing the profits of success in a manner that respects the individual in relation to the group.
- Use profit as a standard for measuring excellence.
- Take pride in the company and its achievements.

speed at which the company could produce and ship products to customers.

This was a crucial time, as Congress had just passed the Medical Devices Act, putting medical device companies under the regulation of the U.S. Food and Drug Administration (FDA). This meant that for the first time Cook had to draft formal design documents and procedures for every product line and every variant of every product within the line. Documentation and control were a big part of being FDA-compliant under Good Manufacturing Practice legislation, and it was also required that the company audit these activities and ensure compliance.

In an effort that represented the start of what would evolve into Cook's quality assurance department, employees were selected to write the procedures and implement document control. Jackie Wikle was shifted from production because of her clerical background, and she helped Cook produce and maintain specifications, procedures and documentation of its processes. She later moved on to become the company's second personnel advisor.

McCullough's main job during this time was to keep communication flowing, to make sure that employees had input on what was happening and that they had respect for the work they were accomplishing.

The changes required by the FDA went beyond the administrative; they also included revisions in production procedures. One of them involved sterilization. For years Cook had sterilized its products and sent them directly to customers after sterilization. But the FDA now required the company to quarantine each load of products from the sterilization process until sterilization could be verified by an independent laboratory. This required Cook to separate orders in production into stock orders (those most commonly ordered by most customers) and floor orders (custom devices) for more efficient delivery to customers. Maintaining stock was crucial when quarantining for several days was required.

In 1977 Cook again expanded its South Curry Pike facility with a finished goods warehouse to quarantine and stock products. This change improved the productivity of employees, greatly reducing delays in the shipment of products.

Jackie Wikle, who joined the company in 1977, played an important role in codifying the quality assurance standards that helped Cook address production problems during the mid-1970s. Later she became the company's personnel advisor.

HONORING EMPLOYEES: DINNER AND A NEWSLETTER

The changes of the mid-1970s made clear the importance of having a happy, productive workforce, so Cook's leaders set out to create an atmosphere in which employees would know that the company appreciated their talent, dedication, hard work, loyalty and—in many cases—long service. Employee turnover cost the company in many ways, not least of which was the loss of their experience in hand-crafting the products.

With this in mind Phyllis McCullough convinced Bill Cook to hold an annual awards dinner that would honor all employees with five years or more of service to the company. The first dinner was held in a small banquet room on Bloomington's east side. But it quickly became a company tradition and grew exponentially,

Angio-Gram

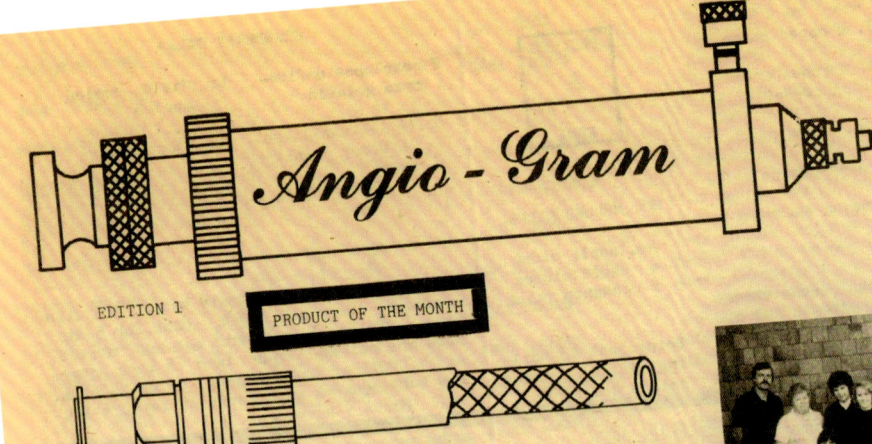

EDITION 1 — **PRODUCT OF THE MONTH** — **DECEMBER 1977**

TORCON BLUE
by Jane Sanders

During the past several months, Cook Incorporated has concentrated mainly on the change-over to an improved Blue TORCON catheter. The necessity for this change came as a result of complaints from our customers that our TORCON catheters were too stiff and would not torque properly. These complaints were primarily from customers in cardiac catheterization laboratories using Judkins coronary catheters.

Due to the tremendous amount of teamwork put forth by everyone at Cook, this change was made possible. Clinical evaluation carried out during the first part of 1977 with the customers who had complained about the old TORCON soon pointed out that we indeed had developed a superior and more competitive product, particularly for coronary catheterizations where our competitors have always had the greatest share of the market. In July, we felt it was time to begin marketing the new product to new customers. I think it will be interesting for all of you to know exactly how these catheters were introduced to various hospitals and how successful the have been, determined by actual sales.

Each of our seven Representatives chose 12 hospitals in their territory which were either Cordis or USCI catheter users. These hospitals would prove to be very beneficial should we be able to convert them to our product. Samples of our new product were sent to the Representatives and taken personally to the hospitals. In most cases the Reps observed the actual procedures and later talked with the doctors about the advantages of our catheter as opposed to either of our competitors.

Below is a list of all of the hospitals which have converted to the Improved Blue TORCON catheter manufactured by Cook Incorporated, and again, this list was compiled by actual sales. Reports at this time indicate that the possibility is very good for the conversion of six additional hospitals not listed.

Hospital	Region	Rep
Vanderbilt U. Hosp.	Southern Region	Wayne Vaughan
Santa Rosa Med. Ctr.	Southern Region	Wayne Vaughan
Hosp. Univ. Penn.	S. E. Region	Tom Bowen
Peninsula Hosp.	Western Region	Jerry Williams
John Muir Hosp.	Western Region	Jerry Williams
D. C. General	S. E. Region	Tom Bowen
Georgia Baptist	Southern Region	Wayne Vaughan
Univ. of Ala.	Southern Region	Wayne Vaughan
VA Hosp. B'ham	Southern Region	Wayne Vaughan
Wash. Hosp. Ctr.	S. E. Region	Tom Bowen
Jewish Hospital	N.E. Region	Staffan Grigholm
St. Mary's, Ks. Cty.	Mountain Region	Frank Longson
St. Paul Hosp.	Vancouver, Can.	Don Wilson
Polyclinic	S. E. Region	Tom Bowen
Latter Day Sts.	Mountain Region	Frank Longson
VA Hosp., Tucson	Mountain Region	Frank Longson
Lackland AFB	South. District	Rick Grenfell
South. Baptist	South. District	Rick Grenfell
Alta Bates Hosp.	Western Region	Jerry Williams
VA Hosp., Dallas	South. District	Rick Grenfell
Pacific Med. Ctr.	Western Region	Jerry Williams
Med. Col. of Ga.	Southern Region	Wayne Vaughan

STANDING LEFT to RIGHT— Jim Heckman, Martha Johnson, Maxine Burch, Nona Flynn, Denice Stephen, Jenny Robertson, Janet Evans, Larry Durnil. SECOND ROW— Dexter Elkins, Sue Zabriskie, Barbara Hanover, Jackie Wikle, Patti Fisher. FRONT ROW— Debi Tosti (editor), Jane Sanders, Teresa Behen, Edna Costello, Linda Kelley, Pam Isom, Carol Miller, Phyllis Maddox.

Seasons Greetings from the ANGIO-GRAM staff. We would like to take this opportunity to explain some of the functions of the paper. Some of the purposes are to open the lines of communications between the various departments of Cook Incorporated, to state the views, ideas, and interests of the employees in different areas. We would like to show you various products that we make, to give you a better understanding of what Cook Inc. is all about.

Please don't hesitate to give us any ideas you might have, such as recipes, advertisements, letters to the editor, gossip, or anything you think might be of interest to others.

We hope you will enjoy reading your paper as much as we enjoy being given the chance to write it.

A CHRISTMAS MIRACLE
by Denice Stephen

All the children at school were excited, it's just one week until Santa comes. But not Tommy, he had nothing to hope for. His mother had told him that Santa only came to visit those who could afford to believe in him. Tommy's family hadn't much money and their home was very little to be proud of. He was always having to withstand the ridicule of the other children. Now it particularly disgusted him to hear the carols about good cheer and christian fellowship. Where was this Christmas spirit? Was it in the brightly lit trees, or in the gayly decorated presents? He had always believed it was much more, but he was beginning to rea-

---

Tom Osborne, opposite, bottom left, with Bill Cook at Cook's first employee awards banquet in 1978, coined the clever name of Cook Incorporated's employee newsletter, the *Angio-Gram*. The newsletter and the annual banquet were among a series of programs introduced to better communicate with employees and boost morale.

along with Cook Incorporated. Although the scale of the event has changed over time, its purpose and central ideas have not. Employees and their spouses are treated to a nice dinner, and honored employees receive a gift. Initially the gift was a Cook keepsake featuring a gemstone; shortly thereafter it included a check from the company honoring the employee's years of service.

The dinner became an overwhelmingly successful way for Cook to recognize the achievements of employees and encourage longevity with the company. By 2007 the Great Dome of the West Baden Springs Hotel and Spa—a Cook real estate property—could barely contain the group, which numbered more than 1,900, including guests.

As part of its effort to better communicate with employees, in December 1977 Cook Incorporated introduced a newsletter. The *Angio-Gram* facilitated communication to a workforce whose diaspora had spread to outposts far remote from the Bloomington headquarters. A relatively new employee named Jim Heckman was tapped to design and produce the publication. A former high-school art teacher, Heckman had come to work at Cook in the summer of 1976 as a draftsman and prototype builder, helping Tom Osborne in the research and development department. It soon became clear that his talent for design extended beyond his initial assignments. When Bill Cook decided that the whole company should have a newsletter, Heckman got the job of starting it up.

Printed in tabloid format on newsprint by a Spencer, Indiana, company, the newsletter spoke compellingly of a company that valued teamwork. The premier issue featured a front-page story saluting the employees who had worked hard in the previous year to retool the Torcon Blue catheters, along with a nod to salespeople who had helped 22 major hospitals across the country convert to the new product. A photo in the *Angio-Gram* showed Heckman and the publication's "staff" wishing all Cook employees happy holidays.

Inside the newsletter was a homey platter of news, recipes, employee birthdays, inspirational advice and classified ads. Future issues would offer photos of—and pats on the back for—employees working together.

Cook workers, above, gathered in Bloomington in 1978 for the company's first employee awards. Every year the banquet pays homage to employees who have been with the company at least five years. In 2008, Cook Incorporated's 45th anniversary, more than 2,200 employees attended.

The *Angio-Gram* was an instant success and was soon followed by an even more concrete demonstration of the company's commitment to honor and reward employees: Cook Incorporated's first employee incentive program. The initial program, launched in February 1978, was based on monthly production; if the company hit the production target, every employee was rewarded with an extra day's pay. But that summer, Cook Incorporated refined the program and replaced the production goal with a monthly sales goal. If company sales exceeded the goal, the company shared the overage with employees. Cook Incorporated also established an annual profit-sharing contribution, with employees' portion based on a ratio of their income as a percentage of the company's total annual payroll.

"We try to find ways to keep people engaged," Bill Cook said, announcing the new plan. "[We try to help] them to be more than they are as individuals."

EMPLOYEES AND MANAGEMENT COME TOGETHER

By the late 1970s McCullough was able to tell *Business in Bloomington*:

> *The employees are willing to work with us, and that eliminates the adversarial relationship. Most of the policies are now in place, are operating, are tied together and interact well. The more an employee is here and working, the greater the opportunities for the employee to increase his or her incentive benefits. The employee has the choice and can control the outcome. Even the pay increases are based on merit. There is an emphasis placed on citizenship: your attitude toward your job and fellow workers. We don't want an employee sitting in the work area complaining to his or her neighbor, because that destroys morale and doesn't solve the problem. We emphasize a positive attitude, cooperation, willingness to work with other people; the employees understand this. It is as important to the job as being a good producer.*

The changes had not come easily, but they could not have come at a better time. The company's initial focus on diagnostic catheterization was about to change, as interventional procedures rapidly became accepted in medicine and the demand for interventional products rose sharply. With that shift in direction, development and sales of Cook products skyrocketed. To meet the sudden demand Cook Incorporated needed a reliable, focused workforce.

The little company Bill and Gayle Cook had founded less than 15 years earlier was on its way to becoming a huge international operation. But it would soon face sweeping changes in the way the U.S. Food and Drug Administration viewed medical technology products—and Cook Incorporated, which had relied on unfettered product innovation as one of its main keys to success, was going to have to play by a whole new set of rules.

The smile on the face of Brenda Akers, building a balloon catheter, says it all: she likes her job. In the mid-1970s, Cook experienced production problems that ultimately led to new programs to incentivize employees and increase morale. Today fully 50 percent of employees have worked for the company for five years or more; 31 percent have been with Cook for ten or more years; and nearly 20 percent have worked at Cook for at least 15 years.

GROWING PAINS   75

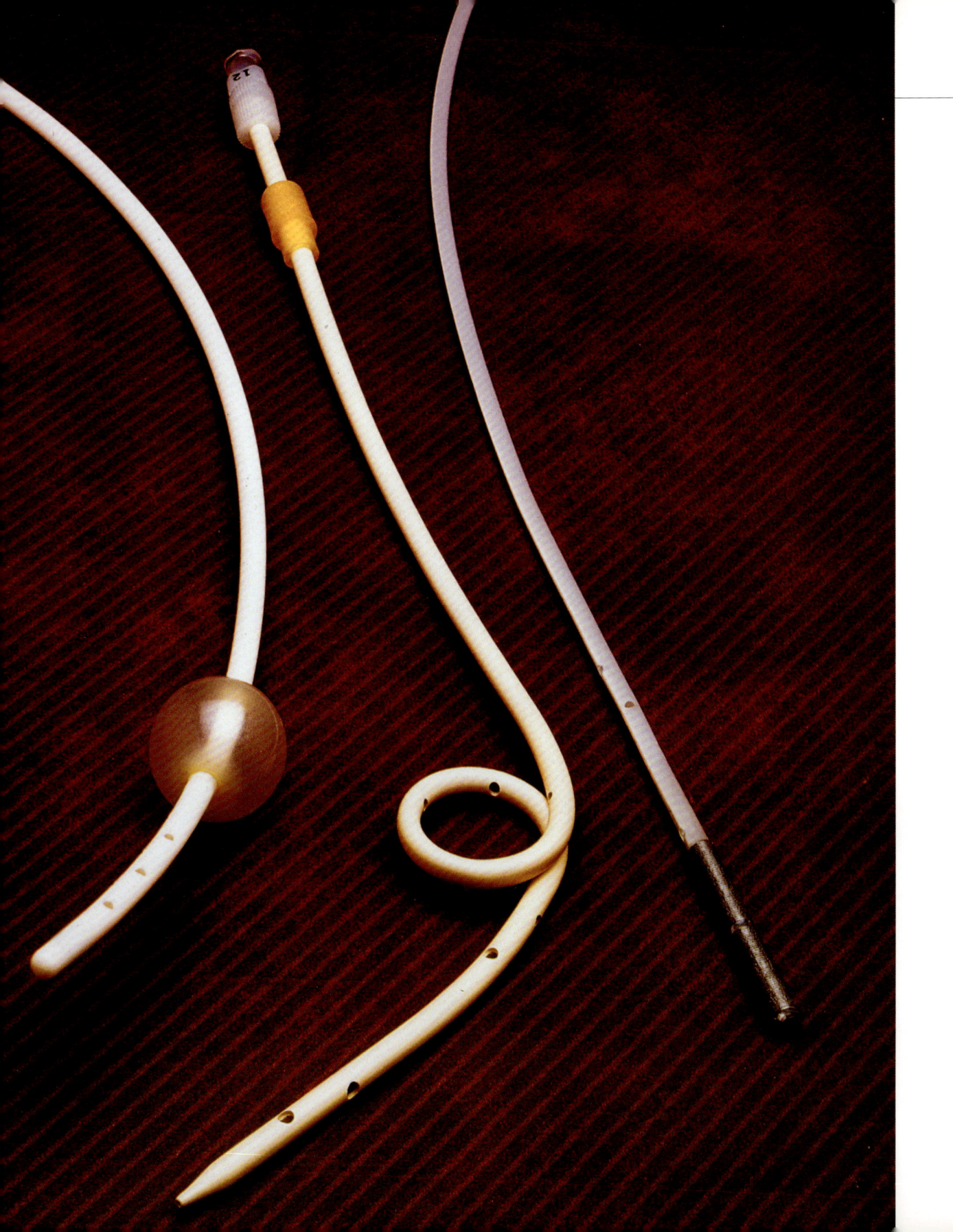

Left to right, the Maglinte
Enteroclysis Catheter Set, the
Wills-Oglesby Percutaneous
Gastrostomy Set and the
McLean-Ring Enteral Feeding
Tube Set are gastroenterology tools developed and
manufactured by Cook
Incorporated.

Chapter Five: 1977–1984

Intervention

An all-hands meeting of employees with Bill Cook in the courtyard of Cook headquarters in the mid-1970s, opposite and right, revitalized the "we're in this together" spirit at Cook. After only a brief pause, the company returned to its pace as a growth juggernaut.

"Cook To Build Plant In Spencer," screamed an eight-column banner across the front page of the *Spencer Evening World* in Spencer, Indiana, on Thursday, March 31, 1977. Accompanying the bold headline was a large photo of key players in the deal transferring 22 acres of land to Cook Incorporated for development on the western edge of the small Owen County community about 20 miles northwest of Bloomington.

Scheduled to open in late 1977, the new facility was expected to initially employ ten to 12 people. Miles Kanne, by then executive vice president of Cook Incorporated, predicted that 100—perhaps as many as 200—might be working there in a decade.

Kanne said the primary reason for the new plant was to separate it from the company's headquarters, reducing the pressure for further expansion of the company's already vast Bloomington facility. Quality-control requirements for Cook's products, he added, were extremely tight, and a small plant like the one planned for Spencer would make it easier to manage such stringent controls. No one at Cook, including Kanne, was saying precisely what would be manufactured there. A subhead in the newspaper article alluded to "special medical devices."

In fact, this was the launch of a new company that would eventually become Cook Urological Inc., an enormously successful entity that advanced Cook Incorporated into a whole new area of medicine—urology (and, later, obstetrics and gynecology)—just as the technologies of endoscopy and laparoscopy were about to revolutionize the field.

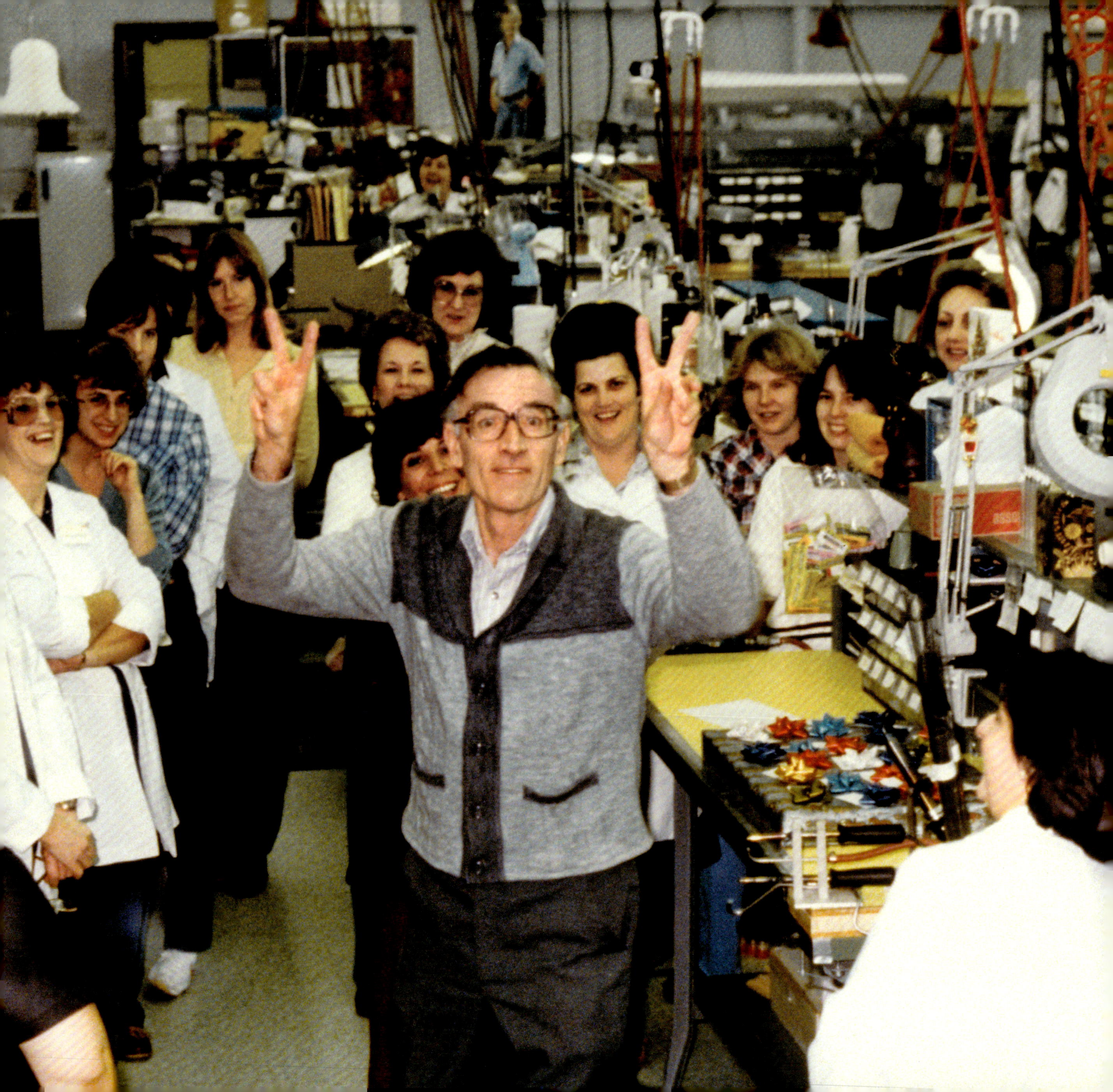

NO REST FOR THE INNOVATIVE

Cook Incorporated's entry into urology began almost accidentally, as a consequence of Bill Cook's heart surgery in 1974. It was while he was recuperating in California that his cousin Van Fucilla introduced Bill to Dr. Al Rutner, a urologist and colleague at El Camino Hospital. Fucilla had heard Rutner railing about the inadequacy of urological equipment more than a few times, and he thought Bill should hear about it. So he brought the two men together at his house.

Fucilla had already talked with Cook about his friend Rutner, and Bill, ever alert to opportunities to expand his company's market, had begun thinking about a tool to percutaneously remove kidney and bladder stones. In fact, Tom Osborne had developed such a tool in 1973. What he lacked was a doctor like Charles Dotter, with whom he could collaborate to design some products to meet urologists' needs.

In Rutner Cook found exactly the man he was looking for. He listened intently as Rutner described ureteral catheters, used to drain kidneys, that were difficult to insert for lack of a flexible tip and that, once inserted, had a nasty habit of falling out—often during the night. While modern catheter equipment, much of it developed and produced by Cook Incorporated, had dramatically improved the quality of care in other medical fields, urology had not been a beneficiary of those advances.

Rutner remembers, "There was nothing on the market." Doctors often fashioned catheters by taping several components together and then used tape to hold catheters in place. "It was all Rube Goldberg," he says. Grateful for Bill's sympathetic ear, Rutner went on at some length, running down a litany of equipment deficiencies. Finally, Rutner remembers, "Bill said, 'Sounds like you have several instruments in mind. Why don't you focus on the three that bug you the most, make some drawings and tell us about the problems and your potential solutions.'"

Rutner took him up on the offer, soon providing Cook with a short list of devices that would make his work easier and improve care for his

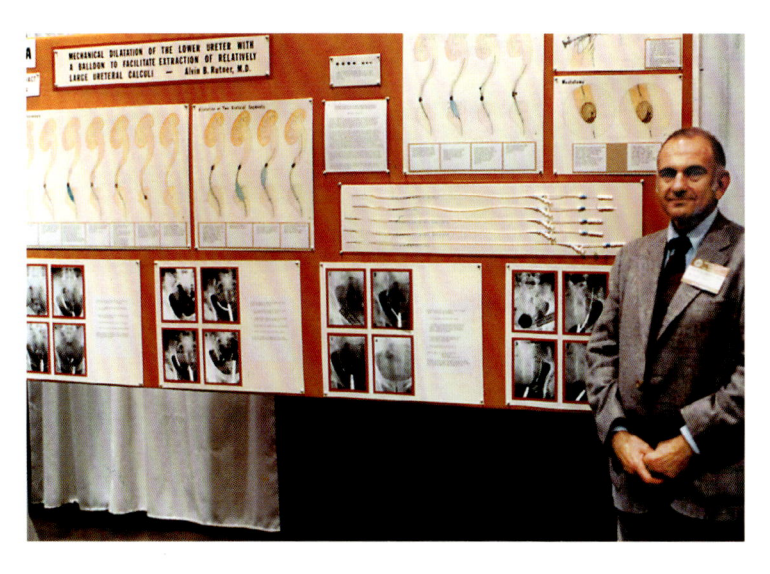

Dr. Al Rutner, a prominent California urologist who was chronically disgusted with the quality of urological equipment, spurred the creation of Cook Urological, which produces products for urological and women's health. Below, Cook Urological employees extend their best wishes to Rutner and his wife, Phyllis, on his retirement in the spring of 2003. Opposite, Bill Cook gives the victory sign while visiting the factory to thank workers for high productivity.

patients. It included a ureteral catheter with a flexible tip; a foolproof package of ureteral catheter connectors; a stone extractor (Rutner says, "There were some on the market, but they were crude, stiff and potentially dangerous. We needed a better way to extract kidney and ureteral stones"); and some sort of gadget for hooking tubes together to make a closed system.

COOK ENTERS THE UROLOGY BUSINESS

Bill sent Rutner's drawings and notes back to Bloomington and asked Dale Chamness to work on possible solutions. Chamness was soon joined by Dick Behen, and together they formed a de facto urology department, the first Cook team dedicated to urological products. As they began work on Rutner's devices, it soon became obvious to everyone involved that there was real potential for the company to prosper serving the urological community. By the time Behen was named to head up Cook's new urological operation at the plant on South Curry Pike, Bill Cook had returned home and Rutner had traveled to Indiana to continue the dialogue they had initiated at Dr. Fucilla's home in California.

Within a couple months Cook Incorporated had developed the first solution for Rutner, a ureteral catheter with a flexible tip. Others would follow shortly. When the American Urological Association held its annual convention in Miami that year, Rutner and Bill Cook were there, and the new devices immediately found such a receptive audience that Cook and Rutner continued to collaborate on equipment needed by urologists.

Over the next few years those innovative urological tools—a percutaneous stone removal set, a flexi-tip ureteral catheter and a universal wedge-tip ureteral catheter—became stock items for Cook. As they became available and more physicians began to employ them, Cook did the same sort of customizing that had characterized the company's early years developing radiological catheters. One of the first beneficiaries of Cook's new urology inventions was Gayle Cook. After she was hospitalized for a week with a kidney stone, a local urologist successfully tried Cook's stone removal equipment.

Cook Incorporated was so successful at providing tools for this new market that by early 1977 Bill Cook decided he needed to spin off a urological subsidiary. The existing sales force could not provide the sales and marketing attention the new product line required. He found the perfect opportunity to develop the new entity that same year when he met Jim Vance, the man whose photo had appeared in the debut edition of the *Angio-Gram*. Vance was the general manager of a company called American Latex, based in Sullivan, Indiana, south of Terre Haute. The company was producing latex-based products for the health care industry, and Vance was interested in selling the operation or merging it.

Cook led a team including Chamness, Behen and Kanne, to meet with Vance and get a sense of the company's potential. Bill wasn't particularly impressed with the facility in Sullivan, but he liked Vance and

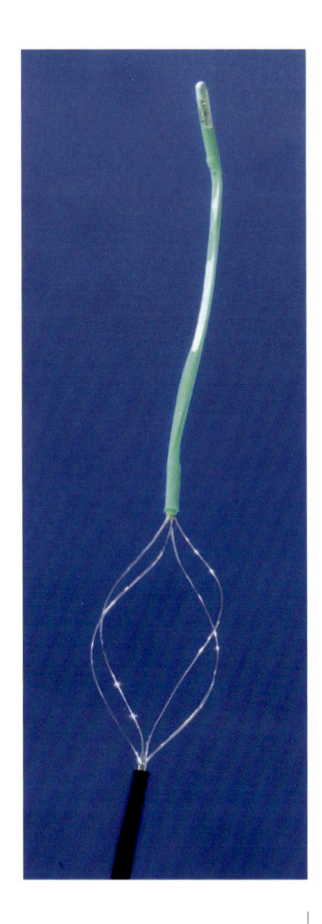

Stricken with a kidney stone, Gayle Cook was a beneficiary of this extraction basket, one of the first products Cook Incorporated developed in collaboration with Dr. Al Rutner.

INTERVENTION 81

In 1977 Cook thanked its employees for their hard work with a picnic held in a park near Bloomington. These photos are from that picnic. The following year, the company held its first employee awards banquet.

THE BLOOMINGTON Y

The Young Men's Christian Association (YMCA) had existed in Bloomington long before Bill and Gayle Cook emigrated from Chicago. With a board of directors affiliated with Indiana University, it had been associated primarily with the school. Few Bloomington residents availed themselves of its services. As times changed and interest waned, the Y—officially known as the Monroe County YMCA—had all but ceased to exist by the mid-1970s. The only sign of life was the occasional meeting of its uninspired board to conduct perfunctory oversight of the organization's financial affairs.

Such was the state of things when Bill Cook joined the Y's board in 1975. Members of the governing body were contemplating the dissolution of the Y altogether, but they thought the voice of the community ought to be heard before they made a decision. Either the Y should assume a broader role in the community, they told Cook, or it should disband.

Across the country many YMCAs were in similar predicaments, most also lacking a unified goal more marketable than following Christian principles and providing a place for recreation. Such traditional values didn't play very well to the rebellious new generation of baby boomers who had emerged from the chaos and social upheaval of the 1960s. Many members of the board felt the Y didn't have a place in such a climate.

Cook had a decidedly different point of view. He had undergone coronary bypass surgery the year before, and, blessed with a new lease on life, he was determined to take better care of himself. If not for that brush with death, he might not have

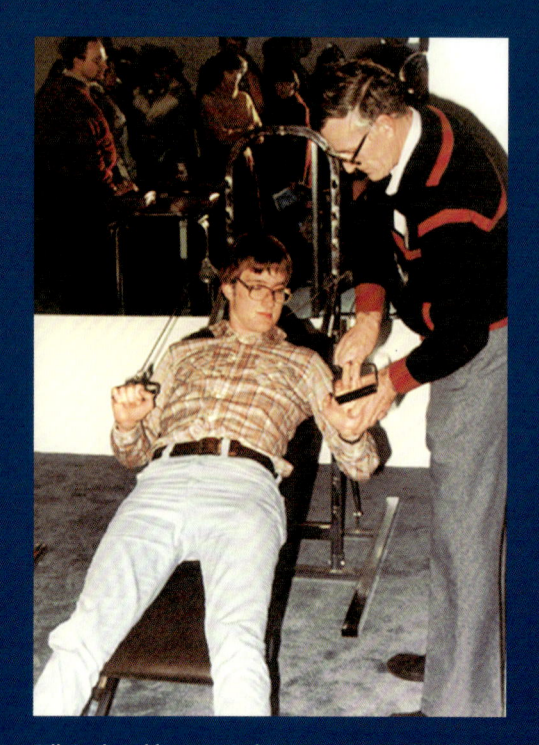

Bill Cook and his son, Carl, try out a piece of equipment at the opening of the Bloomington Y on New Year's Day 1981.

discovered that Bloomington had a dearth of exercise facilities where its citizens could routinely work out and pursue better physical fitness. The Y, he was convinced, could fill that void.

He persuaded the board not to throw in the towel just yet. Rather, he proposed, the community should have an opportunity to respond to the idea of transforming the Y into a family fitness center. With that in mind, the board adopted a revised and expanded philosophy to include promotion of physical fitness and family relationships.

It then asked the national YMCA organization to help conduct a needs survey.

National YMCA headquarters dispatched a team to Bloomington to interview local opinion leaders, primarily longtime members of the business community who were thought to have insight into the collective mind of Bloomington's residents. Their overall take on the concept was not encouraging. Bloomington didn't need a Y, they concluded. Indeed, a reconfigured Y like the one Cook proposed might conflict with such groups as the Boys' and Girls' Clubs, scout troops, Bloomington Parks and Recreation and Indiana University recreation facilities that were already open to Bloomington residents. Moreover, the survey found, the Y would likely undermine the fund-raising efforts of those groups and other charitable organizations.

Bill Cook was undaunted. Suppose the Y was to exist without subsidy, he argued. He was utterly convinced there was a need, and he persuaded the board to stay with the idea for a while longer. Then, characteristically, he took action. His first step was to enlist Drs. Dave Johnloz (now deceased) and Larry Rink, internal medicine physicians at Bloomington Hospital, to become associates of the Y and to create a YMCA–sponsored cardiovascular rehabilitation center at the hospital. Cook put $35,000 behind the effort, the hospital donated a room, and Johnloz and Rink recruited many of their colleagues to help get the project going.

Within months a new cardiac rehabilitation facility and catheterization laboratory were being used to capacity. Sticking to its commitment not to solicit any operational funds from the community for any activities or programs, the board charged user fees and paid for the services rendered by hospital personnel.

Building upon this success, the YMCA board hired Dean Reinke as a full-time director for the cardiac program. In his two years as director Reinke hired a staff and organized a series of popular aerobics classes that were held in schools all over Bloomington. Reinke's successor, Tom Porter, hand-picked by Bill Cook, continued to grow the organization's scope of programming for thousands of Bloomington residents who by now were taking advantage of a service for which the national Y's survey had determined there was no demand. Porter also took the lead in a project to build a new facility for the revitalized Y.

Cook donated land for a new YMCA on Highland Avenue, and with a $1.2 million challenge grant from Cook Incorporated to cover costs, construction got under way in 1980. The 86,000-square-foot facility, featuring a swimming pool, two regulation basketball courts, three racquetball courts, gymnastics facilities, a weight room, a fully integrated cardiac rehab program and preschool programs, opened on New Year's Day 1981. Despite inclement weather thousands of people turned out for the open house. By year's end there were 8,000 YMCA members in a community with fewer than 50,000 residents.

"Bill was absolutely right when he set his goal on building a wellness center," says Porter, who now heads his own successful health products company, Malibu Wellness. "The Y was an extension of Cook Incorporated, a microcosm of Bill's commitment to succeed by making products that improve people's health."

The Bloomington Y is currently the largest independent YMCA—physically and financially—in the United States.

Cook donated land and more than $1 million in seed money to create what is now known as the Monroe County YMCA. It is a model—in both facilities and services—for the kind of health and fitness center that inspires community engagement.

he thought they could work together. What ensued was a series of discussions that culminated in March 1977 with the announcement that Cook would build a plant in Spencer.

As things turned out, Cook decided not to build on the newly acquired 22 acres right away. Eager to launch the new urology operation quickly, the company instead refurbished an old warehouse in downtown Spencer, and the new company debuted in September 1977 as Vance Products Incorporated, with Jim Vance at its helm. Within a year it employed 15 people.

GROWTH IN PLASTICS

If Vance Products couldn't show off a new building that year, another Cook enterprise could. It was Sabin Corporation, Cook's plastics operation. The nine-year-old business had become root-bound in its old space. With a workforce of 15, it needed a new physical plant for its growing operations. Not only was it providing all of Cook's required plastics, it was also supplying half a dozen other medical equipment manufacturers throughout the United States, as well as Cook's European division in Denmark.

The new facility, just north of Cook's South Curry Pike headquarters, proved to be just the room Sabin needed to breathe. By 1978 the company boasted 35 employees and annual sales of $1 million.

At the same time, Cook's sales force continued to grow. In the summer of 1977 the company added two

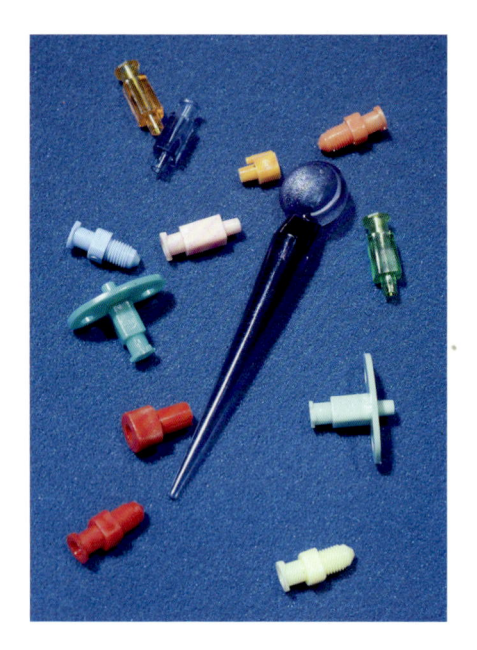

Launched in 1968, Sabin Corporation was Cook's first satellite business, manufacturing plastic tubing and components such as the fittings above. By 1976 it expanded into a new facility next to the Cook Incorporated factory in Bloomington. In 1997 Sabin moved into its current building, right.

new sales representatives, Rick Grenfell and Jerry Williams, to enhance the efforts in the South and the West, respectively.

Williams, a 27-year-old graduate student at the University of Utah, was recommended by Frank Longson, a family friend. At the time, Williams was working on his MBA degree and not immediately certain he wanted the job. Still, he interviewed with Brian Bates, Miles Kanne and Bill Cook, and they all agreed with Longson: his young neighbor had the stuff to be a Cook sales representative.

It was a terrific opportunity. But there was a hitch. If Williams wanted the slot, he had to start right away, and he had to live in California. This would mean delaying his dream of earning an MBA. Williams slept on it. In the end one factor carried more weight than any others: he had been married for three years and was the father of a young child. Family came first, and he needed to provide for them. School could wait. By September the Williams family was living in San Jose, California, and Jerry was hard at work for the only company he would ever work for.

BALANCING STABILITY AND CHANGE

Cook Incorporated had been founded at a time when medical technology companies manufactured and sold products without even having to sterilize them. Quality control was left solely to the manufacturer. That freedom suddenly disappeared with the passage of the Medical Device Act of 1976. This new federal legislation gave the Food and Drug Administration sweeping power to regulate classification of medical devices, compel adherence to a set of stringent standards called the Good Manufacturing Practices (GMP) and control the introduction of products to the marketplace. In short, it imposed significant restrictions upon all medical device manufacturers. For companies like Cook Incorporated, the frontier days were over.

"We had a very large product line by then," recalls April Lavender, currently senior vice president of regulatory affairs, who joined the company in 1976 in customer service. "Now, for the first time, we had to submit a packet of information to the FDA for each product."

Coming as they did during the bicentennial of the nation's Declaration of Independence, the new requirements must have seemed all the more onerous to companies that had been accustomed to unfettered growth and little government oversight. But Cook Incorporated took the matter in stride, with Jennings and Kanne providing their customary leadership, as everyone sought to understand and comply with the new requirements.

Lavender, who would be deeply involved with regulatory compliance both domestically and abroad over the next three decades, was one of the first employees to tackle the often cumbersome process of understanding the new regulations and communicating them to the company's production and engineering departments. She acted as Cook Incorporated's liaison with the government. She spent much of her time interpreting and translating regulations to production and engineering teams, which were becoming increasingly flexible and

April Lavender joined Cook in 1976 in a customer service capacity, but she found her true métier in regulatory affairs, taking on the task of understanding increasingly cumbersome government regulations and interpreting them for Cook's engineering and production teams.

86 SNOWING IN CHICAGO

responsive, and she helped frame the company's overall approach to managing regulatory compliance.

From the outset Cook sought to have a strong presence in the nation's capital in an effort to help define regulations to the best advantage of the company and the medical technology industry as a whole. Many years would pass, however, before Cook's efforts to see that its interests were well represented in Washington began to generate results.

"Stability and change seem like contradictory ideas," says Lavender, who in 1983 became quality control manager, "but they really did define Cook's ability to adapt to this new regulatory environment. We were a solid, well-established company, but we were also flexible enough to evolve."

THE CREATION OF COOK GROUP

Regulation aside, interventional use of the technologies Cook Incorporated had pioneered for diagnosis was rapidly becoming the standard in medical practice. The company's sales were increasing at an unprecedented rate.

By the end of the 1970s "Cook Incorporated was developing more management personnel and restructuring its management for growth," says Phyllis McCullough. "FDA regulations … meant that we needed to better coordinate product development, quality and production efforts." Responding to the need for more senior managers, the company expanded the executive team in 1977. Tom Osborne became vice president of research and development, and Don Hollinger was promoted to vice president of purchasing. McCullough was named vice president of operations.

They would assume their new responsibilities just as Cook Incorporated was acquiring its first computer, a Microdata Reality machine affectionately known as "Fred," which soon proved to be an indispensable asset for sales, inventory control, production scheduling and payroll management. Ever the technology buff, Bill Cook took to computers right away, learning how to program them in order to perform specialized functions for Cook Incorporated.

In short order, as he came to understand how the computer could enhance his business, he bought more, and in 1978 he established a new Cook company called Data Solutions, with Jerry McCullough, Phyllis' husband, as its president. Data Solutions provided computer technology support exclusively to Cook businesses until 1980, then it began marketing its own custom software package to independent insurance agents.

While Cook Incorporated was entering the computer age, the lawsuit in which Bill Cook and Brian Baldwin were entangled from MPL days had a consequence that dramatically reshaped Cook Incorporated's

Don Hollinger, opposite, pull-testing a catheter with a tulip bulb tip, was named vice president of purchasing as part of a companywide effort to beef up the executive team in 1977. The promotion coincided with the acquisition of Cook's first computers, here administered to by Rick Snapp, vice president, systems administration, for Cook Group Incorporated.

holdings; in 1977 Cook formed a new entity as a holding company for all of its increasingly disparate businesses in the United States and abroad. At first idiosyncratically named Muffin Corporation (after Bill's dog), it would soon be recast as Cook Group Incorporated. Cook Incorporated became a subsidiary of Cook Group, specializing in medical technology.

To head Cook Group, the company hired Bob Irie. A retired executive who had worked for Sears, Roebuck and Noble Roman's pizza empire, Irie brought strong management skills to the organization. In the role of corporate vice president, he served as a liaison to the various companies clustered under the Group umbrella.

Irie's responsibilities grew almost immediately. In October 1978 Cook acquired a G. D. Searle syringe plant in Denmark that was selling a respectable $6 million worth of products annually. That company was reconfigured as Asik, Cook's Danish syringe manufacturer, and made Cook a $26 million international corporation with nearly 750 employees. A year later Cook purchased the first of the new companies acquired as a consequence of the extended lawsuit involving MPL. It was Baxa Corporation, a pharmaceutical business Brian Baldwin had created to help ensure safe and accurate doses of liquid medications.

When reporter Bill Schrader interviewed Bill Cook about his company for Bloomington's *Sunday Herald-Times* late in 1978, the title of the story he wrote—"Cook Incorporated: Worldwide and Unnoticed"—was a bit of a stretch. Once "invisible," as Schrader wrote, Cook by that time had outgrown its status as a tiny operation on the outskirts of Bloomington; it comprised 14 different companies and it maintained sales offices in Denmark, Canada, Australia, Great Britain and Germany.

Each Cook company at the time existed as a separate entity, and its key managers reported to Cook Group. As Bill Cook explained to Schrader: "Corporate mobility is stressed, and chain of command reverts directly to the presidents of the various companies from the president or executive vice president of [Cook Group]." Under such a structure, Cook emphasized, "The ability to respond is rapid."

The company's philosophy of growth, Cook told Schrader, had evolved through trial and error, but its key tenets would forever define how Cook Incorporated had succeeded:

- *Maintain absolute control of stock ownership;*
- *Grow through reinvestment of earnings;*
- *Keep debt to an absolute minimum;*
- *Invest in growth situations when a key manager is present and where competition is minimal;*
- *Don't limit growth by trying to concentrate in one field;*
- *Use prototype field testing for all products before marketing;*
- *Don't try to anticipate a market, but grow into it; and*
- *Sell direct whenever possible.*

Acquired from G. D. Searle in late 1978, Danish syringe manufacturer Asik immediately enhanced Cook's European production capacity and presence while also substantially boosting the company's global revenues.

TRANSITIONS AND ADDITIONS

Sabin Corporation, the plastics manufacturer, flourished in its new building. Demand for the company's plastic tubing, improved fittings and adapters and other new plastic materials was skyrocketing.

Unfortunately, Joe Witkiewicz, Sabin's co-founder, did not have long to enjoy the fruits of his labors. Just as his business was finally poised to enjoy dramatic growth, he was diagnosed with terminal cancer in 1979. Don Hollinger, Cook's vice president of purchasing, was dispatched to Sabin to learn the business, becoming president and providing seamless leadership when Witkiewicz passed away. That same year, a young man named Bruce Gingles joined Jerry Williams' team as district sales manager in southern California. A 24-year-old graduate of Indiana University, Gingles was the first Cook sales rep to concentrate mainly on critical care, surgery and anesthesiology.

The Cook Group, meanwhile, continued to grow as it prepared to enter the 1980s. Another European entity—Cook España, S.A.—came into being. And in Melbourne, Australia, Cook Incorporated acquired Hughes Medical, a small company that had been founded by an Australian named Ernest Hughes. Cook changed the company's name to William A. Cook Australia Pty. Ltd. and began manufacturing products in Australia and distributing them to markets around the Pacific Rim and Southeast Asia.

Geoff Reeves, who would eventually rise to hold the top job of Cook Australia, had joined Hughes Medical in 1977 as the company's third sales representative. He was assigned to Western Australia, a vast but sparsely inhabited region comparable in geographic scope to the huge territory covered by early Cook reps based in California.

At that time Hughes Medical was "being run out of a shed in Ernie Hughes' back garden" in Victoria, recalls Reeves, who learned about radiological medicine the same way many U.S. sales reps did—on the job. Ranging up and down the continent's west coast, he

Cook's expansion in the late 1970s extended across the globe. Acquiring Hughes Medical, the company debuted in Australia, able to conveniently reach markets around the Pacific Rim. Geoff Reeves, above, came with the acquisition. In time he would head Cook's Australian operations.

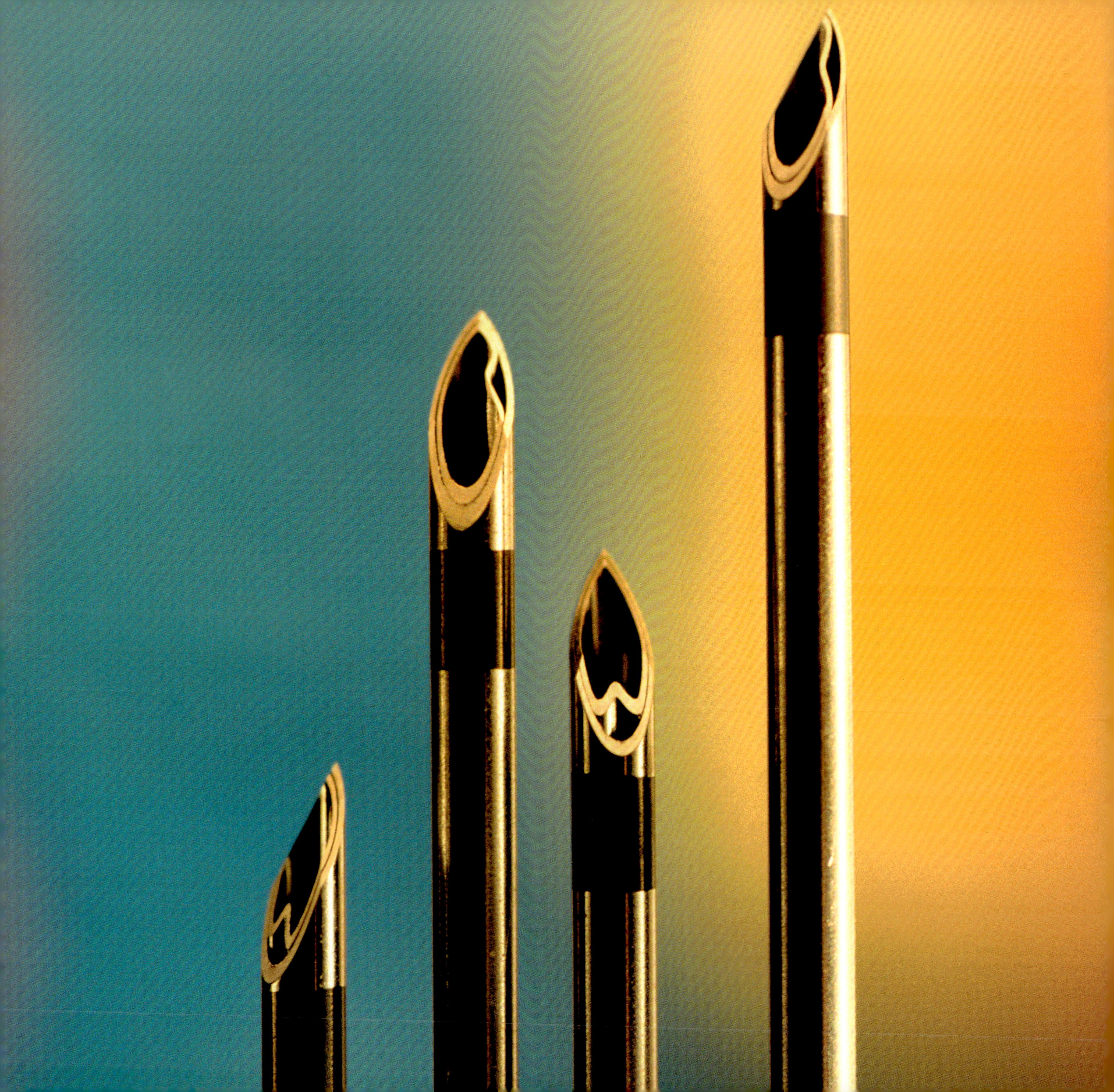

visited about 20 hospitals, where, he remembers, "only a few radiologists performed catheterization. I was lucky in Western Australia to have a very supportive group of people at Royal Perth Hospital who let me into the radiology theaters during procedures so that I could learn the art of angiography."

Reeves says his approach to sales paralleled that of Cook's U.S. sales force. "We produced products to satisfy [the doctors'] procedural requirements. It was a very pleasant time in the industry, as we all felt empowered by the understanding that we were being of assistance to people on the cutting edge of medicine."

In its early years the Australian entity sold a catalog of tools similar to Cook Incorporated's first product lines—radiopaque catheters, sheath sets, needles and wire guides. But it soon was producing interventional devices, as well. While the early years were a struggle, with the company a hemisphere removed from the medical centers where catheter procedures were rapidly evolving, the opening of a new manufacturing plant in Victoria in 1980 changed everything.

In 1981 a U.S. competitor, C. R. Bard, opened a catheter manufacturing plant in Australia, and immediately the Australian government imposed a 30 percent tariff on all imported catheters. This forced Cook to shift more catheter manufacturing for the Australian market than it had planned to Victoria, so the company dispatched Jeff McGough, a former Cook production manager in the States, to Australia to get the most out of the new plant. McGough ran the plant, set up manufacturing as it was being done in the United States and set the stage for Cook's aggressive expansion across the Pacific Rim. (McGough later went on to head Cook Urological Incorporated.)

"The Australian facility came into production just at the right time," Reeves says. "The market was growing, the procedures were becoming more mainstream and the public was just starting to accept new ideas in medicine. The facility lifted both profits and volume." Sales that year amounted to just $770,000, but by 1982 they were topping $2 million, and they would continue to rise.

In time the company also became a leader in the development of technologies required for performing in vitro fertilization and assisted reproduction procedures. By 2000, thanks to collaboration with key researchers and institutions in Australia and elsewhere, it came to be recognized as an innovative world leader in the development of endovascular stent-graft technology used to treat aortic aneurysms.

Cook Australia pioneered products for assisted reproduction—like the Echotip Double Lumen Aspiration Needles, opposite—giving Cook an edge in yet another emerging medical field. Waiting to be shipped, boxes of Cook products, above, sported the company's new logo in the early 1980s.

Left to right, Craig Weeks, Patrick Harty, Enrico Orlandi and Carl Bokkenheuser—Cook salesmen from all over the world—staffed a Cook display at a meeting of the Radiological Society of North America in Chicago in the mid-1980s.

MORE SOPHISTICATED MARKETING

With the Cook Group rapidly spreading across the face of the globe, it became clear that the company's marketing communications effort needed updating. Until the early 1980s Cook Incorporated had produced one catalog annually, each new edition the latest descendent in a lineage that stretched back to the little four-pager that Gayle Cook had designed in 1963. As new products became available between catalog publication dates, the company had supplemented the catalog with product data sheets.

But the industry had become a lot more competitive, and a more targeted marketing approach was needed. Simple product sheets and the one-size-fits-all catalog were no longer adequate. More specialized tools and methods were called for.

Bill Cook realized that, in particular, the company needed new kinds of product literature and more sophisticated trade show booths. In early 1980 he invited company newsletter editor Jim Heckman to lunch and offered him a new job as manager of marketing communications. Cook sketched out the scope of responsibilities on the back of his paper placemat, and Heckman readily accepted the new challenge. In the years to come Heckman became engaged in every aspect of Cook's communications, starting with outreach to each of the Cook Group companies to help them understand how the company stood ready to help them better achieve their unique marketing objectives.

ONE CHAPTER ENDS, ANOTHER BEGINS

Dr. Werner Forssmann—the man whose brazen 1929 defiance of medical taboos had set the stage for the revolution that redefined catheterization in the second half of the 20th century—lived to enjoy redemption. He won the Nobel Prize, watched his visionary idea become standard medical practice and enjoyed a distinguished career, eventually becoming chief of the surgical division at the Evangelical Hospital in Düsseldorf. He was 75 when, on June 1, 1981, in the village of Schopfheim in southern Germany, he died of a heart attack.

In Bloomington on that same day, a young man named Kem Hawkins was embarking upon an unexpected career with Cook Group. Hawkins was a celebrated public-school band leader who had exhibited an uncommon knack for transforming students' lives and inspiring them to achieve. After years of teaching, however, he had decided at the beginning of the 1980–81 school year to make a career change that would offer new challenges, better compensation and more time to spend with his family. He had discreetly put out feelers for a new job and quickly discovered the esteem in which the Bloomington community held him.

He was considering five job offers by the time he met Bill Cook, who had long since sized him up while watching him lead the high-school band in which Carl Cook had performed. Hawkins was amazed to find out how much Cook already knew about him, and he was utterly flabbergasted when, over lunch, Cook offered him a job. It was an offer too good to turn down, though he insisted on fulfilling his teaching obligations for the year before joining Cook Incorporated. As a management trainee, he spent his first ten months on the job learning every aspect of the company before being named plant operations manager in the spring of 1982. Like the job itself, the promotion to a prominent managerial position after less than a year with the company took Hawkins by surprise. But it was only the first in a string of promotions that irrevocably propelled the popular teacher to the top of the Cook organization over the next two decades.

VANCE PRODUCTS BECOMES COOK UROLOGICAL

The company sent out new runners, establishing roots almost everywhere in the 1980s, dwarfing Cook's track record of acquiring and growing small companies during the 1960s and 1970s. In 1980 the company closed Stanco Medical, its last U.S. distributor, and created California Cook Incorporated, a new entity to replace it and absorb Stanco's inventory. A year later Jim Vance left Vance Products, and that company changed its name to Cook Urological Incorporated. Bob Irie, who was becoming accustomed to the role of firefighter, parachuted in to assume the role of president and provide transitional stability.

Vance, in the meantime, went into business for himself just down the road and created a urological technology company that in short order rivaled Cook's. Six years after the founding of Vance's new company, Van-Tec, Boston Scientific purchased it and melded it into their Microvasive division, which was already

"There's one philosophy that pervades everything we do," says Cook President Kem Hawkins, whose motivational style first caught Bill Cook's eye when he was a high-school band teacher. "Always do the right thing for the right reasons."

KEEPING THE HEART SAFELY TICKING

Pacemakers have improved greatly since they were first introduced in the late 1950s—and recent advances in technology and diagnosis have made it possible for younger and healthier cardiac patients to benefit from these medical devices. The problem, however, is that a younger patient can outlive the pacemaker's lead—the wire that transmits electrical signals from the pacemaker to the heart, prompting it to beat, and transmits data from the heart back to the pacemaker. The longer the pacemaker is in place, the greater the possibility that the lead might fail or become infected. Either situation can be fatal.

By the 1980s patients and their physicians were facing lead breakdowns in increasing numbers—and many doctors found that the most desirable way to treat the problem was to remove the entire system, including the lead. But removing a lead can be extremely difficult, as it can become firmly bound to the patient's venous and intra-cardiac walls by scar tissue. Tugging at the lead can cause the wire to break or can tear the patient's blood vessel.

In 1988 Cook revolutionized the extraction process by introducing the first "locking stylet" to help physicians control the cardiac lead throughout the extraction procedure. Designed as an intricate wire with a unique locking mechanism at its distal tip, the locking stylet could be positioned and firmly secured within a lead targeted for removal. The advantages afforded by the locking stylet were magnified by the use of a series of telescoping dilator sheath sets—a concept conceived by extraction pioneer Dr. Charles Byrd.

When used in tandem, the inserted locking stylet transformed the lead into a trackable guide

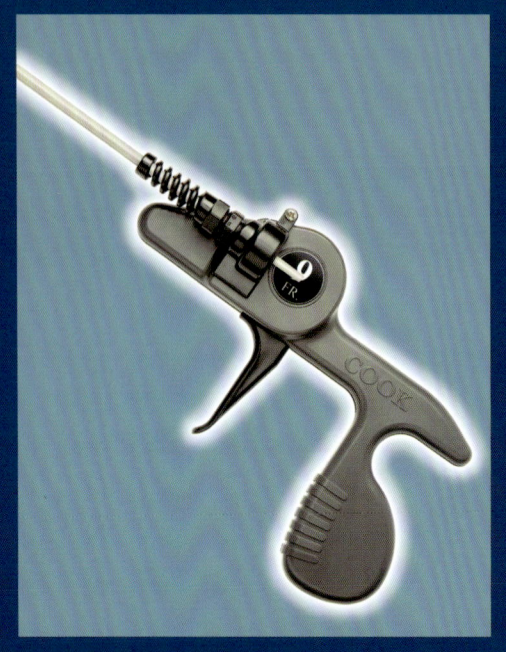

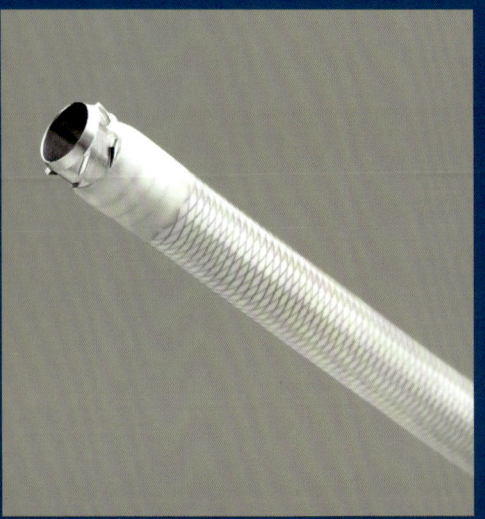

Cook Vascular's Evolution is a state-of-the-art dilator sheath that helps physicians remove pacemaker leads bound to patients' blood vessels by scar tissue.

over which the telescoping sheaths could be advanced in an effort to separate the lead from the transvenous scarred attachments that held the lead within the vein. Cook also developed a variety of femoral lead extraction devices, such as the Byrd Workstation Femoral Intravascular Retrieval Set and the Needle's Eye Snare.

Cook soon established the Extraction Registry, a mechanism to help physicians track the results of extraction procedures. Heralded by leading physicians, the registry was a critical tool in identifying success rates, risk factors and best practices used by physicians to extract pacemaker leads. To this day the registry is widely considered the most comprehensive record of information available about extraction procedures—and it has helped medical device manufacturers improve the technology with which physicians do their work.

Indeed, based on an analysis of data in the registry, Cook Vascular introduced the Perfecta Electrosurgical Dissection Sheath in 2000. This device combines the design of a mechanical extraction sheath like the stylet with radiofrequency-powered energy to dissect scar tissue that can hold leads in place. Perfecta was followed in 2001 by a one-size-fits-all locking stylet called the Liberator, which received attention for its ability to make the extraction procedure less complicated for physicians and to simplify hospitals' inventory management.

Cook Vascular energized the extraction world again in 2007 with the Evolution, a mechanical dilator sheath that rotates past fibrous binding tissue. Early feedback from physicians was highly positive.

producing a successful line of gastroenterologic products.

Not that Cook Urological was resting on its laurels. Irie inherited a company churning out new tools at a blistering pace. Cook products introduced that year included a nephrostomy catheter set, urethral dilator set, percutaneous Malecot nephrostomy set, cystoscopic injection needle, prostatic aspiration biopsy set and a non-adhesive ostomy set. In 1980 the first successful surgery was performed on a human fetus, using a pigtail catheter produced at the Spencer, Indiana, plant.

COOK ENTERS THE PACEMAKER BUSINESS

Carl Cook was about to graduate from Bloomington South High School when Bill Cook founded Cook Pacemaker in Vandergrift, Pennsylvania. The new company was built around the assets of a former manufacturer of a nuclear-powered pacemaker, Arco Pacemaker Company in Leechburg, Pennsylvania, which Cook had acquired.

"My father came up with the novel idea for a rate responsive pacemaker, which was the next horizon in pacemaker manufacturing," recalls Carl. "It took pacemakers to a whole new level."

While pacemakers constituted cutting-edge technology in the 1980s, they were primitive by today's standards. They were programmed for a certain heart rate, and they could be changed only by reprogramming. Bill's idea was to have the pacemaker sense the core blood temperature and respond to greater demand by the patient. "The pacemaker my father envisioned aimed to match the heart's natural function, responding when a higher rate was needed and slowing the heart rate when the patient was at rest," says Carl, who played a major role in the development of Cook's innovative pacemaker. Cook Pacemaker started designing the device in 1981. It would be 1988, however, before it was ready for market.

At Purdue University in 1981, Neal Fearnot, the graduate student who was on hand when Leslie Geddes moved his team from Baylor University, had completed his graduate work and joined the Purdue faculty. He was teaching electrical, mechanical and biomedical engineering in three separate departments. Bill Cook came to Purdue to meet with Fearnot, Geddes and others and discuss his idea for a rate-responsive pacemaker.

With funding from Cook, Fearnot headed up a Purdue team to develop the new pacemaker in collaboration with Cook's new company. In 1983, in office space leased from the Purdue Research Foundation, Fearnot's team became Medical Engineering and Development (MED) Institute Inc., a creative engine established to work collaboratively with Cook Group companies, helping them identify and develop new concepts for medical products. MED Institute went on to generate a wide range of technologies, including drug-eluting stents and a project using induced hyperthermia as a way to treat brain cancer.

While Cook Pacemaker was establishing itself in Pennsylvania, Bill Cook was in the process of acquiring

"The pacemaker my father envisioned aimed to match the heart's natural function, responding when a higher rate was needed and slowing the heart rate when the patient was at rest," says Carl Cook, who played a major role in the development of Cook's innovative pacemaker.

another Brian Baldwin enterprise. K-Tube Corporation, founded in San Diego, California, was the first company to successfully produce hypodermic needle tubing using extremely thin stainless steel strips and laser welding. Cook acquired it as a consequence of the lawsuit in which he and Baldwin were engaged. Stretching on for yet another year, the case had set an unenviable record as the most protracted litigation in the history of Cook County, Illinois. Nevertheless, Cook benefited richly from it in the end. By 2005 K-Tube had become the nation's largest independent needle tubing manufacturer.

In England, meanwhile, another European sales subsidiary, Cook (UK) Limited, was founded. And in Ellettsville, Indiana, a small town halfway between Bloomington and Spencer, Cook Incorporated added production capacity for needles and plastic products by expanding the former McNeely Stone Company building, which Cook had purchased in 1980 to use as a warehouse.

Laser welding, which produces tubing of exceptionally fine precision, such as the samples above, sets K-Tube apart from competitors. The acquisition of K-Tube, the nation's largest independent needle tube manufacturer—founded by Bill Cook's old friend Brian Baldwin—brought Cook full circle, back into the needle industry where he began. Opposite, Cook employee Chuck Wall customizes a plastic component for a medical device.

INTERVENTION 97

A WEALTH OF IDEAS

Scott Eells came to work for Cook in April 1983. A graduate of Indiana University, where he played basketball for legendary coach Bobby Knight, Eells had worked briefly for Cook the summer after his junior year at IU. He demonstrated both an engaging personality and a commendable work ethic—and at a strapping 6 feet, 10 inches tall, he made a lasting impression.

After graduation Eells went to work for Bohn Aluminum & Brass Corporation in Greensburg, Indiana. There he tried his hand at several different jobs before discovering his métier as a quality engineer, managing a team of quality inspectors. It was a good opportunity, but after three years he was ready for a career move. In the fall of 1982 he learned about a sales opening at Cook and applied. The interview with Miles Kanne and Gene DeVane went well, but in the end Eells declined the position. He had a growing family and didn't want to travel as much as the job would require. Instead he accepted a quality control job with Singer Corporation in North Manchester, Indiana.

Kanne was impressed with Eells, however, and that November—just before Eells began working at Singer—Phyllis McCullough called to offer the young man a quality assurance job with Cook. While the proposal was enticing, Eells felt he'd made a commitment to Singer. He said no to Cook for the second time. He'd only been on the job at Singer for about three months when, as he recalls, "I got a call from Coach Knight one day. He said, 'You should be talking to Cook.' I told him I'd already talked with Cook and I'd taken the job with Singer instead. But he was insistent. He said, 'You really need to talk to Cook.'"

McCullough called again less than a week later. She wondered: would Eells be attending any upcoming IU basketball games? When he told her that he would, McCullough asked if he would join her for dinner. Two months later, in April 1983, Eells was back at work at Cook. He filled a newly created position—quality assurance manager—that underscored how important quality control had become at Cook Incorporated. Eells' job consolidated into one position quality-management services previously provided jointly by Kem Hawkins and Dexter Elkins, who was working on product development with Brian Bates.

"My first task was to understand the FDA regulations and what they really meant in terms of production and quality documentation," Eells remembers. "Some of the rules were confusing."

Though he was not an engineer, Eells thought like one. Many of Cook's quality and efficiency problems,

Former Indiana University basketball player Scott Eells turned down two offers from Cook before Phyllis McCullough, left, hired him as a quality assurance manager.

INTERVENTION 99

Phyllis McCullough dons a Cook helmet, above, for a trip around the track at the Star of Indiana Mini Grand Prix, part of HOOSIERFEST, Bloomington's largest festival. As bikers and basketball players and in many other capacities, Cook employees have distinguished the company for years in the YMCA's annual Corporate Challenge event.

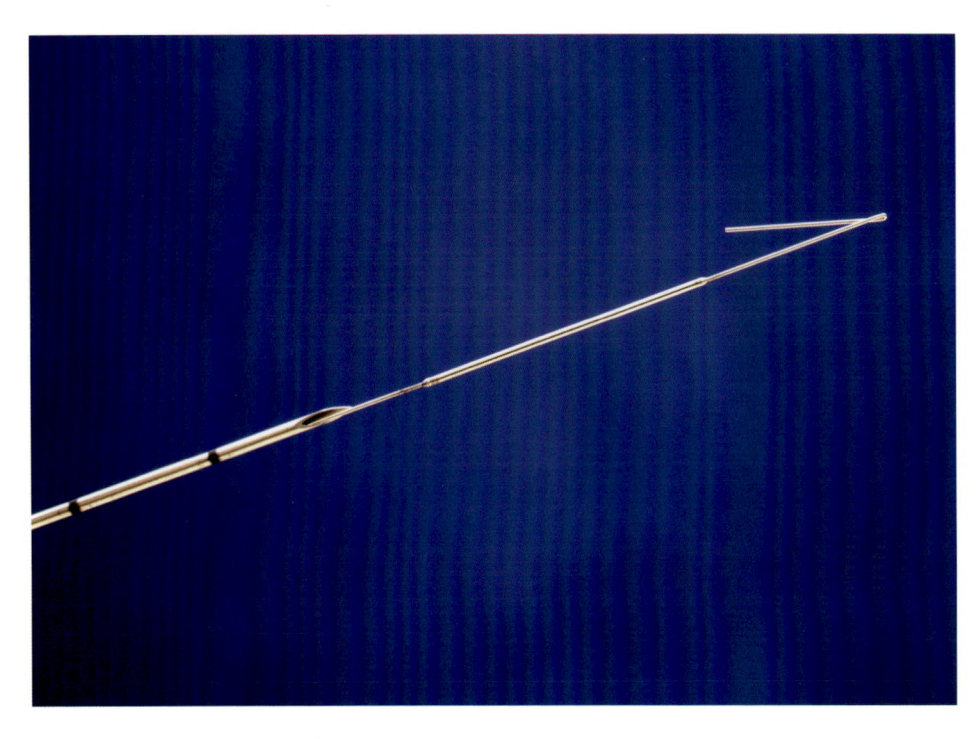

The Breast Lesion Localization Needle, above, and the Chiba Biopsy Needle, below, were among the new percutaneous entry products that Cook introduced in the mid-1980s.

he realized, could be addressed by refining manufacturing—and it was on that process that he focused most intently.

Eells did such a good job at it that, six months after arriving at Cook, he was promoted to the job of operations manager. By 1987, however, he was spread thin and needed help streamlining Cook's manufacturing processes. It was at that point that he hired three production engineers—the company's first. Almost overnight they proved their worth, and Eells spent the next two decades enhancing the company's engineering team. By 2007 Cook employed 20 engineers exclusively dedicated to the production process. Another 80 worked in product development, supported by more than 110 engineering technicians.

Less than a month after Eells came on board, Bill Cook learned that he needed heart surgery again. After the first operation nine years earlier, he had significantly modified his lifestyle, hoping to reduce his likelihood of suffering further coronary disease. But in May he went under the knife again in Indianapolis.

It was a setback, but Cook was not a man easily discouraged. In the aftermath of the operation, he renewed his determination to improve his cardiac health. If anything, his heart problem served as an inspiration to continue developing high-quality medical tools. He was back on his feet by July, when Kem Hawkins left Bloomington for Denmark to spend the next two years managing Cook's new plant in Bjaeverskov and learning the company's European operations from the inside out.

With all of Cook's new subsidiary operations in full swing, the sales of new products exploded, and there came a time in the autumn of 1983 when Cook management had no choice but to mandate overtime for production workers in the Bloomington plant. "It was hard to ask for the mandatory overtime, but the employees responded," Phyllis McCullough told *Business in Bloomington* magazine later that year.

Cook Incorporated was now bursting with more ideas for new products than at any time in the company's history. It was in that context that Brian Bates became the first person at Cook to hold the position of vice president of product development—an appointment that recognized the importance that Cook now placed on well-managed product development and innovation.

As McCullough reflected years later: "Physicians were discovering more and more ways to diagnose and treat patients through the percutaneous entry method, eliminating the need for surgery. Such products as the Breast Lesion Localization Needle and the Chiba Biopsy Needle made those procedures less invasive for patients. At the same time, the Polyethylene Balloon Angioplasty Catheters were allowing physicians to open clogged arteries as well as deliver a stent to prevent reclosure."

In the seven years immediately following passage of the Medical Device Act of 1976, Cook Incorporated introduced 35 new products. The first product for which Cook requested an investigational device exemption, allowing it to be used in clinical studies in order to evaluate its safety and effectiveness, was the Gianturco-Roehm Bird's Nest Filter. The invention was the first effective filter designed for easy, percutaneous placement in the vena cava—the large veins that return blood to the heart from the head, neck and arms—to prevent blood clots from traveling to the lungs. Among the patients to benefit: former President Richard M. Nixon.

The device was a marvel of simplicity, effectively trapping potentially deadly blood clots while allowing the flow of blood without disruption. In an earlier, simpler time, Cook would almost certainly have begun producing it and marketing it to doctors in short order. However, the FDA did not share Cook's opinion that Gianturco's device amounted to a simple procedure. The company was obliged to conduct a clinical trial, a process that began in 1984 and wouldn't end until five years later.

The Cook Incorporated of the mid-1980s was a product development juggernaut, one with an expanding portfolio of subsidiaries and a fast-growing presence outside Bloomington—indeed outside the country—to market its devices, coupled with an entrepreneurial fervor. With only one professional accountant in the entire company, Cook recognized that it needed a certain amount of financial and organizational discipline to successfully manage its growth. At a recognition dinner for the 1984 U.S. Olympic basketball team, several top Cook executives ran into an old friend—John Kamstra, another former member of the Indiana University basketball team (IU coach Bobby Knight was the Olympic coach that year) who had been a Cook employee for two summers while he was a college student.

Kamstra, a certified public accountant who worked for the Arthur D. Young accounting firm and an Indianapolis bank after college, recalls the Cook managers saying, "We could use someone with your background. Come on down." Kamstra signed on, became Cook's second staff CPA and helped Phil Hathaway (the first CPA) and Bob Irie financially manage Cook Group and its subsidiaries.

"It was a challenge to oversee all these operations around the world," Kamstra says. "We were very entrepreneurially based, and we needed to have some semblance of what was going on and keep everybody on the same page." Kamstra is now Cook Group's executive vice president and chief financial officer. But, as he says, "Don't let the title mislead you. Anybody can get involved in anything around here."

As McCullough reflected years later: "Physicians were discovering more and more ways to diagnose and treat patients through the percutaneous entry method, eliminating the need for surgery. Such products as the Breast Lesion Localization Needle and the Chiba Lesion Needle made those procedures less invasive for patients."

Chapter Six: 1985-1992

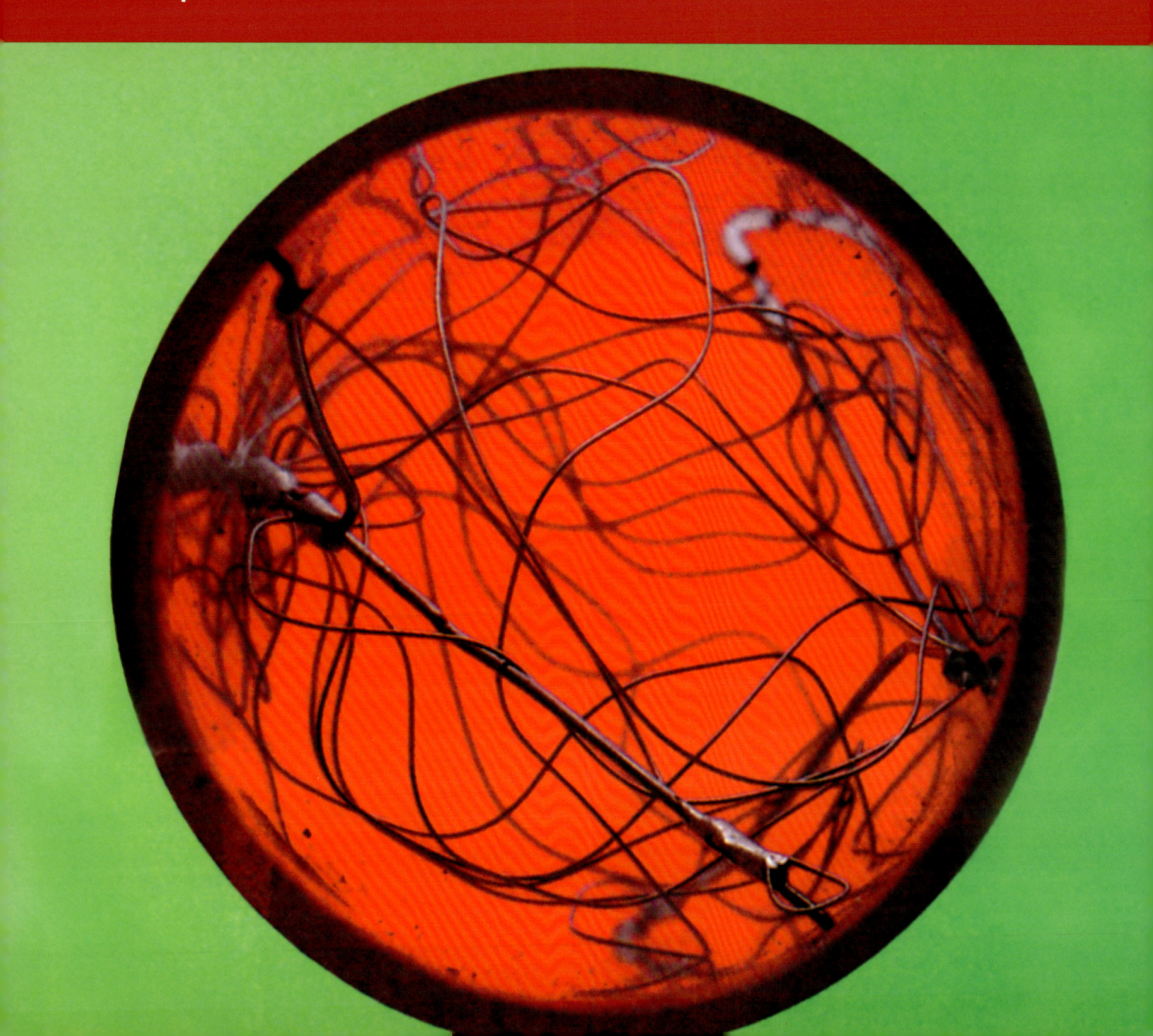

Adapting to Regulation

The Gianturco-Roehm Bird's Nest Filter, opposite, filters blood in the inferior vena cava to prevent pulmonary embolisms. A longtime colleague of Dr. Charles Dotter, Dr. Melvin Judkins, right, invented unique catheters that made it possible to selectively inject contrast dyes into the left and right coronary arteries.

In a decade of consequence in medical technology, 1985 was an exceptionally busy year for Cook Incorporated, but it was an unimaginable coincidence that made 1985 most memorable for the industry. Four pioneers of catheterization died that year—representing a monumental loss of talent and leadership.

Melvin Judkins was the first to pass. He had developed torque-controlled coronary artery catheters and a percutaneous technique that made it possible to selectively inject contrast media—dyes—into the right and left coronary arteries for X-ray and MRI imaging. Dr. Judkins slipped away in his sleep on the night of January 28, seven years after suffering a stroke that left him handicapped but still involved in radiology. Charles Dotter, Judkins' longtime colleague, followed less than three weeks later. He had been ill for several years, but his passing was hastened by complications of bypass surgery. Lung cancer claimed Mason Sones, pioneer of the cutdown procedure for cardiac catheterization, on August 29. Then there was the tragedy of Andreas Grüentzig, the brilliant German cardiologist who was instrumental in the development of the

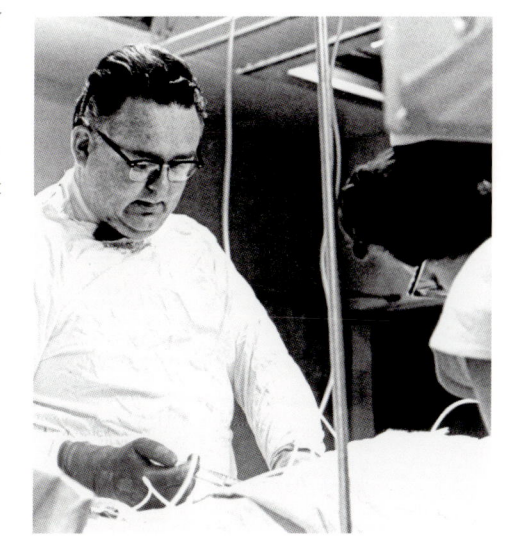

THE DOTTER INSTITUTE

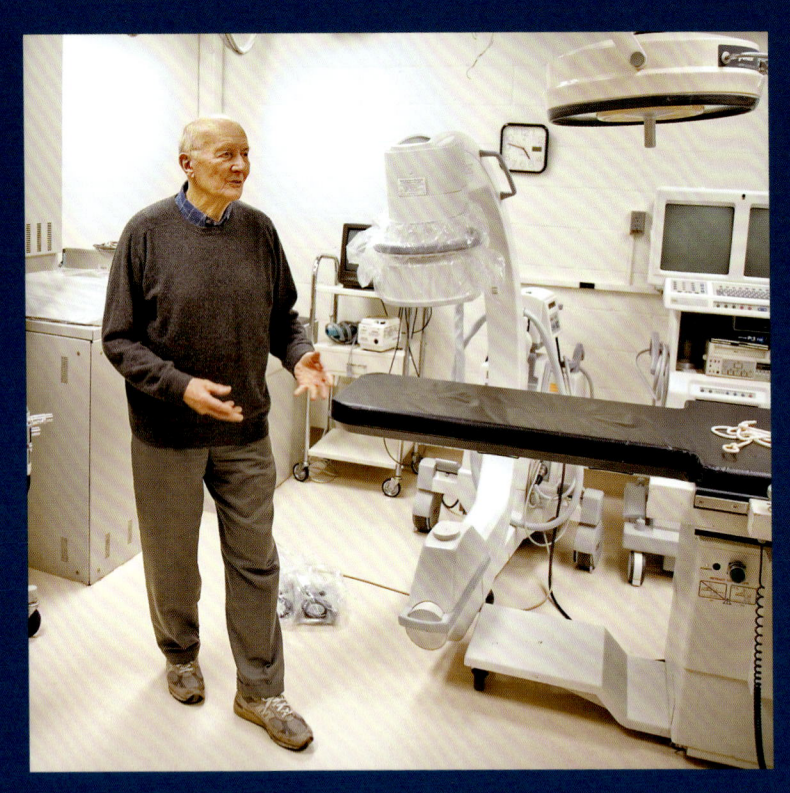

Dr. Josef Rösch left his native Czechoslovakia in 1967 to spend a year collaborating with Dr. Charles Dotter. He ended up staying in the United States and still presides over the Dotter Institute, opposite, which was founded with a large donation from Cook Group to support the institute's work.

In April 1990 the Cook Group contributed $2 million in seed money to establish the Charles Dotter Institute of Interventional Therapy at Oregon Health Sciences University. In total the company has donated more than $20 million to fund the institute's operations.

The institute, observed Leslie and LaNelle Geddes in *The Catheter Introducers*, was "one of the most important developments in the history of interventional medicine." Its purpose had been outlined by Bill Cook a year earlier when he pledged his support during the university's Charles Dotter Memorial Days observation on the 25th anniversary of angioplasty. The institute provided advanced interdisciplinary medical education and research facilities, where patients could receive excellent care and the development of interventional techniques could be carried forth in the spirit of Charles Dotter.

Bill Cook had begun thinking about the idea of an institute for interventional medicine four years earlier. In 1986, the year after Dotter died, Dr. Josef Rösch, Dotter's longtime colleague, and Bill Cook were both speakers at the Western Angiographic and Interventional Society conference in Monterey, California. Both offered talks recounting their respective relationships with the great scientist.

After their presentations the two men spent time walking together and further reminiscing. "Those memories," noted Jan Greene and Otha Linton in the *History of Dotter Interventional Institute: Fifteen Years of Education, Research and Patient Care 1990–2005*, "prompted Dr. Rösch to start thinking about a way to memorialize their late friend and colleague in some permanent, professional way. To that end he wrote to Mr. Cook in October 1986: 'It would be nice to establish a Charles Dotter Research Institute in Interventional Radiology.'"

In March 1991 Dr. Fred Keller, who had spent a decade at Oregon Health Sciences University during the 1970s and early 1980s, returned from the University of Alabama at Birmingham to become the institute's associate director and professor of interventional therapy, occupying a chair endowed by Bill Cook. He simultaneously became chairman of the diagnostic radiology department.

He was the perfect choice for the position. Establishment of the institute had been controversial within the department of radiology, and contention over its creation had created a rift that Keller was ideally poised to repair. A top-notch clinician and inspirational teacher, he was also a visionary interventionalist, and as Greene and Linton noted, "a savvy businessman with strong ideas about the future of interventional radiology."

Under Keller's leadership the institute soon outgrew the former university fire station where it had been housed. In years to come it would fulfill Josef Rösch and Bill Cook's vision of a center where Dr. Dotter's work could be carried forward in perpetuity.

ADAPTING TO REGULATION **105**

106 SNOWING IN CHICAGO

Thousands of lives are saved every year as a result of Dr. Andreas Grüentzig's pioneering work in the development of percutaneous transluminal coronary angioplasty. Grüentzig, below, with a nurse and patient, died in a tragic accident at the age of 46, but the benefits of his work endure today.

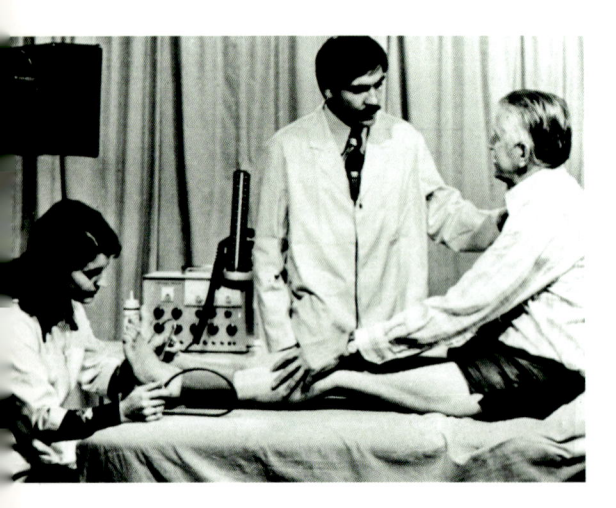

balloon catheter used in percutaneous transluminal coronary angioplasty—nonsurgical catheterization with an inflatable balloon to clear blocked coronary arteries. Grüentzig was just 46 years old when he flew his private plane into an unforeseen storm on October 27 and crashed. His wife died with him.

Bill Cook had known all four of the doctors. He especially counted Dotter as a close friend and one of the greatest men he had ever known. In the 22 years since that momentous afternoon in Chicago when Dotter asked to borrow his torch and some Teflon tubing, the two men had collaborated to create dozens of successful products that had utterly transformed medical practice. Cook Incorporated, Bill knew, would not have been the same company without Charles Dotter.

"He foresaw nearly every interventional product that we use today," Cook reminisced nearly 20 years after Dotter's death, "including catheter arterial dilators, balloon dilators, and self-expanding and balloon-assisted stents. In those early days there was no need to receive FDA approval before using a device on a human, and I am proud to say that even though no federal approval was required, our products were as safe and effective as they are today. In every instance in which Dr. Dotter used a new device, he was thinking of the patient's well-being."

Just before their deaths, Dotter and Grüentzig had been among a growing number of doctors envisioning the possibility of coronary and peripheral stenting to keep vessels open following angioplasty—a notion for which only the adjective "radical" seemed fitting at the time. Further development of stenting by Dr. Gianturco, with support from Cook, eventually shepherded that life-saving idea from the drawing board to the marketplace—against daunting odds—just two years after Dotter and Grüentzig died. Its introduction seemed nothing less than a tribute to those fallen giants.

MORE GROWTH AT HOME AND ABROAD

By 1985 Cook Group had further expanded with the addition of five more European sales subsidiaries: Cook Deutschland GmbH, Cook Group Europe ApS, Cook Italia SRL, Cook Sweden AB and Cook France S.A.R.L.—as well as Baxa Europe Aps, a European extension of Baxa. They also added J. Gardener & Associates, a Bloomington-based manufacturer of sterilization equipment used by the Cook companies. J. Gardener made it possible for Cook companies to comply with the ever tighter control standards of the FDA and the U.S. Environmental Protection Agency.

Cook had also done some thinning. It sold off several subsidiaries—Baldwin & Cook ApS, Hjørring DK, Asik A/S, and Rodby, DK—as the company repositioned itself.

In 1982 Dr. Dotter had asked Cook to explore developing a less expensive, non-ionic contrast medium. Some patients had painful, even life-threatening reactions to ionic contrast agents, limiting the dyes' usefulness. Non-ionic, organic contrast media, which reduced the threat to the patient, had been developed, but they were so expensive that many hospitals didn't buy them. Ever the showman, Dotter had tape-recorded the groans of patients suffering from adverse reactions to ionic contrast agents. It was a singularly unpleasant tape to hear and powerful evidence that the new product was needed.

To tackle Dotter's latest challenge, Bill founded Cook Imaging Corporation. He built a multi-million-dollar plant in Bloomington to develop a non-ionic product. In addition to conducting pharmaceutical research and developing radiographic contrast media, Cook Imaging operated Cook Pharmaceutical Solutions, which provided formulation development, production runs and clinical trial runs for Cook Imaging products.

If Bill Cook could have guessed how long it would take to create the non-ionic medium and get it approved, he might not have undertaken development of the new product. It was 1994, and Chuck Gifford was at the helm of Cook Imaging by the time the FDA approved Cook's product, called Oxilan. By then Dr. Dotter had been dead for nine years, his tape of agonized patients long lost, and competing companies had developed their own products, driving the price of Oxilan down.

By 1996 the Cook Imaging plant was sitting idle. Not only was Oxilan not selling, the company had a $35 million inventory. Undaunted, Cook recruited Jerry Arthur to help reconfigure Cook Imaging. Before taking early retirement from Eli Lilly and Company, Arthur had run a sterile filling operation—the process of packaging filled vials and syringes—and Cook representatives had consulted with him when Cook Imaging was being launched. When the company approached him about moving to Bloomington to help turn the moribund imaging operation into something productive, he agreed right away. He missed the challenges of the workplace.

In September 1996 Arthur reduced Cook Imaging's Oxilan production so the business could be built around the capabilities of the Cook Pharmaceutical Solutions unit and the plant could be converted to contract manufacturing—filling vials and doing formulations science for other drug companies. The changeover was a model of efficiency. For a short time 40 of the company's 60 employees were dispatched to Cook Incorporated to work in medical device production. They were brought back the following spring when Cook Imaging reemerged under the name Cook Pharmaceutical Solutions.

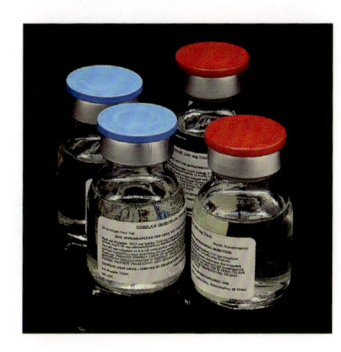

"We identified early on that there was a market niche for a responsive,

Cook Imaging, established in the early 1980s to develop a non-ionic contrast dye, ran into a regulatory quagmire that held up release of its product Oxilan, left, for so long that Oxilan was no longer commercially viable by the time it was approved. Under the leadership of Jerry Arthur the business reemerged in the late 1990s as Cook Pharmaceutical Solutions. Its headquarters is shown above.

"MY LUCKY DAY"

Cook Incorporated has always had wings. The company bought its first plane two years after Bill and Gayle Cook arrived in Bloomington, and by 1979 it had two aircraft—a single-engine Cessna 210 and a twin-engine Cessna 340—and a good pilot. The pilot was Russ East, and he'd been flying for Cook for several years. He had started as a machinist back when the company had just one plane and Bill Cook only needed him to fly occasionally. Now East was busy all the time, and the company was growing rapidly.

Bill knew there was going to be greater demand for aviation at Cook, so he started looking for another good pilot. He interviewed a few people, but he hadn't found the man he was looking for. Then one day that summer, he and East were at Bloomington Airport when a potential disaster unfolded. An inbound corporate pilot had a problem with his forward landing gear. The plane was unquestionably going to nose over on touchdown. How bad things would get after that was anybody's guess. Television crews and print journalists, hearing about the situation on their police scanners, arrived to find fire trucks on the runway as the plane descended with its front landing gear dangling and useless.

People held their breath. The plane touched down, and the pilot somehow managed to wrestle it to a halt uneventfully. And that was that—almost.

"Who's that?" Cook asked East.

"Bob Harbstreit," East said.

"How come I haven't talked with him?" Cook asked.

Harbstreit already had a job, and East didn't think he'd be interested in moving. Cook wanted to talk with him nonetheless. They had lunch a week later. Harbstreit had never met Cook, though he knew who he was, and the meeting went so smoothly he didn't even realize he was being interviewed. By the time dessert was served, he'd agreed to come to work for Cook. "I guess that day with the damaged landing gear was my lucky day," he now says.

His arrival signaled the commencement of a new phase for the company's aviation services, which always had been a hallmark of Cook's success. The two pilots were soon flying on almost a daily basis. "Bill called the planes 'weapons,'" Harbstreit recalls. "They were essential to the company's sales effort. Field representatives would set up a tour of the plant, and we would fly out to a remote location," often to the West Coast, "and bring the customers back to Bloomington. After the tour we'd fly them home. Other times the company might have a problem with a product. We'd fly someone out to meet with the customer the same day the call came in. Sometimes we'd bring the defective product back to Bloomington,

Bill Cook discovered that flying gave his company a competitive edge from the very beginning. Many of Cook's early salesmen zipped to and from meetings with customers in their own planes.

and it would go right to R&D. It was a big advantage over competing companies that didn't have aviation support."

Bill Cook realized the power of aviation right from the start. In the 1980s he told a number of his young sales reps that he would purchase airplanes for them if they would take flight lessons and get their licenses. Jerry Williams, Brian Bates, Craig Weeks and Rick Grenfell took him up on his offer, and they, like Gene DeVane, were soon using planes to visit customers and to fly customers in from remote locations. Only when the cost of insurance became prohibitive did Cook stop providing his field sales force with planes.

"We utilized the aircraft to deliver product on short notice, bring physicians to the plant for product development sessions, and for humanitarian missions," says Phyllis McCullough.

By 1987 the company's airplane service had evolved into a full-fledged business. Cook Aviation provided aircraft refueling and a fixed-base operation at Monroe County Airport along with general customer service. By 1990 Cook had purchased three British Aircraft Corporation BAC 1-11 planes, which are the size of Boeing 737s but outfitted to hold approximately 25 passengers.

Bob Harbstreit—who learned to fly when he was a boy in an old Piper Cruiser that belonged to his dad—had flown all over the world by the time he retired in 2004. His son Nathan followed in his footsteps, becoming a chief pilot for Cook a year after his father's retirement.

Flying was such a core part of Cook's way of doing business that its aircraft department evolved by 1987 into a full-fledged subsidiary, providing refueling and other general aviation services at Bloomington's Monroe County Airport.

high-quality operation that would provide complete service, quick turnaround and accomplish all of this at a reasonable cost," Arthur said.

Cook Pharmaceutical began with a single customer—Arthur's former employer, Eli Lilly. But syringe filling was eventually added to the product line, and by 1998 Cook had invested an additional $25 million to expand the capacity for high-speed syringe filling. That move in turn led to more business and a second multi-million-dollar expansion in 2000 to handle high-speed vial production for freeze-drying capabilities.

"Suddenly," says Arthur, "a business unit that looked to be on the brink of disaster four years earlier had become one of the top contract manufacturing operations in the industry." It was so successful that Baxter International, an Illinois-headquartered global health care company, purchased Cook Pharmaceutical for $250 million in 2001. A year later Baxter sold the rights to manufacture Oxilan to Guerbet LLC, a French medical imaging company with U.S. headquarters in Bloomington.

In Winston-Salem, North Carolina, Cook established Wilson-Cook Medical Inc. in 1983 to provide innovative products for gastrointestinal endoscopy. Wilson-Cook was a new collaboration with Bill Cook's old ally Don Wilson, head of Cook Canada. In the years to come its development followed the now familiar Cook template. By working closely with prominent gastroenterologists Wilson-Cook became a worldwide leader in the design, development and manufacture of devices used in gastrointestinal endoscopy, bronchoscopy and surgery and in the treatment of esophageal, stomach, pancreatic, liver and colon disorders.

In 1984 Cook Incorporated refined its international presence. It founded Cook Group Europe to coordinate the plethora of European sales organizations. This in turn enabled William Cook Europe to renew its focus on product development and production. Similarly Cook's Asian subsidiaries and distributors in Singapore, Taiwan, Malaysia and Hong Kong began to purchase products directly from each Cook manufacturer. This took pressure off Cook Australia, which had served as the primary supplier for all Cook products throughout the Pacific Rim. The Australian company could now spend more time and resources on its in vitro fertilization products, for which the market was expected to grow, and on development of other technologies.

"WE'RE EXPANDING SO FAST, IT'S HARD TO KEEP TRACK"

Early in June of 1985, just after Carl Cook graduated from Purdue University with a bachelor of science degree in electrical engineering, seven-year-old Cook Urological announced plans to more than double its 22,000-square-foot plant in Spencer. The expansion would

In 1983 Cook launched Wilson-Cook Medical Inc., its headquarters shown above, in Winston-Salem, North Carolina. A partnership with Don Wilson, head of Cook Canada, it developed products for gastrointestinal endoscopy, another consequence of the catheterization revolution Cook fomented in the 1960s. Two years later Cook expanded its Cook Urological unit, right.

allow the company to boost production of its products—kidney stone retrievers, balloon dilation devices and other urology tools—in order to meet demands that had increased by 100 percent in only the past year and were projected to increase by an additional 50 percent in 1985.

The company had debuted in 1978 with just five employees. Now it had 115, and its president, Jeff McGough, told Bloomington's *Sunday Herald-Times* reporter Bill Strother, "We're expanding so fast it's hard to keep track." An Indiana native, McGough was the man who had helped to launch Cook Australia's manufacturing operations in 1980. He replaced Bob Irie as head of the urological subsidiary in 1983. He had worked his way up the ladder at Cook, spending time at the company's facilities in Denmark and Australia before returning home. Company sales, he said, had been driven up by the serendipitous convergence of two trends: national demand for more efficient and less expensive health care and the introduction of "increasingly sophisticated medical techniques that utilize Cook products."

In 1985 Kem Hawkins returned from Denmark to manage the Critical Care Division of Cook Incorporated, which addressed the unique needs of emergency and critical care medicine, anesthesiology and other related specialties. Critical Care was selling many different kinds of central venous catheters, and the products were being used in so many specialties that problems with catheter perforations and erosions were on the upswing, including incidents in which patients were seriously injured or even killed.

A new Medical Device Reporting mandate from the FDA at this time required hospitals and physicians to report incidents that occurred during procedures in which a device was being used. In addition to requiring the hospitals and physicians to report device malfunctions or procedure problems to the device companies, the new rule required device manufacturers to keep monthly reports and examine them for trends. It was from such a report that leaders of the company identified the recurring problem of perforation of a vessel during the use of Cook central venous catheters. This was brought to Bill Cook's attention.

"It wasn't a statistically high number," says Dexter Elkins, vice president of marketing at Cook Urological, "but when Bill Cook learned about it he put the matter on the front burner and turned the heat up to high." Bill Cook took immediate action to address this problem, engaging McCullough, Elkins, Hawkins, Rick Mellinger and Brian Bates in organizing a day-of-learning event at which leading radiologists and critical care physicians came together to assess the matter and recommend solutions. "Bill saw it as greater than just a problem for our company," says

A large group of Cook sales representatives and managers posed for this photo at a company sales meeting held in Park City, Utah, in the mid-1980s.

A FLOWER THAT SAVES LIVES

Surgery and trauma patients often require a filter to keep them from suffering pulmonary embolism—obstructions caused by clots in the vessel that carries blood from the heart to the lungs. There are about one million pulmonary emboli every year in Europe and the United States, and 30 percent of them prove fatal.

Until the advent of Cook's Günther Tulip Vena Cava Filter, the filter had to remain in a patient's body for the rest of his or her life—but many patients require a filter only temporarily, while, for example, they are unable to take anticoagulant drugs because of potential complications from bleeding.

In the 1980s Professor Rolf Günther from Aachen, Germany, began working on a device to prevent pulmonary embolism. The device, called a vena cava filter, sits in the inferior vena cava (IVC), the vein that returns blood to the heart. Günther learned that a cone-shaped wire filter placed within a vessel creates the least amount of obstruction while supporting the vessel. Even if a captured clot fills 70 percent of a conical filter, the filter can still allow 50 percent of the blood to flow through it. Furthermore, clots trapped in the center of such a filter will dissolve more quickly than in other products.

The delicate, flower-shaped Günther Tulip Vena Cava Filter first became commercially available in Europe in 1992. The device's specially designed barbed "feet" are bent at 55-degree angles to create a solid hold on the vein wall while causing little or no damage. It also features a small hook on the top that makes it easy to retrieve when it is no longer needed, using a minimally invasive procedure. To do so a physician uses a "snare" to grab the hook and then pushes a plastic catheter over the filter to collapse it, detaching its legs from the vein. The filter can then be removed from the patient's body in much the same way it was originally implanted.

The Tulip is made of a durable, biocompatible alloy that was chosen to be compliant with magnetic resonance imaging (MRI), a procedure that was proving to be an important diagnostic tool at the time of the Tulip's invention. Since the Günther Tulip was introduced, more than 50 physicians have published papers about their work with the device.

Cook has sold more than 100,000 Tulips worldwide, including in the United States where the device was approved in 2001. In 2006 the Tulip became the top-selling filter in the world, and since then it has been the fastest growing product in Cook's Peripheral Intervention business unit—solidifying the company's position as an IVC filter leader.

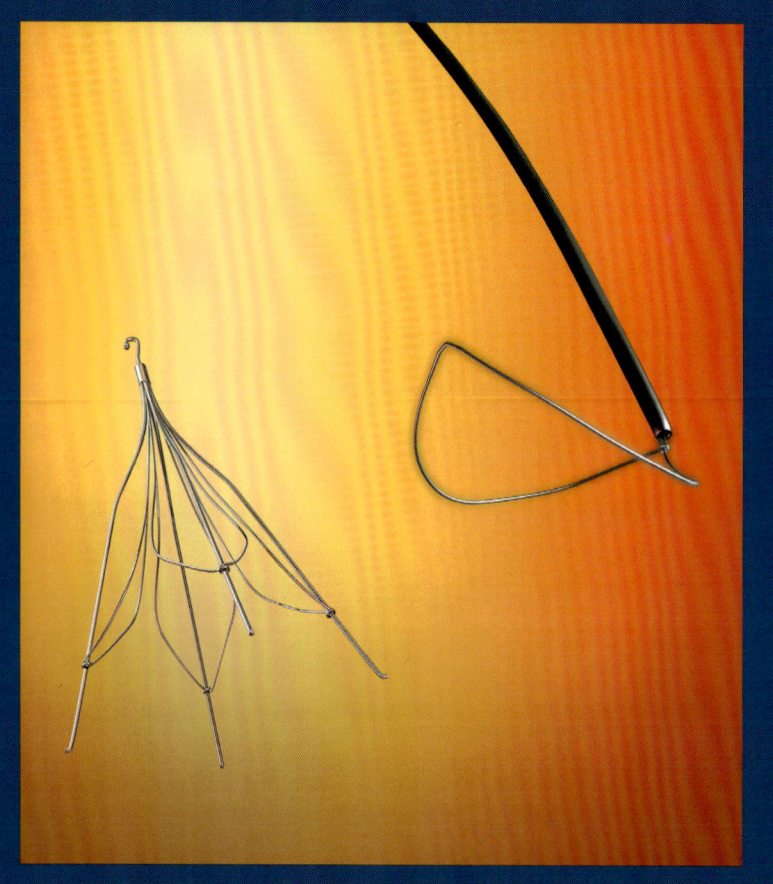

Named for Dr. Rolf Günther, the Günther Vena Cava Filter was the first device that could be implanted temporarily in the vena cava to prevent pulmonary emboli. Ingeniously designed, it is easy to install and easy to remove.

Elkins. "If we were having these problems, he thought, other companies that manufactured similar products might be having similar problems. He wanted to do something to improve patient care."

The conference was held in Indianapolis, and Cook used it to launch a campaign that featured dissemination of new educational materials, including an informative poster for display in laboratories, to the medical community. Hawkins continued to help Critical Care refine its product line and focus its product development. Under his leadership sales would increase throughout the balance of the decade and into the 1990s.

"Ironically," Phyllis McCullough observed, "the FDA was invited to participate in the conference, but it declined. Only after Cook's recognition of the problem and the success of its educational materials did the FDA convene a panel of industry experts to assist in this endeavor."

PERSISTENCE IN A REGULATORY ENVIRONMENT

Cook had indeed continued to enjoy success creating products during the new age of regulation, but its interaction with the Food and Drug Administration had not gotten any easier. In fact, the tedious process required to test Dr. Gianturco's Bird's Nest Filter seemed to portend a level of contentiousness with the agency that Cook had never experienced before.

It seemed that the FDA required more changes with every quality inspection of the company, and every time Cook submitted a product to the agency for market approval, the process took longer. An incident from 1984 reveals how difficult it had become for Cook to work with the agency. Dr. Gianturco had invented a pump that would deliver chemotherapy drugs to patients in small pulses. Cook developed it, as always, with an eye toward improving patient care. By pulsing the drugs, Dr. Gianturco reasoned, the device would spread out administration of the drugs. This would be less traumatic to the bloodstream and the vascular system of the patient and would reduce many of the negative side effects that accompanied delivery by more conventional means. But the FDA would not allow Gianturco's pump on the market unless Cook obtained a New Drug Application (NDA) for every drug that might be pulsed through the tubing—even though the pump never came in contact with the drug.

That requirement taxed credulity. Since Gianturco's invention might have been used to pump countless drugs, testing it for every drug that could possibly be pumped through it was a virtually unachievable requirement for approval. The FDA essentially doomed the product.

Cook Critical Care experienced a similar problem when it developed a product called an intraosseous needle. The needle was used to deliver medications through the bone when children's blood vessels collapsed in trauma situations because of blood loss. The FDA took the position that, like Gianturco's pump, it needed an NDA for every drug the needle might be used to deliver. The requirement was absurd, and a parade of pediatric specialists came to Cook's aid to convince the agency that the needle was a not only a life saver but

Different as they may have been in personality, Charles Dotter and Cesare Gianturco were two of a kind when it came to invention. Both were visionary thinkers and tireless workers who made enormous contributions to the advance of health care.

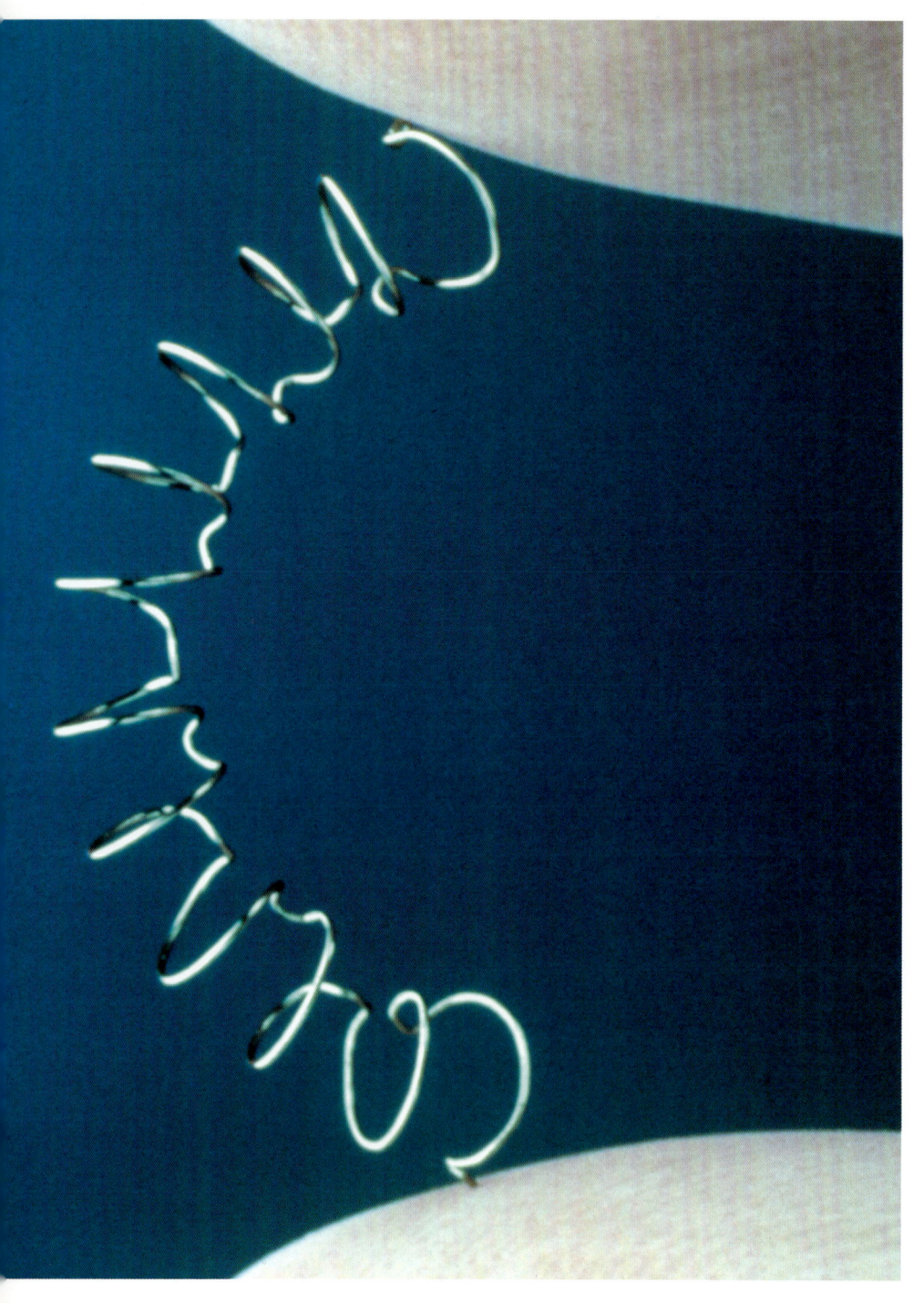

absolutely essential medical technology—a fact that the FDA eventually accepted.

Cook's struggles with the new regulatory environment continued past the tenth anniversary of the Medical Device Act. Cook wasn't alone. Even those in the industry who agreed that some level of regulatory oversight was necessary could see that the FDA's application of the rules was often autocratic and inflexible. But Cook stuck with it, learning from every encounter with the agency, becoming much more savvy about utilizing gentle persuasion and lobbying for change with both the FDA and Congress, determined to find a way for the FDA to oversee development of medical devices without the interminable, costly delays.

"THE HOTTEST THING IN MEDICAL DEVICES TODAY"

In 1985 Dr. Gianturco unveiled yet another innovation, a device designed to keep coronary arteries open after angioplasty procedures. It was the Gianturco-Roubin Coronary Stent, and he had been working on it in his basement since 1978.

Although Dr. Dotter had experimented with the use of nitinol as a stent material, it was Dr. Gianturco who ultimately invented a practical design for a stent that was mounted on a balloon, earning him recognition as "the father of stenting." Gianturco had conceived of stents in the mid-1970s, and at about that time he showed Bill Cook a prototype for the first balloon-mounted and self-expanding stents. This was the venerable Z stent design, an important product platform and the forerunner to Cook's current AAA device and product family, which are among Cook's most successful products.

By 1979 Gianturco had developed a balloon-expanded stent that he tested on laboratory animals, but he began working on the product in earnest with Andreas Grüentzig in 1985. When Dr. Grüentzig died, a colleague, Dr. Gary Roubin, stepped in to help Gianturco bring the idea to fruition.

Years later, in an article published in the journal *EuroIntervention*,

Roubin recalled the challenges coronary interventionalists faced in 1985: "Many groups, including Grüentzig's team at Emory, were exploring the path into more complex, diffuse, calcified tortuous and bifurcating disease, and multi-vessel disease," he wrote. "It was becoming very clear to all involved, however, that advances into more complex diseases came at the high cost of an increasing incidence of abrupt closure of the artery either during the procedure or within 48 hours." Roubin asked readers to imagine stenting in:

> . . . an environment where most if not all cardiothoracic surgeons were at best paranoid about the progress of percutaneous transluminal coronary angioplasty (PTCA) and at worst openly hostile about loss of status and clinical volume to interventional cardiologists. Imagine an environment where cases could only be scheduled if there was an O.R. and surgeon available to "back you up," where cardiothoracic surgeons could "veto" PTCA attempts on any patient, and imagine the professional challenge and hazards knowing that, depending on your patient selection and technical skills, 1 in 10 caths could end up as an emergency bypass, myocardial infarction or death.

It was in that context that Roubin and Gianturco, their research underwritten by Cook, persevered with their coronary stent work. Over the next few years the device was taken through clinical trials, and a pre-market approval application was submitted to the FDA in June 1991. Further delays followed before it was finally presented to the FDA panel in 1992 and unanimously recommended. "It's a very big event," Phyllis McCullough told *Indianapolis Star* staff writer David J. Shaffer. "We think it's not only a life-saving but a cost-saving device. If patients are prevented from going to bypass surgery, that's a major cost savings. The mortality for patients that either have a heart attack or have to go to emergency bypass surgery is very high. If this can be prevented and the patient is not required to go to bypass surgery, or can go to bypass surgery later in a controlled environment, the likelihood of survival is much higher."

To the *Bloomington Herald-Times*, she added: " … there definitely is a niche for this. Stents may be the hottest thing in medical devices today."

Remarkably, even after a nationwide clinical study at 13 leading medical centers, including the Mayo Clinic, Stanford University, the University of Michigan and St. Vincent Hospital in Indianapolis, unanimous recommendation still didn't assure Cook of the FDA's permission to market its new product. That took more than another year—causing considerable tension between Cook and the FDA—and it might have been further delayed if it hadn't been for Howell Heflin, the senior U.S. Senator from Alabama, who was a fortunate beneficiary of Cook's pre-market approval testing.

Heflin had checked into Bethesda Naval Hospital near Washington, D.C., in early May 2003, undergone a PTCA and was experiencing chest pain and fluctuating EKG readings when Dr. Gerry Pohost, chief of cardiology at the University Alabama-Birmingham, had him flown home.

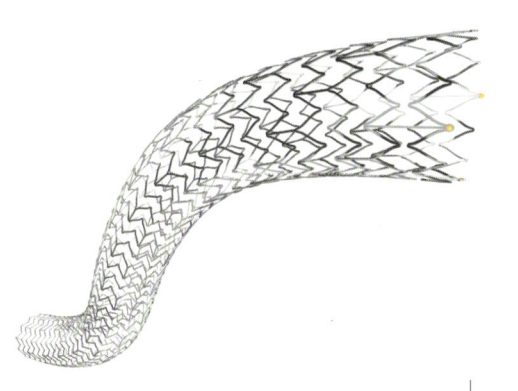

In 1969 Charles Dotter began experimenting with devices called tubular prostheses, designed to enlarge blood vessels blocked with plaque. But Dotter's early models were flawed, and it would be another 16 years before Cesare Gianturco unveiled the stent he had been tinkering with since 1978. Flex-stents, opposite, and Z stents, above, evolved from Gianturco's research.

> *Since existing products could not be adapted for alternative uses without further testing, product development was stifled. The prospect of enduring the FDA approval process meant many products that could significantly benefit small populations of patients never got developed at all.*

On May 17 Gary Roubin inserted a Gianturco-Roubin Flex-Stent in Howell's chest at UAB—one of the only places in the country where the procedure could be performed. Within days Heflin was back in Washington, where he recuperated over the Memorial Day break. Word quickly got out that Heflin was going to sing the praises of the stenting procedure on the Senate floor when the session resumed in June and that Heflin's son was going to hold a news conference doing the same and blasting the FDA for holding up approval of the Gianturco-Roubin stent for almost a year.

But the FDA preempted the Heflins and avoided bad press when the agency sent April Lavender at Cook a letter—dated May 28—informing the company that pre-market approval for the stent had been granted. Days earlier FDA Commissioner David Kessler had distributed a press release over the news wires, and representatives of the FDA had made phone calls to McCullough—and local news media—alerting them that approval was on its way.

On June 7 Heflin addressed the Senate, saying he was "delighted to be back in the Senate chambers after missing a few days due to some problems with my heart," and describing the stent, its development by Gianturco and the procedure in some detail. There was no criticism of the FDA, and Heflin's son never held his news conference.

COOK AND THE FDA

Cook Incorporated had endured an epic approval process in order to market the coronary stent, which became standard medical equipment by the turn of the century. The experience fueled the company's determination to exploit any opportunity to compel the FDA to streamline its cumbersome procedures. "Though [Bill] Cook agrees with the need for FDA regulatory control assuring patient safety and product effectiveness, he sees [many] problems with the current FDA structure," reported Brian Werth of the *Bloomington Herald-Times* in 1987, observing that, "in the past year, only 72 … medical devices nationwide received the FDA's pre-market approval …"

Bill Cook's assessment of the FDA's deficiencies was pointed and specific. The agency's review panels, he said, were overwhelmed by the pace of innovation. Participation on the panels obligated members to regularly put their medical practices on hold, and they were so widely dispersed geographically that the logistics of travel to Washington made it extremely difficult to coordinate meetings. While the FDA was underfunded, medical manufacturers' costs to comply with their requirements were astronomical, especially when the approval process was protracted. Class III products, such as the Gianturco-Roubin Coronary Stent, which offered the greatest potential to save lives but were considered high risk by the agency, typically took the most time to approve. Since existing products could not be adapted for alternative uses without further testing, product development was stifled. The prospect of enduring the FDA approval process meant many products that could significantly benefit small populations of patients never got developed at all.

On top of all those issues, Bill Cook accused the FDA of standing in the way of sick people who might want to help themselves. "A patient having a 50-50 chance to live or improve life quality should have the opportunity to assess the risk himself with his doctor," he told Werth.

When Congress took up the charge in 1990, Steve Ferguson became a fixture in Washington, playing a major role in drafting new regulations and legislation that began to reshape the FDA's regulatory process. Seven years later he worked with Congress again as it further refined the process, making extensive and long overdue changes in the way the FDA works with the medical technology industry.

In the late 1980s Cook made a significant donation to enable Bloomington Hospital to build a new, state-of-the-art cardiac catheter laboratory. Bill and Gayle Cook, below, attended the opening of the new facility.

MORE NEW COMPANIES, GROWTH AND PROMOTIONS

Cook Incorporated and the Cook Group continued to grow during the last half of the 1980s. Cook Southeast Asia Pte. Ltd., Cook Belgium NV/SA, Cook (Switzerland) AG, and Cook Urological Switzerland Ltd. all began business in 1986. Cook Nederland B.V. was founded a year later, Cook Asia Ltd., a year after that, and Cook Taiwan Ltd. in 1989. Cook Canada in Stouffeville, Ontario, and Cook Australia in Queensland, Australia, both dedicated new facilities that same year.

In March 1988 Jeff McGough announced that Cook Urological would be adding another 26,000 square feet, expanding its physical plant in Spencer to some 76,000 square feet by the fall. It was the second major addition in three years, and there was no telling how soon another would be needed. Cook Urological was now growing by nearly 30 percent every year.

Cook Incorporated was employing some 650 people at its plants in Bloomington and Ellettsville by June 1988. That month, precisely 25 years after Bill and Gayle Cook set up shop in Bloomington, Phyllis McCullough was named president, CEO and chairman of the board of Cook Incorporated. Jackie Wikle, who was then in the role of the company's personnel advisor, and Jim Heckman, the draftsman who had become Cook's first manager of marketing communications, were named vice presidents.

The company's most senior managers—Bill Cook, Miles Kanne and Ross Jennings—now joined Bob Irie and Phil Hathaway in Cook Group. They would focus on the growth of all the Cook companies and help direct the ongoing expansion of those companies to meet specific needs.

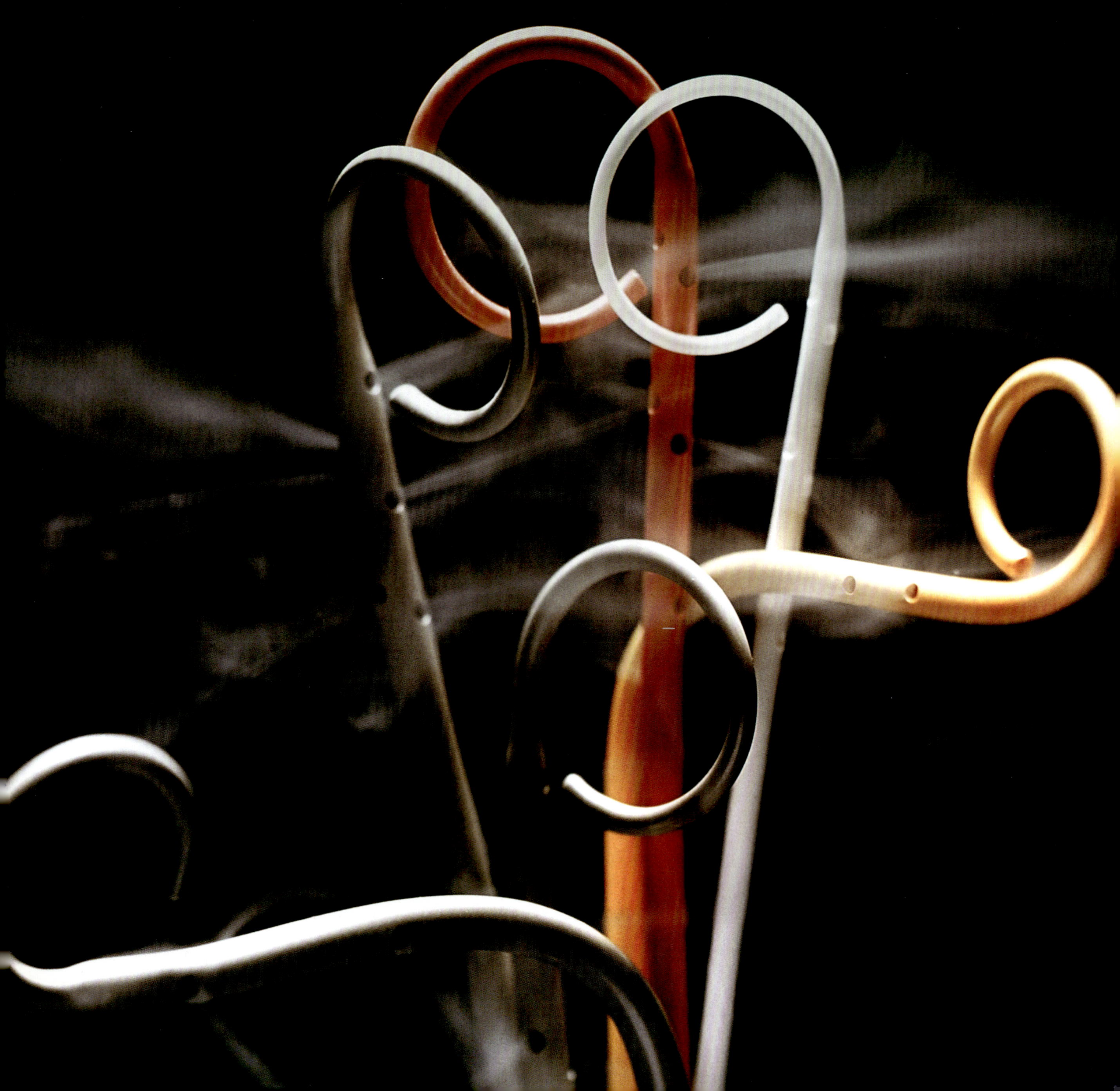

In 1989 a new, state-of-the-art research and development facility opened in Bloomington. Housing a team bolstered by the hiring of additional technicians, specialists and four new engineers, the $2 million R&D operation allowed Cook to significantly expand its research capabilities. "We're always looking for new materials—exotic alloys, which require new fabricating methods," said Tom Osborne, vice president of research and development. "New machining and welding techniques are being developed all the time."

BATTLING THE COMPETITION WITH NEW PRODUCTS

Not only was Cook saddled with regulatory challenges, the competition was increasingly fierce. More and more the company was forced to patent its products and manufacturing processes to protect itself from piracy. This was an expensive legal task that called for additional skilled personnel in almost every part of the organization.

Notwithstanding these legal and regulatory impediments, Cook Incorporated still managed to find innovative solutions to the challenges doctors faced every day. The impetus for those developments had not changed in nearly 30 years.

Between 1985 and 1990 the company managed to introduce more than 40 new and extraordinarily diverse products, including catheters for shock-wave lithotripsy, the use of sound waves to pulverize kidney stones; obstetrics and gynecology tools, including a fallopian tube catheter set and an intrauterine insemination catheter; and a new body-temperature-regulated pacemaker called the Sensor Model Kelvin 500. They were exactly what hospitals needed—affordable "tools of the trade" that got the job done. Inspiring nearly every one were doctors who, like the first physicians Cook had worked with, needed new and better equipment to better serve their patients.

There was nothing glamorous about these new tools, but they were state-of-the-art and probably the most diverse array of devices Cook had ever generated in a single five-year span. Still, none of them came close to matching the uniqueness of the product Neal Fearnot was about to unveil.

Cook had been licensing from Purdue University the rights to produce and sell a promising biomaterial called small intestinal submucosa (SIS), which Fearnot and Leslie Geddes had stumbled upon almost accidentally while they were doing research on stents for Cook during the 1980s. It turned out to be an astonishing discovery. Geddes and Fearnot thought the collagen-based material, harvested from the lining of pig intestines, might make a good coating for stents. In reality it had infinitely greater potential. SIS has the capability to duplicate almost any tissue it comes in contact with when it is placed on or in the body.

So great was the new discovery's potential that by 1995 it would lead Cook to create an entirely new business. Within a decade scientists would be developing a constantly expanding array of new products based on SIS with no real limit in sight.

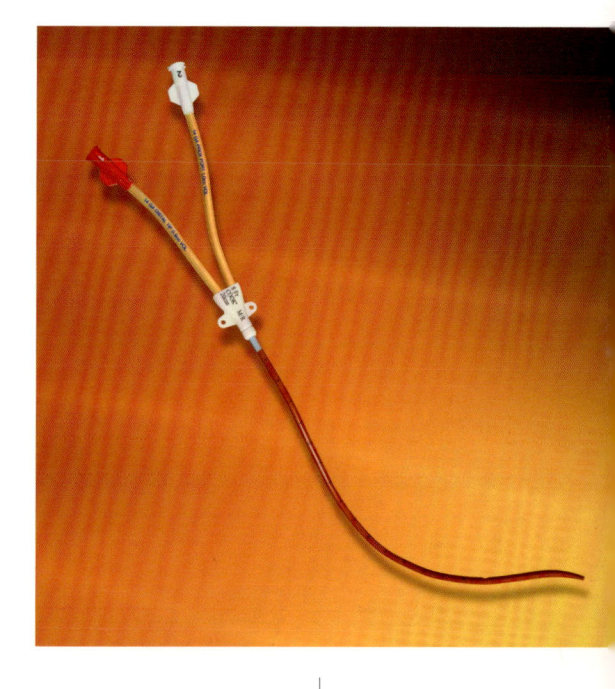

The Central Venous Pressure Monitoring Catheter, above, and a bouquet of "pigtails," opposite, were among dozens of new or improved products that Cook, battling increasingly fierce competition, introduced during the second half of the 1980s.

Chapter Seven: 1993-1997

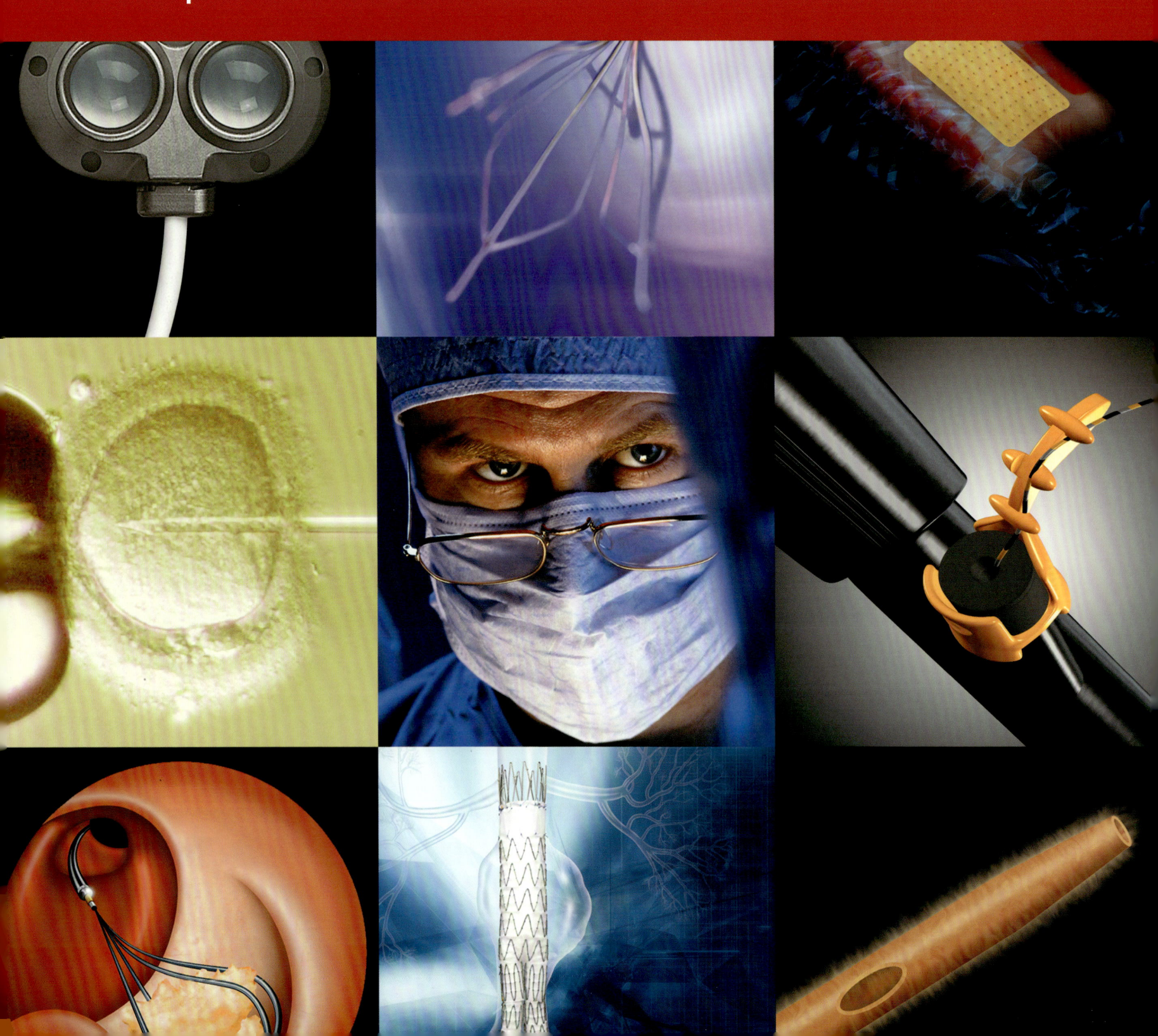

The World's Largest

Dr. Cesare Gianturco and Dr. Andreas Grüentzig were designing a balloon-expanded stent when Grüentzig died in 1985. With Cook support Gianturco and Dr. Gary Roubin introduced the Gianturco-Roubin Coronary Stent, right, in 1991. A physician, opposite, is surrounded by Cook technologies that have changed the face of health care.

Cook Incorporated's fast expansion continued into the 1990s. In 1993 the company established Cook Ireland Ltd. in Limerick to meet the needs of clinicians in the fields of gastroenterology, urology and obstetrics and gynecology throughout Europe. The company provides local product development, manufacture of urological and gastrointestinal devices and distribution for Cook Group companies. It also functions as a shared service center for all Cook strategic business unit sales activities in Europe.

In Bloomington that same year Cook Incorporated opened a primary care health clinic for Cook employees. Cook management was convinced that the clinic could deliver quality care to employees while containing the rising costs of health care. The company would accomplish that by owning the facility and offering workers an after-hours alternative to the emergency room at Bloomington Hospital or the walk-in clinics, which tended to be more expensive than family physicians.

Cook was the first business in the Bloomington area to offer such a service. Nationally it was in good company, joining a growing roster of large corporations, such as Gillette, Goodyear, Adolph Coors and John Deere, that had successfully set up their own clinics as one way to try to contain rising health care costs.

BRINGING THE STENT TO MARKET

Cook worked hard in the early 1990s to educate health care professionals about the uses of the Gianturco-Roubin Coronary Stent. Since it was a totally new product, the pre- and post-treatment of stent patients was deemed as critical to the success of the procedure as the actual placement of the stent. Consequently entire cardiology staffs were trained along with physicians. Only after training and certification did the full market launch of the product

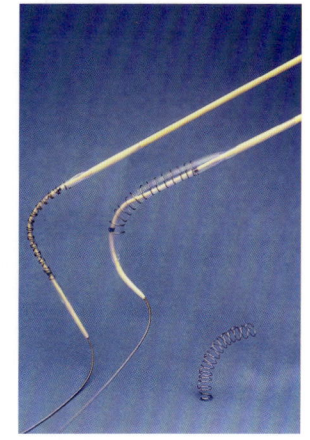

Cook Urological leaders Fred Roehmer, Jerry French and Jeff McGough, left to right, are suited up in the early 1990s, preparing to watch a procedure using Cook products. Cook sales reps often don scrubs with the company logo to observe medical procedures and learn firsthand how their products are used.

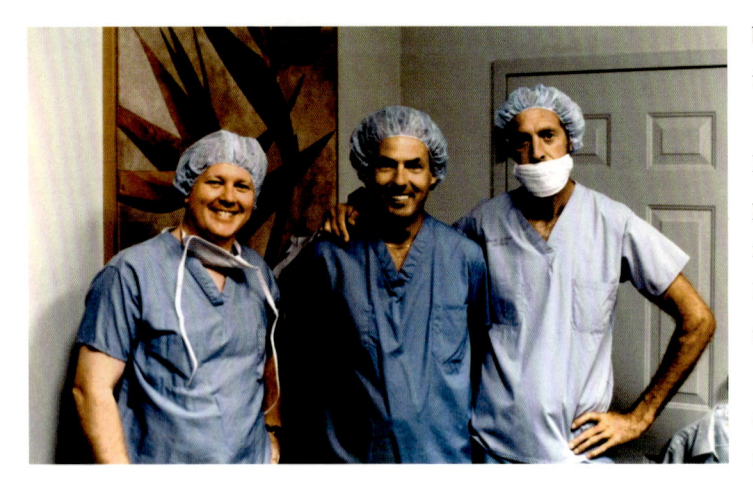

begin in the United States. Some stents were being sold abroad, and in each country the same training was required to assure success.

The stent quickly caught on, but it was approved only for a limited application. It could be used just for acute or threatened closure of a vessel following failed angioplasty. It was not approved for use as an adjunct to angioplasty or as a primary treatment of previously untreated blockages. So even as the company was awaiting the FDA go-ahead to commence marketing, it began refining the stent's design in order to pursue approval for broader applications.

In the meantime, Johnson & Johnson (J&J) acquired the rights to an alternative device, the Palmaz-Schatz Coronary Stent, designed by Dr. Julio Palmaz of the University of Texas Health Science Center. While conducting clinical trials on its stent, Johnson & Johnson announced that it had also acquired Cordis Corporation, Miles Kanne's former employer. By the time of the acquisition, Cordis had established strong credentials in the cardiology field. With a line of angioplasty balloon catheters, guiding catheters and related products for use in coronary angioplasty, Cordis had a leg up on Cook, which still had to develop its own guiding catheters and other products.

Once Johnson & Johnson received pre-market approval from the FDA for the Palmaz-Schatz stent, the company promptly sued Cook for patent infringement, alleging that Cook had violated Palmaz's patents on stent design and use of balloon catheters to deliver stents. Cook, however, had also worked with Dr. Palmaz. He had approached Cook Incorporated after the company began supporting Dr. Gianturco's research, and Cook, impressed with his concepts, had underwritten portions of the cost of his research and had even paid for the patent over which J&J sued Cook. The litigation quickly descended into a squabble over which company had established its stent designs first. It dragged on for three years, draining Cook resources until—with FDA approval of Cook's second-generation stent approaching—the two companies settled their case early in 1997. Cook didn't want the lawsuit to jeopardize approval of its plans for extended applications on the stent.

THREE-CONTINENT SOLUTION TO A LIFE-SAVING CONDITION

Two heads are better than one, says the old adage. Sometimes three are even better. That was certainly the case when Cook developed a stent-graft that revolutionized the way surgeons treat an abdominal aortic aneurysm (AAA)—a potentially fatal swelling of the artery that supplies blood to the abdomen, pelvis and legs. Three Cook teams on three different continents worked together to develop a life-saving device.

Abdominal aortic aneurysms are the 13th leading cause of death, taking at least 15,000 lives every year and affecting more than 1.7 million people, in the United States. Until the advent of AAA stent-grafts, treating an AAA required an open procedure. A long incision was made from the patient's sternum to the pubis. The intestines were lifted and laid to the side in order to access the aneurysm and insert a graft—a polyester fabric tube used to line the blood vessel's damaged walls. Not only was this major, invasive surgery, it often invited complications. After one year, morbidity rates related to hernias and chronic pain were significant, while as many as 5 percent of patients died—in part because many of those undergoing the graft were over age 65.

The development of Cook's AAA stent-graft is a sort of triple play dating to Dr. Cesare Gianturco's development of the Z stent in the 1970s. While Gianturco never adapted his Z stent for AAA repair, others experimented with doing so in the early 1990s. Meanwhile, in the early 1990s Argentine physician Juan Parodi published a paper describing his own success performing endovascular AAA procedures, entering the patient's circulatory system through a small incision in the leg, using an entirely different technology based on balloon expanding stents. Parodi's paper generated positive attention in the medical and popular media around the world. The third piece fell into place when

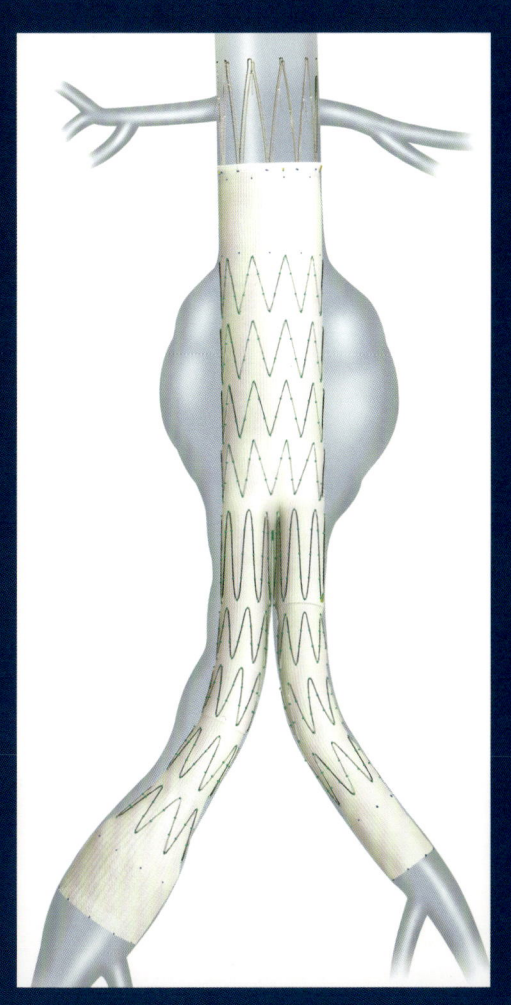

Cook research teams in the United States, Denmark and Australia played roles in creation of the life-saving Zenith abdominal aortic aneurysm stent.

Cook researchers in Australia combined Gianturco's self-expandable Z stents with polyester surgical graft material to create what evolved into the company's Zenith line for the endovascular treatment of abdominal aortic aneurysms.

The genesis of Zenith was research by Dr. Tim Chuter in Rochester, New York, who began designing an AAA stent-graft in the early 1990s. After Chuter visited the Cook team in Perth, Australia, those researchers became excited about such a stent-graft and soon began their own development. A similar thing happened with the Cook team in Denmark after a visit from Chuter. In 1997 the three teams got together to share information about their developments. It was clear that Cook could not develop, engineer, manufacture, pass regulation and market three stent-grafts intended for the same purpose.

As a result of that meeting, one product, which relied most heavily on the Australian group's findings, came to market. In 2003 the FDA approved the Zenith stent-graft, and it soon became the industry leader. Its highly flexible, three-piece modular design makes it useful on more patients than other stent-grafts. Once in place, Zenith's innovative barbs and structure reduce the risk that the graft will migrate—and this in turn minimizes the time-consuming and potentially dangerous need to go back and adjust the stent-graft while increasing the chance that the damaged vessel wall will shrink closer to normal size.

The Zenith line has been a huge success for Cook, contributing to a major growth in gross revenues for Cook's Aortic Intervention strategic business unit.

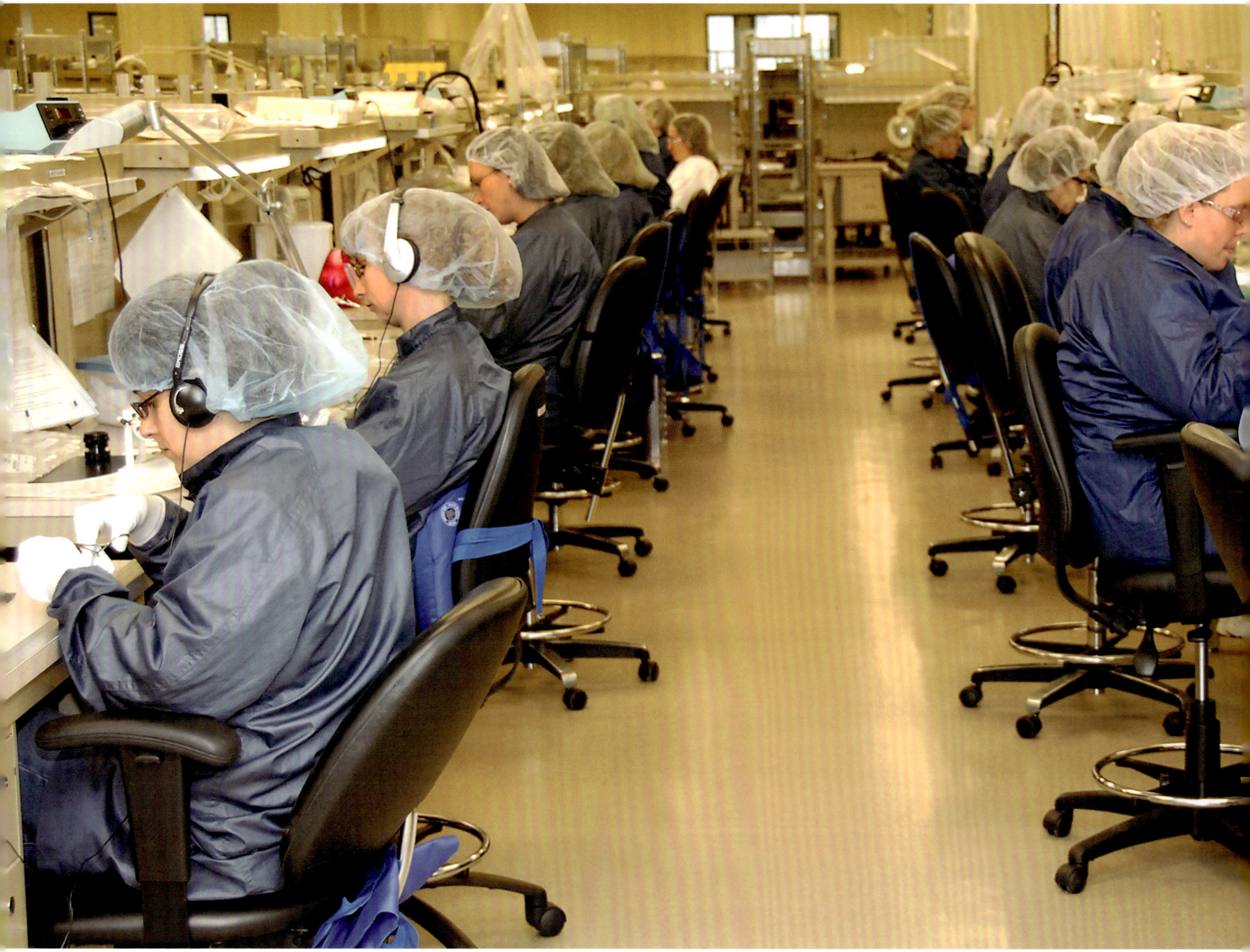

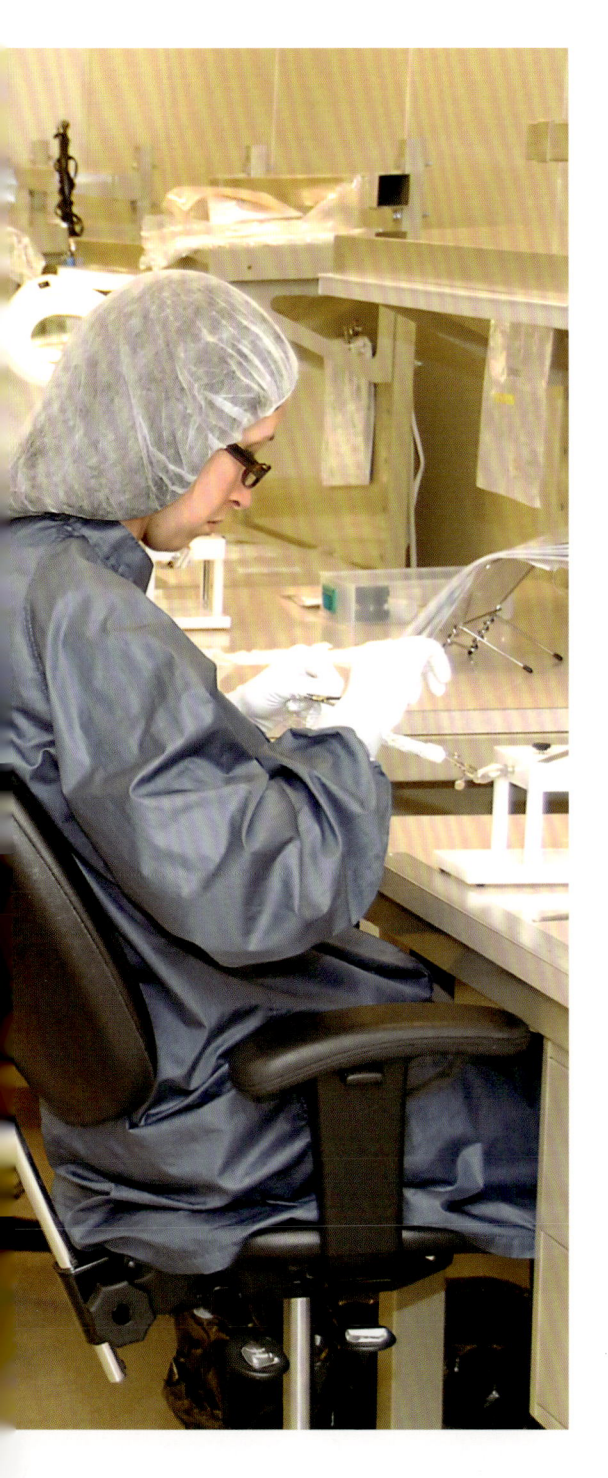

By then Dr. Gianturco had been dead for two years. It was not lost on Cook's team that Johnson & Johnson had all the time in the world to develop its stent, while most of a decade ticked away between the unveiling of Gianturco's device and the FDA's belated approval. It was emblematic of the travails Cook had endured during that difficult regulatory period.

Brian Bates is quick to leap to Dr. Gianturco's defense, asserting that his role in the invention of stents was enormous and remains largely unappreciated. It was also galling to think of the lives that might have been saved had Gianturco's device been available to doctors sooner. His death, before the Gianturco-Roubin Coronary Stent finally began to garner the acclaim it deserved, would have seemed just one more sorry episode had he not been one of the very greatest inventors in the field.

In Winston-Salem, North Carolina, while the saga of the Gianturco-Roubin Coronary Stent was playing out, a different drama was unfolding that would also have a profound impact on the company. Mike Hughes, a seasoned sales professional who had joined Cook in 1991 and worked in Chicago and Tampa, joined Wilson-Cook in 1994 as national accounts manager. He hadn't been on the job very long before he observed a growing, and disturbing, trend.

"Up to that point, Cook had never experienced any price pressure," Hughes says. "We had always been committed to making the best products possible. History had taught us that, as long as we did that, we could name our price." But that was about to change. In response to the managed care revolution, hospitals in large numbers were joining or forming group purchasing organizations to leverage their buying power. By the early 1990s, says Hughes, this phenomenon had achieved a critical mass.

He convened a meeting of senior Cook officials, who concluded that changes were inevitable. "We've never taken our eyes off clinical product development," says Hughes. "But we realized that purchasing was

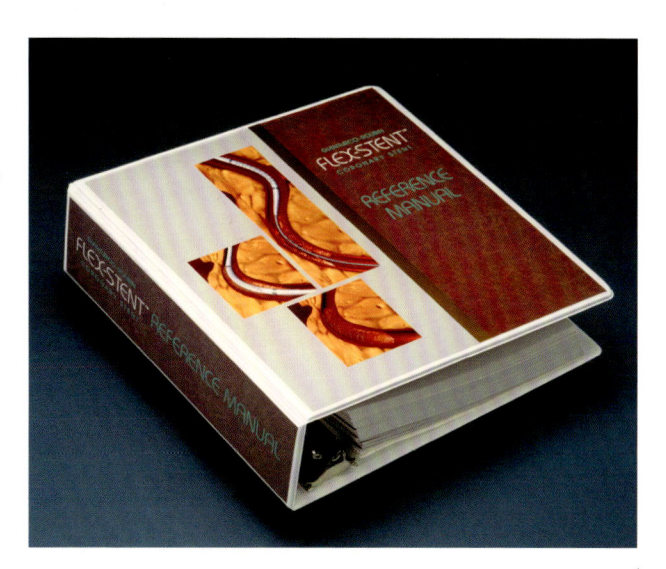

Workers assemble Cook's AAA (abdominal aortic aneurysm) stent-grafts, opposite. The AAA stents are fabric tubes that reinforce aneurysms, weak spots in blood vessels. Above, Cook provides this massive reference manual to all physicians when they receive training on the use of the Gianturco-Roubin Flex-Stent Coronary Stent.

"NO LOSERS IN HISTORIC PRESERVATION"

When they first moved to Bloomington in 1963 and money was tight, Bill and Gayle Cook would occasionally enjoy an evening dining out. Their restaurant of choice was usually McDonald's. Their recreational budget was tight. Even when his company made money, Bill put it back into the business—ensuring Cook Incorporated's growth.

On weekends, to get away from the pressure of work—especially in those early days when they were the company's only employees—the young couple enjoyed going for leisurely drives through the countryside, exploring the old back roads that stitch across the hills, river valleys and limestone outcrops of southern Indiana. Gayle Cook began to chronicle their expeditions, and soon her accounts of the whereabouts of off-the-beaten-path treasures and historic landmarks had become a book, *A Guide to Southern Indiana*, the definitive resource for anyone who wanted to get to know the Hoosier State's lower half.

But another avocation was born in those simple automobile trips, one that the Cooks have pursued with increasing joy as the fruits of their labors have given them the wherewithal: historic preservation. What they found on those Sunday afternoons was often both inspirational and heart-wrenching. The landscape, even in Bloomington, was dotted with fine old buildings, homes and commercial facilities, often of great historic significance, that were disintegrating from neglect. What should have been community assets were often ugly deficits.

They decided to do something about it. As funds became available, they began purchasing and restoring many historic buildings and homes in southern Indiana. Their first foray into preservation, in 1976, was the Cochran House, a beautiful old home built circa 1850 by James Cochran, a prosperous local businessman. Once restored, it became the first Bloomington home of Cook's Monroe Guaranty Insurance Company. It later housed CFC Inc., a Cook company founded in 1973, and then Cook Group itself.

It was also in 1976 that the Cooks restored the Colonel William Jones house in Gentryville, Indiana. Jones, the house's original owner, was a Whig representative in the Indiana state legislature and owned a store in which young Abraham Lincoln worked as a clerk. Lincoln slept in the house one night in 1844 after making a campaign speech for Henry Clay, the Whig presidential candidate that year. After the restoration, the Cooks donated the house and property to the State of Indiana.

Among the many beneficiaries of the Cooks' restoration work have been Richard and Charles Pritchett, contractors from Bedford, Indiana. The

Bill and Gayle Cook, opposite, strike a relaxed pose on the porch at Cedar Farm, the elegant antebellum plantation on the Ohio River that they rescued in the 1980s. The Cooks' weekend getaway sprawls over 2,500 acres and includes Indiana's largest privately owned contiguous native forest.

brothers started a long-term relationship with Bill Cook when, at no cost, they built him the workbench on which he and Tom Osborne created catheter products when Cook Incorporated was still a spare-bedroom operation. Grateful for the gift, Bill has included them and their sons in nearly every Cook construction and restoration project for more than 40 years.

The Cooks are strong believers in the idea that many refurbished buildings can also become commercially viable, rather than simply standing as museum pieces that require ongoing subsidization. Their restoration work in Bloomington has included Graham Plaza, Allen Court, the Illinois Central railroad depot, the Grant Street Inn, the Bloomington Antique Mall, Fountain Square Mall and many other buildings, most of which now house successful businesses. Almost single-handedly the Cooks wrested those buildings from potential destruction and in the process bestowed both architectural beauty and economic vitality upon downtown Bloomington, which, like many downtowns, had suffered from retail movement to the suburbs.

"Historic preservation is a business," Bill Cook said in 1985. "Restoration is one of the best ways to be profitable in real estate. The cost of new construction far outweighs the cost of preservation."

His greatest resource in that effort has been CFC Inc. When credit unions offered an alternative to the low-interest loans CFC had provided to employees, CFC evolved into Cook's real estate development and management company. It was through CFC that Bill and Gayle purchased Cedar Farm, an antebellum plantation built in 1837 on the Ohio River near Corydon, Indiana. The Cooks, who spend most weekends at the estate, opened it to the public for two days in 1985 after they had completely restored it. Twelve thousand visitors found themselves taking a trip back into the past. The 2,500-acre complex includes not only the magnificent main house but a cookhouse, milk house, ice house, schoolhouse, tenant dwellings and livestock and tobacco barns. The extensive woodlands, which are being preserved and replanted, comprise Indiana's largest privately owned contiguous native forest.

In 1996 CFC collaborated with the Historic Landmarks Foundation of Indiana to stabilize and partially restore the West Baden Springs Hotel, a national historic landmark in West Baden, Indiana. Once described as the "eighth wonder of the world," the grand old hotel, built around a central atrium with a towering dome, is recognized as one of the nation's most important preservation projects. Then, when CFC became involved in the restoration of nearby French Lick Springs Resort and the development of the French Lick Resort Casino, CFC resumed work on the West Baden Springs Hotel—which reopened to acclaim on May 23, 2007. In addition to his many other responsibilities with the company, Carl Cook has overseen these and several other restoration projects from the beginning.

"Saving landmarks great and small is an investment which benefits everyone," Bill Cook wrote in 1999. "From the artisans hired to lay brick and re-plaster walls, to the neighborhood revitalized by having a restored property where once a vacant eyesore stood, to the local governments receiving new tax revenues as business grows, there are no losers when it comes to historic preservation. And that's the best reason of all for doing it."

French Lick Springs Hotel, left, and the West Baden Springs Hotel are both Cook restorations benefiting southern Indiana's economy and exemplifying the goal of preserving fine old buildings and returning them to productivity.

THE WORLD'S LARGEST 129

Steve Ferguson was a young lawyer in Bloomington when he met the Cooks in 1966. In the 1980s and '90s, he played an important role in government and regulatory affairs. Today he is chairman of the board of Cook Group.

an entirely different side of the health care picture. It had become as important to understand purchasers' needs as it always was to understand clinicians' needs."

When Kem Hawkins came to Wilson-Cook in 1997, he lent support to Hughes' efforts to spread this message across the Cook organization. Ten years later Hughes had risen to the role of vice president of corporate accounts, and he headed an organization made up of 11 corporate account executives (CAEs) in Europe, 20 CAEs and key account managers in North America and two CAEs in Australia. All of them were devoted to understanding the needs of health care purchasers and finding ways to ensure that Cook meets those needs without conceding the product quality that has always been the company's hallmark. Today some 75 percent of all purchases are made via contracts with buying groups.

"WE WANT TO BE READY"

In 1995 small intestinal submucosa research created the need for a new company—Cook Biotech Inc. The company, jointly owned by Cook, the Purdue Research Foundation and Methodist Hospital/Clarian Health Partners, was founded to develop and manufacture commercial products made from SIS and, hopefully, other biomaterials from natural tissue sources for use in medical products.

Headed by Neal Fearnot, Cook Biotech was based in West Lafayette, Indiana, near the Purdue campus, and it conducted research, development and manufacturing operations in a state-of-the-art facility befitting the potential of its singular discovery. It also operated its own processing and production line, where natural tissues were transformed into acellular biomaterials.

The next year, Cook Pacemaker changed its name. Founded in 1981, the company had initially been involved in the development of cardiac rhythm management and vascular access products. Now the company abandoned pacemakers, refocusing its business objectives to zero in on the opportunities presented by a growing market for vascular products. In its new incarnation, Cook Vascular Incorporated, it soon introduced such devices as a Doppler probe and monitor for short-term invasive monitoring of blood flow through grafted vessels, a jumbo vascular access port, dual valve catheters, noncoring needles for port access and tools to assist in the extraction of indwelling catheters and cardiac leads.

They were excellent examples of the rich diversity in Cook's product lines. By 1997 Cook Group was a conglomerate of 42 companies. They manufactured more than 140,000 different products and combinations of products for diagnosis and treatment of disease, and they were shipping a whopping 60-plus million units (primarily wire guides and catheters) every year. The company boasted some 1,300 employees, having added 120 hourly workers since the beginning of the year with plans to add another 70 by year's end.

"Our whole company is based on getting new products," Steve Ferguson, Cook Group's chief operating officer, told the U.S. Senate that year. "We are going to see an exponential explosion of new devices and techniques in the medical world over the next decade, and we want to be ready to make them available to Americans."

Ferguson had traveled to Capitol Hill to try once again to convince Congress of the need for FDA reforms. He told the U.S. Senate Labor and Human Resources Committee that Cook and the Medical Device Manufacturers Association believed that the FDA went far beyond its statutory mandate in reviewing the effectiveness of devices. The FDA's overzealous evaluations caused lengthy delays in bringing life-saving products to market, he said.

Ferguson told the Senate panel about the 12 years it took Cook to get FDA approval for its coronary stent. Many companies, he said, were now doing most of their product development in Europe, even though labor costs there were significantly higher, because regulatory approval was much quicker. By the time the Cook device was approved in the United States, he noted, competitors' products had been available in Europe for years. The coronary stent situation, he said, was a good example of what was happening in the international medical technology marketplace.

"In the U.S. the only stents available are the stent we introduced in 1992 and the stent manufactured by Johnson & Johnson, which came on the market soon after ours," Ferguson said. "In Europe physicians can choose from 32 stents which are approved… The score is 32–2, Mr. Chairman. Patients and doctors have no choice but to use old technology in the U.S. This is wrong, and we cannot allow this to continue."

Ferguson, who had been working on this problem for nearly ten years, acknowledged that the FDA had taken some important steps toward modification of the regulatory process. But, he added, the agency needed to exempt from lengthy Class III regulatory reviews a number of devices that had only undergone minor changes from their original models. He said other changes should be made in the pre-market approval process and in streamlining other product reviews.

It had been a long stretch, but by 1997, thanks to hard work and persistence, Ferguson had helped to eke out some small changes in FDA regulations. The next time would be different.

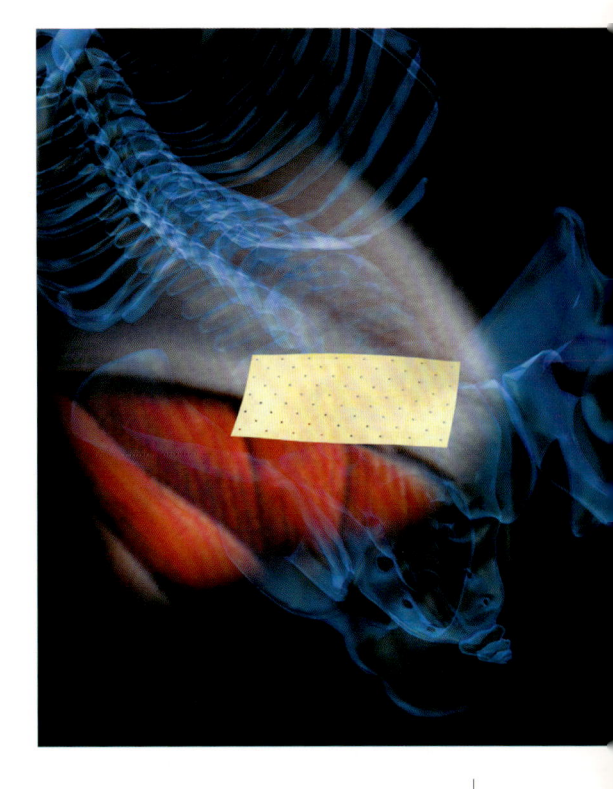

The discovery of small intestinal submucosa (SIS) by researchers at Purdue University led to the creation of Cook Biotech Incorporated. The product, shown above for inguinal hernia repair, is a naturally occurring "scaffold" that dramatically propels healing.

REDUCING CATHETER-RELATED BLOODSTREAM INFECTIONS

For treatment of a wide range of conditions, many patients require a venous catheter—a tube placed through the skin into which medicine, blood or nutritional supplements can be injected quickly into the bloodstream. Unfortunately central venous catheters—especially those used in critically ill patients—present a serious and potentially fatal threat. Infections occur in about 3.5 percent of lines placed, and up to 20 percent of infected patients die. The rates are even higher when the patients are children.

In 1986 Cook marketed the first anti-infective vascular catheter. Branded as Bio-Guard AB, it was coated with tridodecylmethylammonium chloride, a surfactant that helped to bond antibiotics to the catheter surface. A randomized trial proved those catheters effective in reducing infections, but surgeons complained that they were inconvenient since the catheter required soaking in an antibiotic solution for up to ten minutes before use. The heat was on for Cook to develop something even better.

Cook launched the Spectrum catheter in 1997. It used a combination of two antibiotics, rifampin and minocycline, which researchers found to be highly effective in preventing infection. The solution permeates the entire structure of the device, allowing the antibiotics to remain active on the internal and external surfaces for more than three weeks (first-generation catheters impregnated with antibiotics were effective for a mere three days). Furthermore, Spectrum Glide's slippery hydrophilic coating facilitates access through even the toughest tissues.

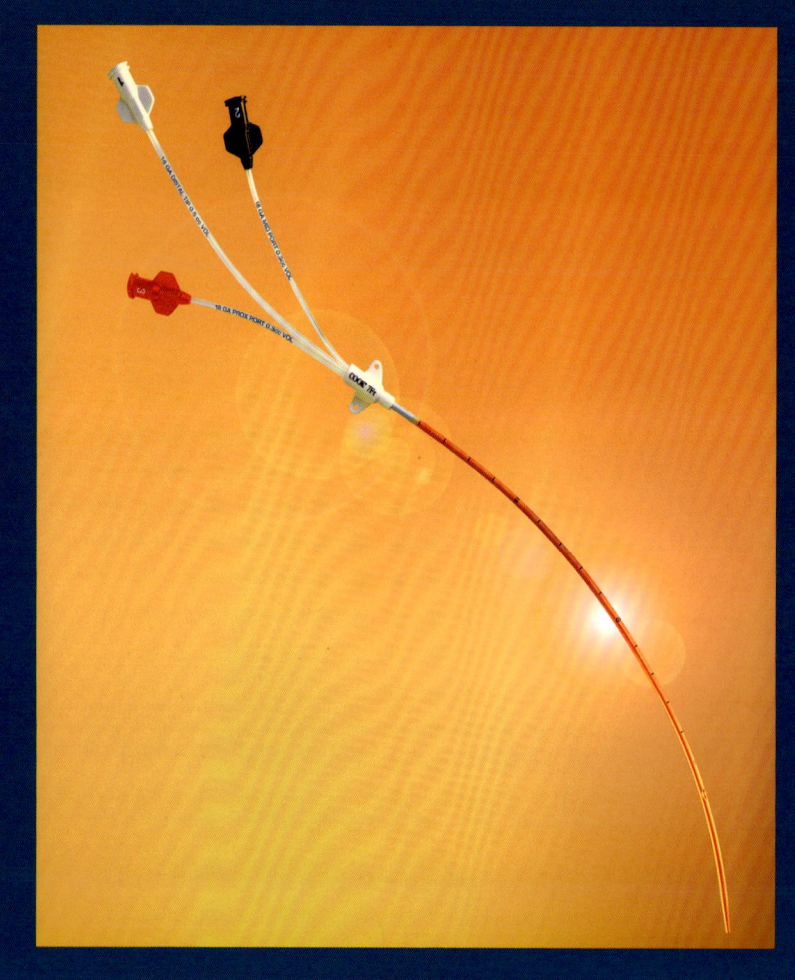

With the development of Bio-Guard AB, a venous catheter coated with a surfactant to bond antibiotics, Cook declared war on potentially fatal catheter-related bloodstream infections. While Cook has struggled against regulatory resistance to the use of its antibiotic-infused catheters, the stage has been set for a breakthrough.

Use may increase even more with increased public and scientific scrutiny of hospital-acquired infections. Industrywide best practice standards are being established, and, thanks to Cook's lobbying efforts in Washington, Congress passed CMS-1533-P, a change to the Medicare and Medicaid programs that denies federal payment for catheter infection costs that could be reasonably prevented by following certain guidelines. Those guidelines include the use of antibiotic or antiseptic catheters in cases where catheters are required for prolonged periods of time or where other methods fail to achieve infection targets. The law went into effect on October 1, 2008.

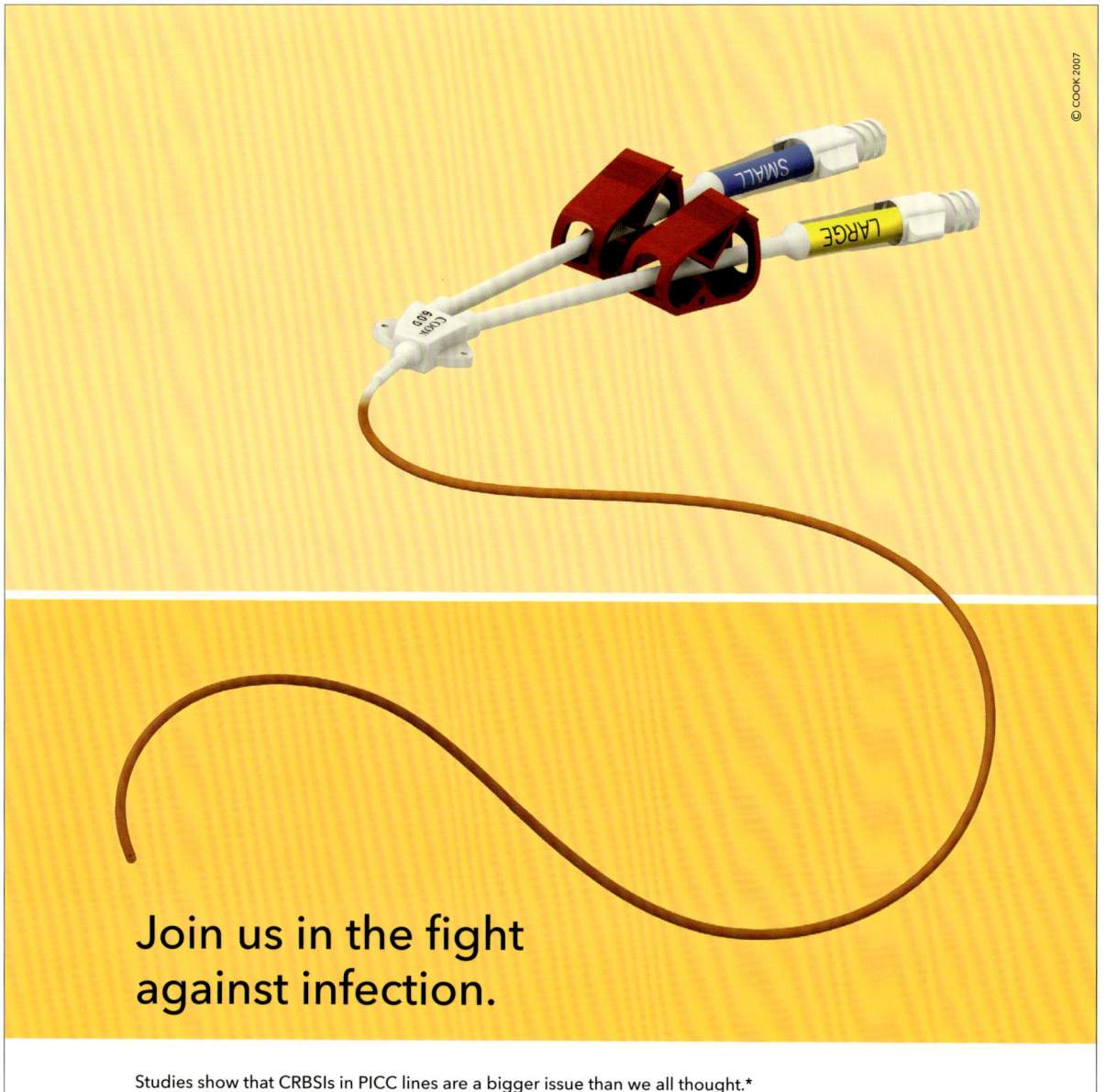

An ad for Spectrum PICC highlights the many benefits of Cook's antibiotic-impregnated catheters. Not only do they prevent bloodstream infections in patients requiring venous catheters, their use also significantly decreases the need for systemic antibiotics.

Join us in the fight against infection.

Studies show that CRBSIs in PICC lines are a bigger issue than we all thought.* As the creator of the first and only antibiotic PICC, it's our responsibility to keep you not only informed, but prepared. That's why Spectrum PICC is infused with an antibiotic compound that breaks down and destroys bacteria. To learn more about Spectrum PICC and how you can join us in the fight against CRBSIs, visit cookmedical.com.

COOK MEDICAL
Spectrum® PICC
ANTIBIOTIC-IMPREGNATED CATHETERS

*Data on file.

| AORTIC INTERVENTION | CARDIOLOGY | CRITICAL CARE | ENDOSCOPY | PERIPHERAL INTERVENTION | SURGERY | UROLOGY | WOMEN'S HEALTH |

While Ferguson was in Washington, Cook Incorporated was creating yet another new business entity called Cook Endovascular. Based in Bloomington, the new division would deliver core Cook technologies and products to physicians and other health care professionals in endovascular therapies, vascular surgery and neurosurgery.

INTRODUCTION OF THE GR-II

In May 1997 *Bloomington Herald-Times* reporter Brian Werth noted that "Cook's new GR-II Coronary Stent is the first new coronary stent cleared for clinical use in the United States in three years. Cook's earlier stent—the first cleared for use in the U.S.—has been commercially available since 1993, with more than 100,000 U.S. implants."

Cook's new stent was referred to as "low-profile," which meant it addressed a real need that Cook's earlier stent could not fulfill. The GR-II's design enabled it to easily pass through another stent already placed in an artery. With the GR-II, doctors could now reach new trouble spots in narrower sections of coronary arteries or even in smaller side branches of the blood vessels.

"We greatly underestimated the animosity that had grown in the cardiology market against Johnson & Johnson, due to the high cost of their Palmaz-Schatz product and the lack of continuous development and enhancements," Phyllis McCullough says. The market shifted practically overnight. Between June and July 1997 Cook sold 50,000 of the new stents, and sales continued to be brisk right through the autumn, climbing from about $14 million per month to upwards of $40 million.

Several other companies were soon nipping at Cook's heels and eyeing the long-established frontrunner, Johnson & Johnson, which was also going through clinical trials with stents of its own. Guidant Corporation (later part of Boston Scientific) completed clinical trials for a coronary stent called the Multi-Link and gained FDA approval in September. As Guidant prepared for full launch, Arterial Vascular Engineering, Inc. (AVE) and Boston Scientific received approvals for their products.

By September sales of the new Cook stents topped 75,000. A month later—less than a week after Guidant launched the Multi-Link—McCullough made a bold prediction. Based on sales to date, she said, Cook expected to ship 200,000 GR-IIs in the United States in its first year.

Cook and Guidant were making deep inroads into Johnson & Johnson's share of the U.S. stent market. Both companies' stents offered striking advantages over Johnson & Johnson's. Much more flexible, they could be used in smaller arteries. Cook's device, at about $1,300, had a $250 edge on Guidant's. Guidant also had the benefit of a

Striking as this nighttime shot of Cook's headquarters in Indiana may be, the sun never sets upon the Cook empire.

STATE OF THE ART IN ASSISTED REPRODUCTION

According to a 2006 report from the European Society of Human Reproduction and Embryology, more than three million babies have been born since 1975 using assisted reproductive technologies (ART). Many of those children and their parents can thank Cook, a global leader in the field. The company's breakthrough technologies in egg retrieval; embryo fertilization, culture and storage; and embryo transfer have helped pave the way for assisted reproduction to become one of the fastest growing segments in medicine.

One of Cook's breakthroughs came in the early 1990s, when Andre Van Steirteghem from the Flemish university Vrije Universiteit Brussel in Brussels identified a revolutionary technique for injecting a single sperm into a mature human egg—a process known as intracytoplasmic sperm injection (ICSI). Professor Van Steirteghem worked with Cook to develop the specialized, minute glass pipettes that make this procedure possible. These extraordinary pipettes, manufactured by hand under high magnification, are 1/40th the diameter of a human hair and are used by embryologists to capture and inject the sperm, as well as to hold and manipulate the egg.

Van Steirteghem's procedure made assisted reproduction available to a new range of parents, particularly those with severe male infertility. In addition to assisting with ICSI, Cook's micropipettes have opened up research and technology options for a host of other assisted reproductive technologies.

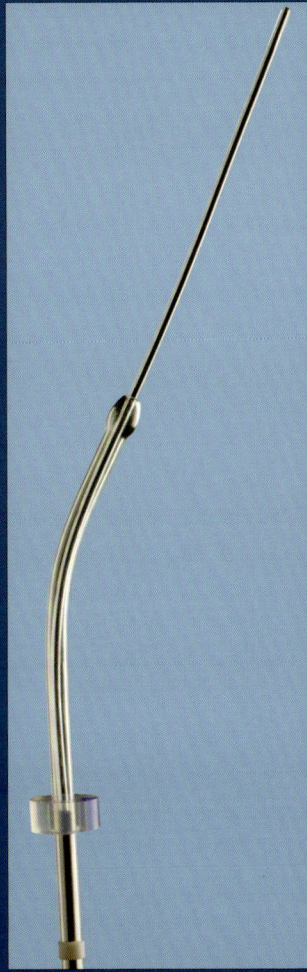

Cook's global leadership in assisted reproductive technologies (ART) has evolved largely from research and development efforts with Sydney IVF, a world-renowned in vitro fertilization (IVF) center in Australia. Devices like the Sydney IVF Embryo Transfer Catheter, left, have improved embryo implantation rates while also enhancing ART procedures for patients.

Cook's other contributions to ART include the world's first truly sequential IVF culture media suite for the efficient culture and development of human embryos. The suite was the culmination of many years of research and development by Sydney IVF, one of the largest and most innovative IVF groups in the world.

The first generation of the sequential media suite was commercialized in 1998, and it comprised a series of balanced solutions that were optimized for the key steps of oocyte fertilization and subsequent embryo development—up to and including the implantation stage. The second generation of the system, which tries to more closely mirror in vivo physiology, was released in Europe and Asia in mid-2007 and soon thereafter in the United States.

Cook also has designed and manufactured the only incubator specifically developed for IVF/ICSI. Because of its ability to reproduce a stable physiological environment for the egg and embryo, the MINC Benchtop Incubator has been shown globally to improve the conditions of embryo culture and the results of implantation.

Another Cook innovation has involved the development of specialized embryo transfer catheters, which due to their design aid in the efficient and safe placement of embryos after culture into the delicate environment of the uterus. One of the major breakthroughs in this field came about when Cook researchers saw that implantation rates improved when technicians used ultrasound to guide the transfer of embryos, improving the accuracy of placement. Out of this discovery, in 2000 Cook introduced the Echotip Soft-Pass Embryo Transfer Set, which married the new transfer technology with that of a soft catheter.

At the same time, Cook, again working with Sydney IVF, developed the Sydney IVF Embryo Transfer Catheter. It combines a unique bulb-shaped tip to ease passage through the patient's anatomy and reduce tissue trauma with technology that lowers the amount of fluid used during the transfer—again improving implantation rates in patients. This catheter has proved globally to be one of the most successful among a full line of ART products offered by Cook's Women's Health business unit.

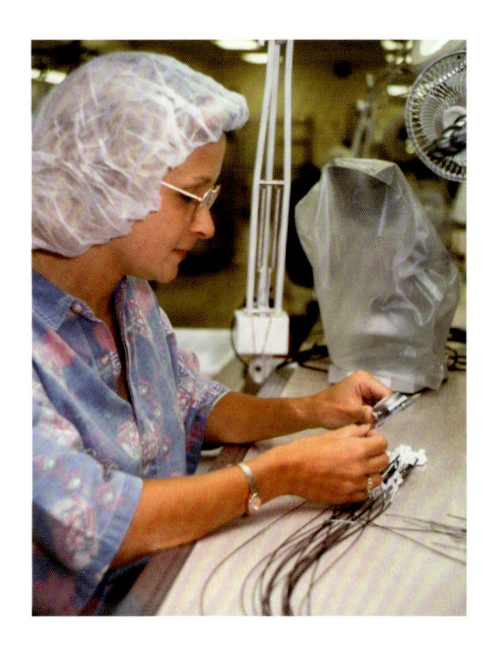

patented rapid-exchange balloon catheter, which meant that physicians didn't need an extra technician in the lab to assist them with the procedure. But the blush was not to last. While the GR-II continued to enjoy the popularity that had attended its debut, Cook began to hear that all might not be right. The new stent was experiencing higher than acceptable rates of restenosis—reclosure of the vessels that had been stented.

When it also became clear that Guidant and AVE's products functioned better than the GR-II, Cook was left with no fallback position. The company had neither an alternative stent nor the requisite ancillary products. It was a setback, and Cook was left with only one option. Announcing a policy that allowed doctors and hospitals to return GR-II devices for credit, Cook simply withdrew from the market in October.

It was not entirely a bad month, though. On October 9 the company learned that the FDA was finally overhauling the way it approved new drugs and medical instruments. Both houses of Congress approved the streamlining, and a new plan was expected in a few weeks. For Steve Ferguson, the news was especially sweet. His tireless efforts to reform regulation had not been in vain.

BOLD PLANS

In August 1997, while the company was still enjoying the success of the GR-II, Cook announced plans to build a new, multi-million-dollar headquarters. It would be a complex on 70 acres of land in the north end of the Park 48 industrial park, west of Bloomington and about a mile from the South Curry Pike address, where the company had been a fixture for more than three decades. At some one million square feet, the new facility would house Cook Incorporated's five divisions: cardiology, radiology, critical care, surgical and endovascular products. Construction was expected to begin in a year.

"We hope to create an industrial campus that will be on a scale of a Microsoft or Nike headquarters," said Dave McCarty, Cook's director of public relations. It was an effort to modernize and consolidate facilities that had become too spread out for efficiency and effective communications. That the new complex was projected to have parking for 1,700 to 1,800 employees was a sign that Cook expected to grow even more and significantly increase its workforce. Thus, despite the setback with the GR-II, Cook looked toward 1998—and the new century that loomed just around the corner—with optimism.

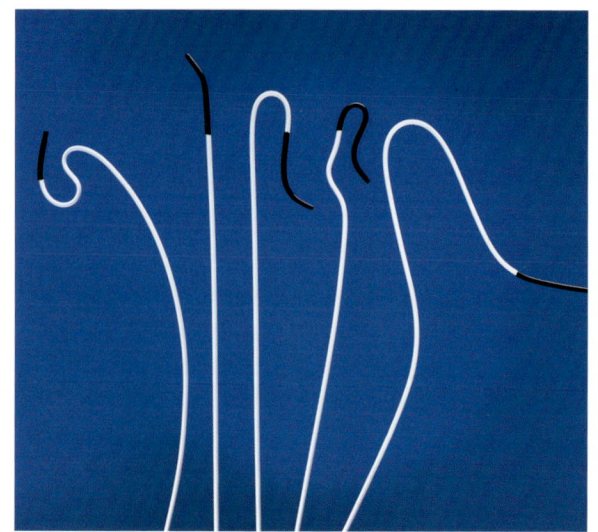

Cook Incorporated's first catalog offered three kinds of catheters for percutaneous catheterizations. Today's Cook catheter tips, right, come in many shapes for cerebral, visceral or multipurpose applications. Even though the product line has grown dramatically, Cook's commitment to quality has never wavered, as the worker inspecting catheters, above, demonstrates.

THE WORLD'S LARGEST   **137**

"We hope to create an industrial campus that will be on a scale of a Microsoft or Nike headquarters," said Dave McCarty, Cook's director of public relations. That the new complex was projected to have parking for 1,700 to 1,800 employees was a sign that Cook expected to grow even more and significantly increase the workforce.

Chapter Eight: 1997-2009 and Beyond

Evolution

The smiles on the faces of this group of Cook employees say it: Cook is a great place to work! Pam Edwards, right, agrees. A 30-plus-year veteran of the company, she says, "I just love coming to work"—and she's done it, without fail, for more than 8,000 days.

Following the incandescent moment of success and rapid nose-dive of the GR-II stent, Cook Incorporated was not deterred. The company dug in to research new stent designs and explore the use of drug coatings to help forestall restenosis, the problem that had doomed the GR-II.

In 1997 the company acquired co-exclusive rights with Boston Scientific to an anti-restenosis drug called Paclitaxel, a derivative of the cancer drug Taxol. Both companies had confidence in the new drug, but Cook was now tasked to find a stent design that would accommodate the drug without infringing on the myriad of stent patents already owned by other developers.

With that goal in mind, Cook acquired Global Therapeutics in 1998. It was a small Colorado company, but it already had a coronary stent on the market in Europe and it was on the verge of launching another. Joe Horn, Global's president, joined Cook Incorporated as a vice president and oversaw the integration of Global's second-generation device, the V-Flex, with a Cook model called the Supra-G. The consequence of this technological fusion was Cook's Logic Coronary Stent, coated with Paclitaxel, trials of which got underway in Asia in 2000. Almost simultaneously Cook started European trials of a Paclitaxel–coated V-Flex.

It was an anxious time. The purpose of the studies was to evaluate the stents' safety and effectiveness as well as various dose densities of the drug coating. Cook's licensing agreement for Paclitaxel specified milestones, and the company was intent on meeting its obligations.

The stent wars were only one front on which Cook companies were hard at work. Demand for interventional products continued

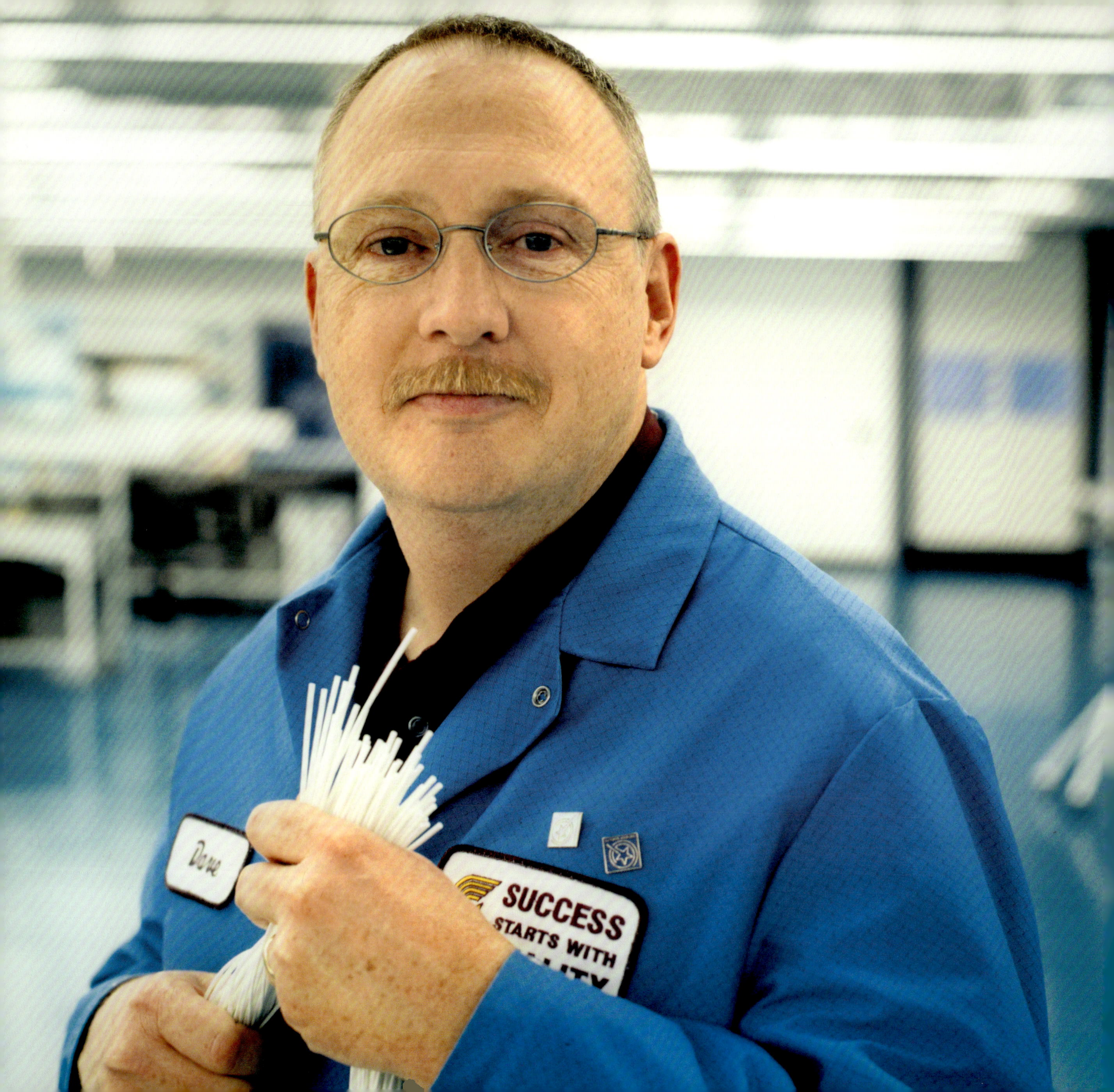
Dave
SUCCESS
STARTS WITH

to increase, and there was an ongoing need for new and more effective critical care products, too. There was, for instance, pressure to eliminate infections related to the use of central venous and other indwelling catheters. The quest to solve that problem resulted in a process to impregnate catheters with antibiotics. The company's Critical Care division was soon developing enhanced airway management products and Spectrum, the first line of antibiotic-impregnated central venous catheters.

Worldwide, Cook was abuzz with industry and invention.

MOTHER NATURE'S SCAFFOLD

Then there was Cook Biotech. SIS was no longer merely a promising idea. By 2000 the newly retooled FDA had cleared five applications of Cook's small intestinal submucosa for use, and, as Mark Bleyer, then executive vice president of Cook Biotech, reported, initial sales of the product "have been going very well." He predicted that SIS "has the potential to be a true breakthrough technology."

Though researchers were still uncertain how SIS worked, they had no question about what it was capable of doing. Rich in proteins and other growth factors that seemed to "switch on" high-speed healing without regard for the nature or severity of the injury or the location, it quickly earned the nickname "Mother Nature's scaffold for healing." It bonded with any tissue to which it was applied, almost instantly signaling the body to start creating healthy new tissue. Then it aided in the development of the new blood vessels that would be needed for the healing process to continue. There seemed to be no limit to its compatibility with the body's array of highly differentiated cells. Indeed researchers had used it to cure chronic sores, to repair internal organs, to treat urinary incontinence and to successfully treat wounds so severe and so deep that no treatment other than amputation would have been available in the past.

Dr. Matthew Parmenter, a Bloomington podiatrist who had used the product, which Cook was marketing under the name Oasis, called it "phenomenal." Parmenter was eminently qualified to make such a claim. He had used Oasis to treat more patients than any other doctor, and he had successfully treated injuries as severe as chain-saw accidents and shotgun wounds. "I used this stuff to reconstruct ligaments and tendons," he told *Indianapolis Star* reporter Jeff Swiatek in 2000. "This is a whole different ball game with this product."

By 2004 Cook Biotech had extended SIS's rapidly expanding utility to include a prototype SIS–coated

Mark Bleyer, above, currently president of Cook Biotech, addresses guests and employees at the dedication of Cook Biotech headquarters in 2004. Opposite, when doctors were having difficulty inserting a central line catheter in Dave Drewes' elderly mother, the Sabin employee urged them to try a TurboFlo PICC he helped design. It worked the first time.

venous valve designed so that, once implanted, it eventually became absorbed into the native lining of the vessel in which it was implanted. "We see enormous potential for devices incorporating SIS," said Bill Cook, "ranging from replacement heart and vein valves to endovascular devices that remodel the aorta and other blood vessels."

A NEW PLAN FOR GLOBAL CENTRALIZATION

The management changes that took place as the 20th century wound down were like an intricate dance. While the Cook Incorporated executive group was again expanded, other Cook managers were deployed to fill management needs at various company outposts.

"In an effort to maintain consistency in the production processes, employee policies and management culture, Cook Incorporated became a breeding ground for new management personnel for other Cook companies," Phyllis McCullough recalls. Don Hollinger took over the leadership of Cook Urological, while Dave Heine became president of Sabin. A few years later, when Sabin needed to grow once again, Bob Lendman replaced Heine.

With Cook out of the pacemaker field, Cook Vascular shifted gears and repositioned itself as a developer of pacemaker lead extraction devices and vascular access ports. Cook Group's Chuck Franz served Cook Vascular as interim president until Louis Goode was named to that post.

On the East Coast Don Wilson, Bill Cook's old friend from Canada, was about to retire from Wilson-Cook. Carl Dickie was named to replace him, but that relationship didn't work out, and Kem Hawkins was dispatched to Winston-Salem to become Wilson-Cook's operations manager for a time. Ron Mobley, an experienced Cook Incorporated production manager, was tapped to join him, and together they oversaw the improvement of Wilson-Cook's production, quality and engineering capabilities.

Hawkins became president of Wilson-Cook, replacing Wilson when he retired, and Mobley became vice president of operations. Hawkins remained in North Carolina until 2001, when Bill Gibbons was appointed president of Wilson-Cook.

Meanwhile, Gene DeVane, the inveterate airplane pilot who had joined the company as a Midwest sales representative in 1973, concluded his career with Cook in an unlikely setting. In the late 1980s DeVane made a business trip to Japan with Ross Jennings. When Jennings had to return to the United States suddenly, DeVane, who couldn't speak Japanese, was left on his own. Interacting with Japanese clinicians, he found that his years of experience successfully communicating with American doctors had provided him with a way around the language barrier. He began traveling extensively to Japan on behalf of Cook, and in 1999 he moved there for an extended stay to shore up the company's Asian operations. It was his last assignment for Cook before he retired.

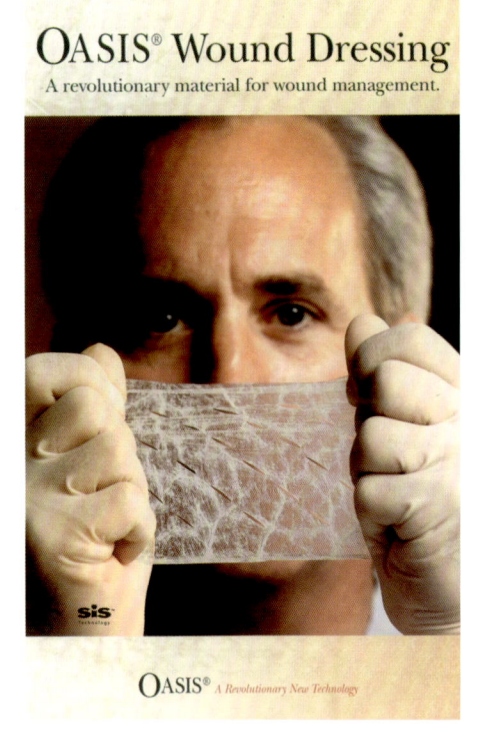

Oasis wound dressing is one of an increasing array of SIS-based products being created by Cook Biotech. SIS speeds healing of superficial injuries, and Cook anticipates many internal applications, as well.

FUSION: A BETTER WAY TO PERFORM ERCP

Cook's Fusion, introduced in 2004, is a family of advanced devices with which physicians can better perform endoscopic retrograde cholangiopancreatography (ERCP). It's an important product that has made it possible for physicians to potentially reduce the trauma to patients while performing a complicated procedure.

In ERCP a physician inserts an endoscope through the mouth to diagnose and treat problems in the liver, gallbladder, bile ducts and pancreas. This allows the physician to see inside the digestive tract and inject dye into the ducts of the biliary tree and pancreas so they can be viewed by X-ray. Meanwhile, the physician can use a catheter to perform sphincterotomies of the biliary and pancreatic sphincters, muscles that lie at the juncture of the intestine with the bile and pancreatic ducts.

Fusion—developed in collaboration with Dr. Stephen Deal, a North Carolina gastroenterologist—dramatically increases the efficiency with which doctors can access areas of the biliary system for diagnosis and treatment. Fusion is also a superior platform for draining bile from blocked ducts and treating various abnormalities of the pancreas.

One of the Fusion system's innovative features is the intraductal exchange, or IDE, which simplifies and improves many areas of treatment, including the complicated task of placing multiple biliary stents. Traditionally this required that the stents be preloaded on a very long wire and then inserted. Access without an inserted wire guide can be difficult if not impossible. The Fusion Oasis stent introducer allows the physician to quickly and safely disengage the wire from the catheter within the ductal system—eliminating the need to withdraw and reinsert a wire guide and reducing concerns about initial or subsequent access when placing multiple stents. Fusion Oasis also allows the physician to easily reposition stents. It is designed to be an advanced ERCP platform that redefines ERCP techniques and even allows it to be converted back to the more traditional long-wire system if the physician chooses.

Fusion's OMNI Breakthrough Channel technology gives the physician complete control of the wire guide while assistants maintain control of the devices during the procedure. It allows for flushing and accepts any diameter or length of wire guide. Other benefits include DomeTip technology, which enhances access and reduces the potential of patient trauma during cannulation.

Fusion has quickly become a major product line for Cook, ending a competitor's former monopoly on short-wire technology and contributing significantly to Cook's position in the critically important area of ERCP.

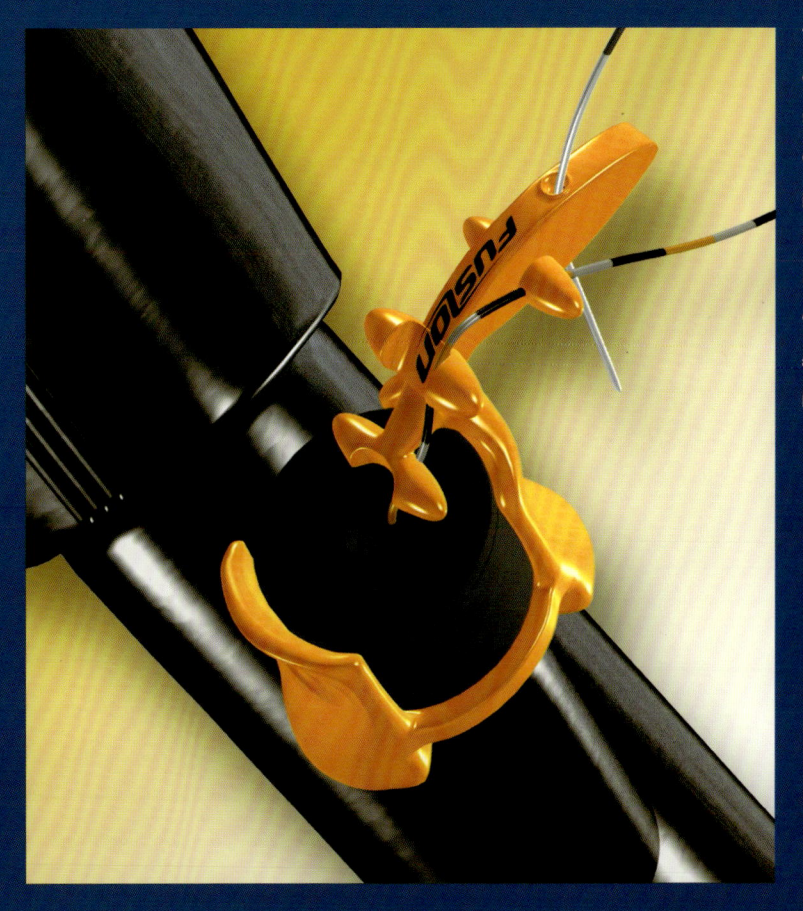

This wire guide locking device is part of Cook's successful Fusion family of devices to help physicians perform ERCP, a procedure in which an endoscope is inserted into the mouth to diagnose and treat liver, gallbladder, bile duct and pancreas problems.

Carl Cook, right, was an infant when his father attended his first professional convention. Today Cook's trade show booth, opposite, is house-sized, and Carl is vice president of Cook Group. He also is president of Cook MyoSite, a company developing autologous cell therapies to promote healing. PVA Foam Embolization Particle, below, is used for permanent embolization of hypervascular lesions and arterio-venous malformations.

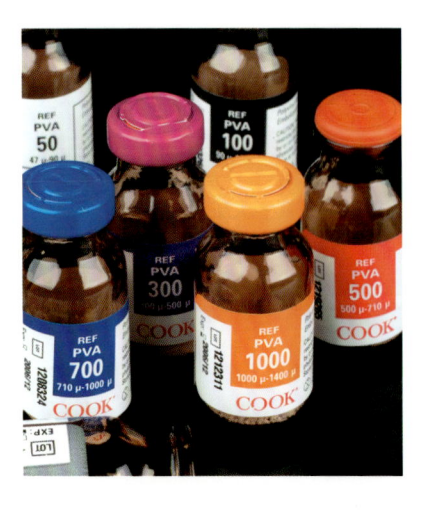

In 2000 Carl Cook, just a toddler when Bill and Gayle had launched the business, was named a vice president of Cook Group. He had already played important roles in the development of Cook Vascular and Wilson-Cook. In 2001 he would be involved in the creation of another new business, Cook MyoSite, of which he would become president.

Dedicated to research that in many respects paralleled Cook Biotech's, Cook MyoSite had at its foundation pioneering University of Pittsburgh research on the use of autologous cells—cells taken from a patient, modified and then reimplanted to promote growth of healthy new tissue. This therapy is used to treat conditions such as urinary incontinence, where natural muscle tissues have grown weak or lost their capacity to function normally. Like SIS, autologous cells may also have the ability to repair many other damaged tissues.

When Cook sales and management personnel converged for a worldwide sales and marketing meeting in 2000, the focus was on the adjustments that would be necessary to accommodate the changing marketplace. Bill Cook set the tone, asserting that the company's size meant that careful planning and coordination of growth were more important than at any time in the company's history.

Once a canoe, the company had become a supertanker. Phyllis McCullough understood that steps needed to be taken to keep it from losing its bearings. She gave her full support to reorganize its business and replace its traditional company-specific sales organizations with strategic business units (SBUs), each with responsibility for marketing to a specific industry segment worldwide. McCullough felt this structure would allow SBU heads to better direct the sales and marketing of all diagnostic and interventional, gastroenterological, urological, in vitro fertilization, critical care, vascular and wound care products. Cook Incorporated also began to streamline its product line. With each Cook facility offering a large variety of products for every segment of the market, manufacturing had become inefficient, and profits were eroding.

To reaffirm the identity of Cook as a whole, the graphic imagery used by each subsidiary changed. Many of the Cook companies had developed their own look over the years, and there was nothing about the logos that suggested a unified company. Now the business began marketing almost everything under the unambiguous name—with capital letters—"COOK." Though the changes were often difficult, the upshot was a new structure that enhanced the capacity of each business segment to boost sales and much more efficiently develop new products.

McCULLOUGH STEPS DOWN

Few people had ever imagined that Bill Cook would sell his company. He had practically built it brick by brick. Some offers are too attractive to ignore, however. In 2000 Cook seriously entertained an offer for a

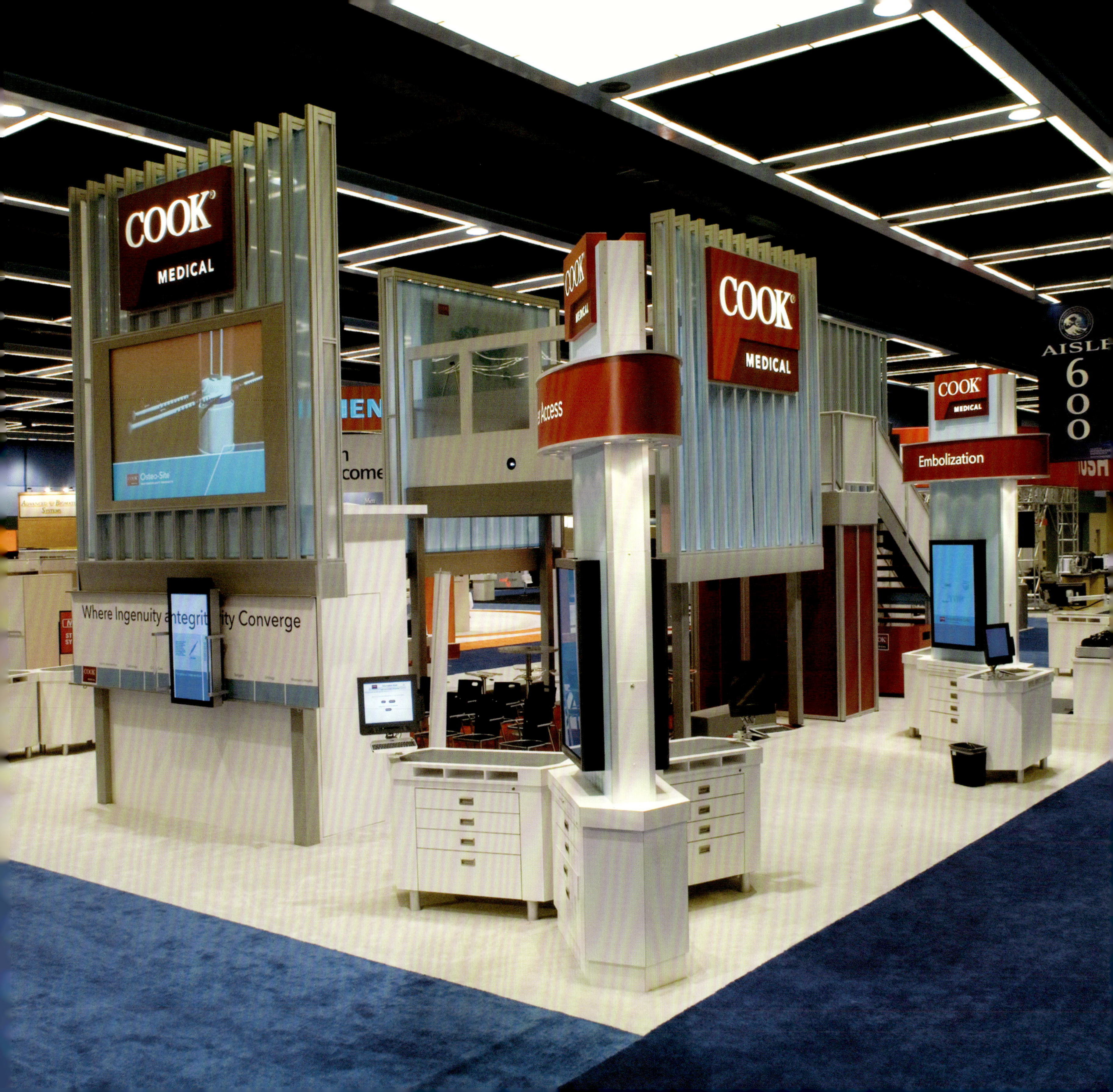
COOK
MEDICAL
COOK
MEDICAL
Embolization
AISLE
600

NCIRCLE: REDESIGNING KIDNEY STONE EXTRACTION

About one in ten people will experience kidney stones, which can be profoundly painful. Many of those stones eventually pass on their own, but some must be removed surgically.

In the past, physicians used stainless steel "stone baskets" in the procedure. Wire was formed into a basket-shaped device that came together in a tip. This was usually formed into a small ball to reduce trauma to surrounding tissue during use. The baskets featured wire leaders, which made it easier to pass the basket beyond the stone and deeper into the body in order to open the basket, capture the stone and pull it out. Moving the basket beyond the stone presented one of the biggest drawbacks to these devices. The procedure was hardly flawless, and damage sometimes occurred.

Another limitation of the baskets was their inability to retain shape. When physicians apply lasers to break up the stones before removal, they sometimes must make multiple attempts to remove the stone fragments. Early stone baskets did not hold up well after multiple uses. Further, as flexible ureteroscopes became more advanced, the metal stone basket often limited endoscope visibility.

In 1998 Cook Urological introduced NCircle—the first stone extractor made of nitinol, a new alloy of nickel and titanium. Nitinol has excellent shape memory and can withstand multiple stone removal attempts. But NCircle also overcame two other major limitations of previous models: first, it is tipless, making the NCircle basket much gentler to surrounding tissue; second, the new design eliminates the need to move the basket beyond the stone. Doctors can align the device next to the stone and use flexible wires to grab it.

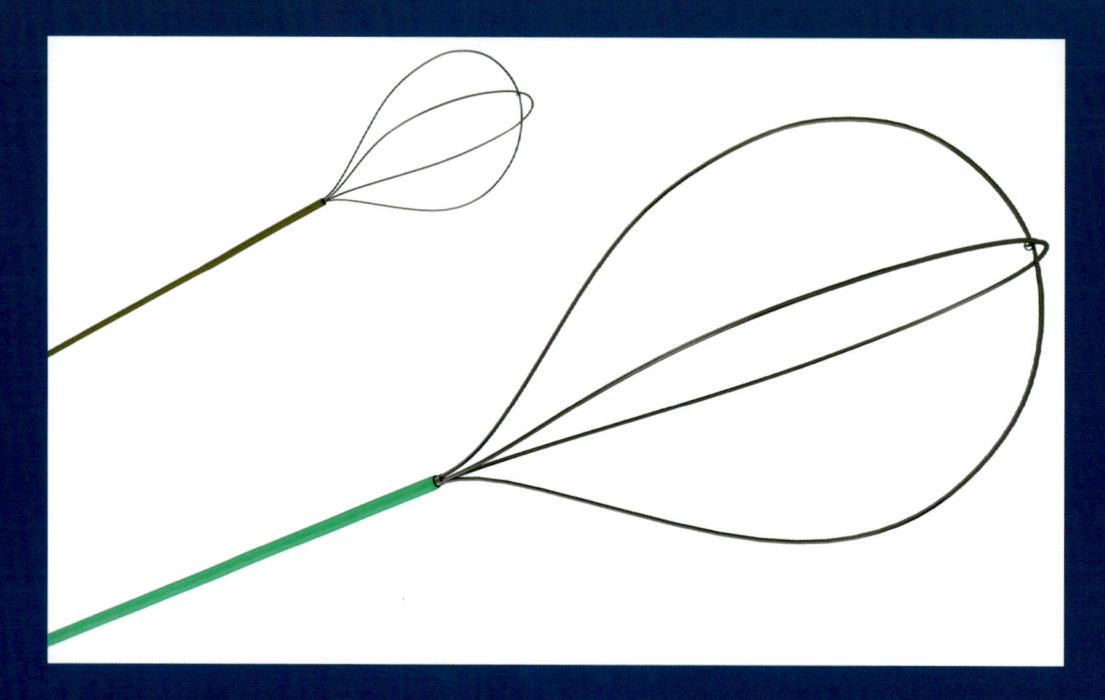

Previous best practices dictated the use of non-invasive shock wave therapy to fragment stones from outside the body, allowing them to pass naturally. However, current research shows that stone recurrence with this therapy is high, and stone-free rates are low. The introduction of NCircle technology, along with improved endoscopes and intra-corporeal lithotripters, allows physicians to render their patients completely stone-free—and to do so in a procedure that is minimally damaging to the patient's body.

Sales of historic stainless steel extractors decrease each year, while the popularity of nitinol stone devices grows at a double-digit rate. Today NCircle is considered the gold standard for kidney stone extraction.

In the late 1990s Cook introduced NCircle, a kidney stone extractor made of a nickel and titanium alloy called nitinol, that is noted for its capacity to retain its shape. A significant technological advance, NCircle addressed several problems with old-generation extractors, and it has rapidly become the surgical tool of choice.

buyout by Guidant, the giant cardiovascular products company whose Multi-Link device had followed Cook's GR-II into the coronary stent market back in 1997.

What Guidant wanted, says Steve Ferguson, was the cardiovascular side of Cook's business. For legal reasons, however, Guidant needed to purchase the entire company. Had the deal gone through, Cook would have been able to subsequently reacquire all the other parts of the company from Guidant.

For the better part of a year, while lawyers hammered out the details, Cook managers took as a given that they would soon be working for Guidant. In the end, though, the merger fell through. "While the deal never happened, other companies learned a lot about and formed a respect for Cook," says Phyllis McCullough. "We also learned a lot about what we needed to do to continue our growth and focus on the impressive products in the pipelines of all the Cook Group companies."

Cook did indeed have lightning in a bottle. Preliminary results from clinical trials for coronary stents coated with Paclitaxel looked positive. New technology was greatly expanding Wilson-Cook's product development capacity. In vitro fertilization products, a specialty of Cook Australia, had finally been approved for use in the United States. William Cook Europe had invented a detachable embolization coil system, a new intravascular filter and microcatheter technology. The future also looked extraordinarily bright for Cook Biotech's SIS product.

"We had a full plate," says McCullough, "and we needed to get our organization working together to take full advantage of those opportunities." She would not be the person to lead that charge. After 27 years with Cook and with a track record of exceptional accomplishment, she was ready for a change. Early in the summer of 2001 she stepped down from the presidency of Cook Incorporated. Wishing to remain involved, she retained her positions as chairman of the board of Cook Incorporated and vice president of operations management at Cook Group, a position she had been appointed to in 1998.

"THE FUTURE IS BRIGHT"

In the autumn of 2001 Scott Eells, who had been with the company for nearly 20 years, most of them in operations and manufacturing, was promoted to chief operating officer of the company. Kem Hawkins, the onetime teacher whose managerial potential had caught Bill Cook's eye while he was leading a high-school band in Bloomington, stepped in behind McCullough as president.

Hired as a managerial trainee in 1981, Hawkins experienced a rise to the top of the organization that was every bit as meteoric as McCullough's had been. As president of Cook Group and Cook Incorporated, he could put to use managerial skills and vast knowledge of the company that he had gathered over 20 years. He would now be charged with leading an effort to better organize and manage product development and sales across all Cook Group companies worldwide.

Cook's Zilver stent is becoming the standard of care for cardiovascular patients with narrowing of their peripheral arteries.

148 SNOWING IN CHICAGO

EVOLUTION   149

"There was just no consistency," he says of the challenge he faced. "In Europe we had ten different subsidiaries and, when we put them together, most of their stock was different. We had managing directors and sales managers in every country, and each country's sales operation functioned independently. When we had new technologies to market, we had to go to each of these long-established companies individually."

Hawkins, with full support from McCullough, pulled together a team of high-level Cook executives to map out a strategy proposing to restructure the company into strategic business units (SBUs). "Putting that structure in place wasn't easy," says Hawkins. "Change is always difficult, and this was no exception, because it broke up long-established territories and redirected responsibilities." There was understandable resistance—in fact, two years of it, complex and sometimes tempestuous, before the new structure was finished.

By 2003 Cook's strategic business units emerged as significantly more sleek and efficient global operations. The company consolidated its product lines and unified them across the globe for company and customer benefits. "Today we attempt to treat every customer in every country the same," Hawkins says. "We have the same customer service, the same regulatory approval efforts, the same representation and knowledge.

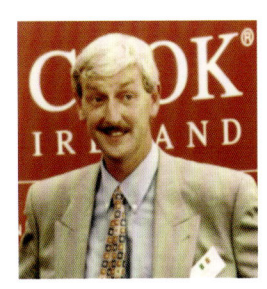

Kem Hawkins, left, addresses hundreds of employees gathered under the enormous dome of the West Baden Springs Hotel for the company's 2004 employee award dinner, opposite and below. Bill Doherty, above, is the managing director of Cook Ireland.

GIVING BACK

When Northwestern University wanted to build a new materials and life sciences building, the Cook Group didn't hesitate to help. Their $10 million donation made possible the creation of William A. and Gayle K. Cook Hall, the new materials and life sciences (MLS) building at Bill Cook's alma mater, which opened in 2003. Significantly expanding Northwestern's science facilities, the new building leveraged natural linkages between diverse technologies to help broaden the university's educational and research horizons.

The gift was generous indeed, but it was hardly the first time the Cook group of companies had supported Northwestern. An earlier gift of $2.5 million had established an endowed professorship, the Bill and Gayle Cook Chair in the Biological Sciences and associated research funding; and Cook Group had also given Northwestern an additional $100,000 to establish a scholarship in memory of Joseph Fucilla, the father of Dr. "Van" Fucilla, Bill Cook's cousin and the radiologist who initially encouraged Bill to begin making medical devices.

The Cook Group's support of education has not been restricted to Northwestern. Since 1995 they have established faculty chairs at Indiana University (Gayle's alma mater), the Indiana University School of Medicine, Rose-Hulman Institute of Technology, the Dotter Interventional Institute, Purdue University, the Miami Vascular Institute, the Society of Cardiovascular & Interventional Radiology and a fellowship at the University of Pennsylvania. Most of those chairs have been in science and technology. Investment in education, the Cook Group learned early on, is one of the best ways to accomplish their goals of improving patient care and giving something back to those who helped them achieve success.

The Cook Group's largesse has extended well beyond the sciences. Longtime sports fans, they supported creation of the Cook Athletic Stadium at the Rose-Hulman Institute of Technology. When Indiana University sought to equip its 52,000-seat football field, Memorial Stadium, with outdoor lighting, the Cook Group provided funding for that, as well.

The Cook Group also has been a supporter of youth education and music, as evidenced by the company's passionate support for the Star of Indiana Drum and Bugle Corps, a competitive corps founded in Bloomington. Between 1985 and 1993 Star of Indiana competed all over the United States, winning the Drum Corps International championship in 1991 and placing in the top three in 1990, 1992 and 1993. After 1993 Star of Indiana left the competitive circuit and transformed itself into *Brass Theater* and then *Blast!*, a Broadway production. In 2001 *Blast!* won a Tony award for "Best Special Theatrical Event" and an Emmy for "Best Choreography."

Cook Group also provided the funding to create the William and Gayle Cook Music Library, which integrated the Indiana University library's renowned collection of printed and recorded music with a computer classroom, a media editing center, multimedia workstations in reading areas and a central computer room linking the IU School of Music to the world.

Investments like these, the development of the Monroe County YMCA and the Cook Group's commitment to preserving and revitalizing historic properties throughout southern Indiana, have enriched the communities in which Cook Group is located. But as Cook's success provided the company with the means to behave philanthropically, it discovered that having the wherewithal to change the world, rescue it and reshape it in bold and beautiful new ways was, well, enjoyable.

Over 40-plus years Cook has invested nearly $200 million in making the world a better, healthier, smarter and more beautiful place. It's been, as Bill and Gayle Cook will quickly confirm, a lot of fun.

Cook Hall is Northwestern University's materials and life sciences building, built in 2003 with a donation from the Cook Group.

Cook's investment in the quality of life goes well beyond its businesses and employees. Over the past 40-plus years, the company has committed more than $200 million to countless facilities and programs, including the football and track stadium at Rose-Hulman Institute of Technology, opposite above, and the Star of Indiana Drum and Bugle Corps, above, which evolved into *Brass Theater*, right, and later, a Tony and Emmy award-winning Broadway production called *Blast!*

Delivery is consistently timely. It's made a tremendous difference in how we do business."

By the time the new strategic business unit structure was operational, Cook's new million-square-foot headquarters complex was complete. It had taken four years to build, and it was worth the wait.

One day in 2002, as construction was nearing completion, Hawkins stopped by with local newspaper reporter Brian Werth to survey what would soon become his new office and to reflect on his own history with the company and Cook's unique culture. Cook employees, he told Werth, shared a special awareness of the impact the company had on medical technology and the importance of every product that Cook has manufactured for people in need of medical care.

"That's a foundation that was laid by Bill Cook," Hawkins said. "The people here are special. Our technology is driven by people who use their talent and experience to achieve success. Decisions here aren't made by committee. They are made by people who are ultimately responsible for that decision. Sometimes it takes years for a concept and a product to emerge as a marketable technology. We try to be in a position to let that happen."

He looked around the cavernous new facility, soon to be populated with high-energy people, and he said, "We hired 300 people in 2001 and added 200 more in the first five months of this year. I don't expect that to slow down at all. The future is bright. We're in the process of filling these buildings with technology and expertise that cannot be duplicated elsewhere."

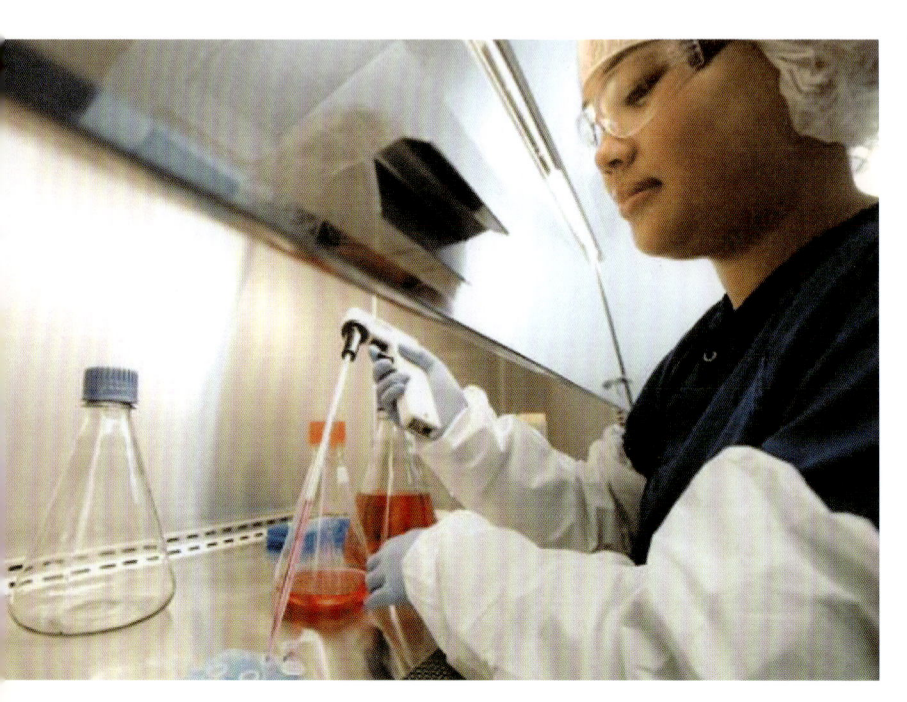

Working in a laminar hood, Melody Lao, assistant scientist, cell culture process development, takes the first step in the cell expansion process, growing small volumes of cells to create a larger volume for manufacturing in Cook Pharmica's small-scale cGMP (current Good Manufacturing Practice) plant. Opposite, winter turns Cook Group's Bloomington headquarters into a striking composite of contrasts.

EVOLUTION 153

SURGISIS TO THE RESCUE: RELIEF FOR TROUBLING COLORECTAL CONDITIONS

People with inflammatory bowel diseases like diverticulitis, colitis and Crohn's disease are at high risk of developing anal abscesses, as are those with immune-compromising conditions such as diabetes, AIDS and cancer. When an anal abscess develops, a tunnel called a fistula forms between the internal anal canal and the exterior of the skin. The fistula remains in about half the cases, even after the abscess has healed. It's rarely a highly dangerous condition, but it can be painful, is often irritating and it does present a risk of infection.

Anal fistulas are most commonly treated with a complex surgical procedure called a fistulotomy in which an incision is made to open the fistula tract and merge it with the anal canal, allowing the tissues to heal from the inside out. While smaller fistulas can be treated in a physician's office, larger wounds require surgery under spinal or general anesthesia. About 30 percent of fistulotomy patients later complain of incontinence, and 20 percent develop recurrent fistulas and/or abscesses.

Deeper fistulas may require a seton, or a piece of suture material that is passed from the external skin opening along the fistula tract through the internal opening in the anal canal, exiting through the anus. The suture is gradually tightened over a period of weeks, opening the fistula tract in an effort to allow it to heal. In other cases the lesion is closed by the injection of a clotting agent called fibrin glue. More complex fistulas may be treated with an endorectal advancement flap, whereby the doctor dissects and lifts a flap of the rectal wall next to the fistula's internal opening, pulls it over the internal opening and sutures it into place to close the opening.

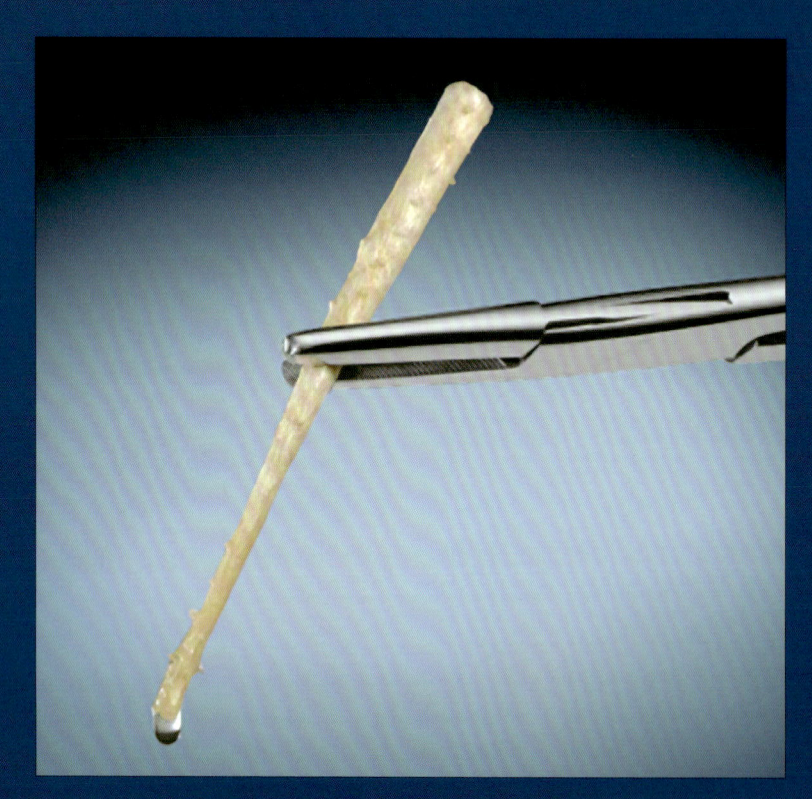

This small conical object represents hope to thousands of people afflicted with inflammatory bowel diseases. It is a Surgisis Biodesign Anal Fistula Plug, invented by Cook and introduced in 2005. Made from Cook's naturally occurring "scaffold," SIS, the plug promotes rapid healing of anal fistulas that result from abscesses.

In the spring of 2005 Cook introduced an alternative to those remedies called the Surgisis Biodesign Anal Fistula Plug—a cone-shaped device made of an advanced, Cook-developed tissue repair graft that promotes tissue healing. In a minimally invasive procedure the plug is drawn through the fistula tract and sutured in place.

The plug is made from small intestinal submucosa (SIS), a complex collagen obtained from the small intestines of pigs. Doctors Neal Fearnot and Leslie Geddes discovered SIS in the 1980s, and Cook has been developing it for a wide range of uses ever since. Since Surgisis Biodesign and human tissue are so similar, the patient's tissue and blood vessels easily grow into the Anal Fistula Plug. This allows the patient's immune system to protect the Anal Fistula Plug from infection while it acts as a scaffold for rapid healing. Eventually Surgisis Biodesign completely remodels into the patient's own tissue. A further benefit is that the procedure for placing the Anal Fistula Plug is unlikely to cause either incontinence or the pain associated with other procedures.

The Surgisis Biodesign Anal Fistula Plug has been an important product for Cook and a godsend for many people suffering from anal fistulas. Cook is now developing many new devices for the colorectal surgery specialty.

In 2004—with the transition from the old South Curry Pike offices to the company's sparkling new headquarters well under way—Cook Group announced plans to invest $45 million in a new biotech drug development company. Based in Bloomington, the company, called Cook Pharmica LLC, would be housed in a 430,000-square-foot warehouse Cook had purchased and was already renovating. In the sterile laboratories within Cook Pharmica, employees would focus on growing small batches of bioengineered mammalian cells—building blocks of the future for both health care and Cook.

There was speculation that the new operation might create 150 to 200 new high-tech jobs immediately. But no one who knew anything about the history of Cook bet money on that number. People around Bloomington, where Cook Incorporated was once referred to as a "best-kept secret," knew all about Cook now. Again and again they had seen the company spin off new business entities with employment projections that later proved to be significantly short of reality. Cook, they knew, was the very exemplification of success. Its annual sales were now estimated at some $700 million. It employed 2,500 people in Indiana. Whenever it launched a new business, lots of jobs soon followed.

"The only way that Cook can survive in this new century is to continue developing and marketing new breakthrough products," Bill Cook told *Endovascular Today* in 2005, "—products that will help to reduce medical costs, save lives and improve patient quality of existence."

"PROMISES"

No one could have agreed more than Rick Mellinger, vice president of marketing. Even as Bill Cook spoke those prophetic words, the company's vice president of marketing was already deeply involved in a multifaceted refinement of Cook's worldwide marketing efforts that paralleled the SBU restructure.

"Historically Bill has been frustrated with the fact that we haven't gotten the kind of recognition we deserve," Mellinger notes. "Well, in the past few years, a tremendous amount of work has gone into providing clarity to Cook. We have eight strategic business units, 15 distinct medical entities, and over 7,000 employees worldwide manufacturing our products on three continents. Yet many people only know us from a single technology. So we're leveraging the scope of this company around the Cook name. Our message going forward is that maybe Cook isn't the company you thought it was. Maybe it's a lot more.

"We want people to understand that the scope of what Cook does is very broad," Mellinger says. "We're in critical care medicine, urology, endoscopy, assisted reproduction, obstetrics and gynecology, interventional radiology, cardiac catheterization and vascular surgery. We want to make it clear to physicians that if you have an idea, you should be talking to Cook because we have vertically integrated all of these organizations."

Not only does the company have a solid track record in each of the areas of medicine Mellinger referenced, but expertise garnered from more than 40 years of experience has also positioned Cook to provide

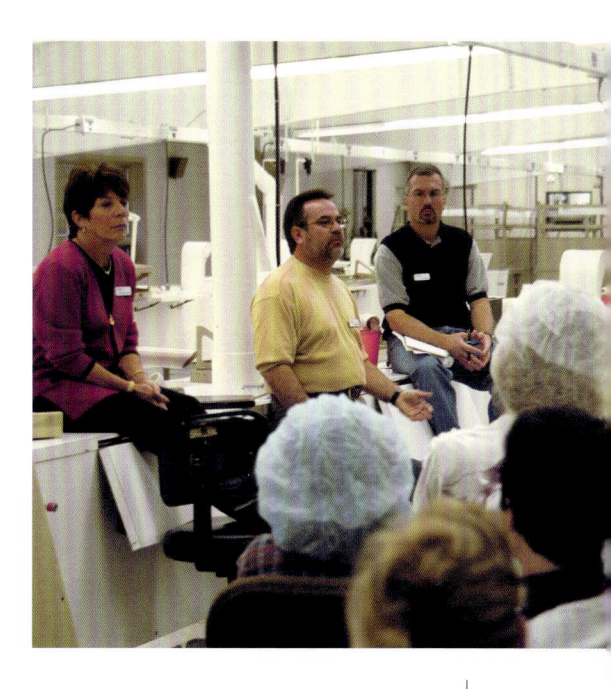

Rick Mellinger, center, and Dan Peterson were among Cook executives who joined Phyllis McCullough. left, for face-to-face meetings with the Cook workforce in early 2000 to address employee concerns and boost productivity across the board.

Bill Cook has been a health care innovator for more than 40 years, and his mind remains a fertile medium for bold ideas. Moreover, his quest for excellence—permeating the diverse enterprise that bears his name—is as unrelenting as it was four decades ago, when he casually asked his soon-to-be wife, Gayle, "What would you think about starting a company?" Among the proud employees of that company are, opposite, from left, Randy Wrightsman, Angel Jackson, Tyler Bunch and Matt Terwiske—all members of the research and development department at Cook Urological Incorporated in Spencer, Indiana.

guidance to anyone interested in bringing new medical technologies to the market. The hard years during which the company struggled to get new products approved by the FDA taught the people at Cook many valuable lessons. Those lessons take on added meaning when one considers that the Cook empire currently covers nearly 30 regulatory regions around the world.

Cook's creation of MED Institute in 1983 now seems especially prescient. With a complete staff of research, engineering, legal and technical consultants, the institute is ideally poised to provide the complete scope of new product development services, including Good Laboratory Practice testing, animal testing, clinical trial monitoring and preparation of regulatory approval submissions. MED Institute has developed a global regulatory system capable of handling the arduous Class III-type submissions. This has allowed Cook to more efficiently move through the approval process everywhere in the world.

As Cook Incorporated enters its fifth decade, the company is an evolving tribute to the values, ethics and principles that Bill and Gayle Cook committed to when they first began assembling medical devices in their Bloomington apartment in the 1960s. Their first and most important principle back then was, as Bill Cook articulated it, "Build a quality product in a timely manner." At Cook Incorporated 45 years later, that still is the most important principle—and success indeed has followed.

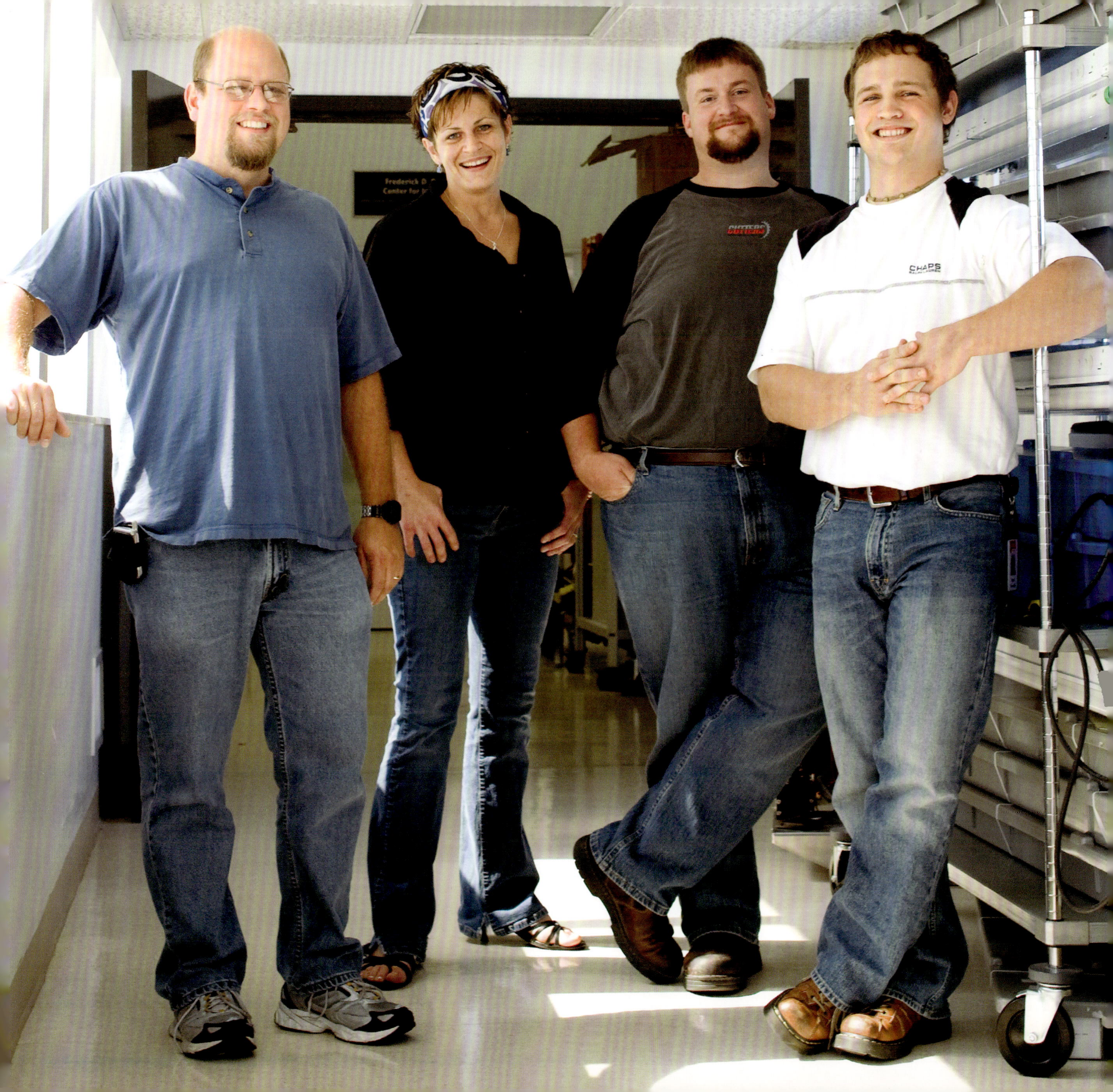
CHAPS

Acknowledgments

Writing is often thought to be a lonely task. It's a claim that seems to imagine the writer, neck-deep in his or her psyche, wrestling with words, presumably in a dank garret room somewhere. I suppose there's some kernel of truth in that stereotype. Sooner or later, every writer has to sit down to the keypad or the notepad or the granite slab and—"by himself, all alone," to borrow a wonderful redundancy from the great writer James Jones—hammer out the story.

Long before sitting down to write a book like this, I start by meeting a lot of people and talking with them about their memories of how the company evolved. Because Cook Incorporated is still a relatively young company, I was very fortunate to be able to spend time with many of the original players. Brian Baldwin, Dr. Van Fucilla, Tom Osborne, Miles Kanne, Ross Jennings, Gene DeVane and Phil Hathaway were a uniformly gregarious crew, each with marvelous "campfire" tales to tell.

Gayle Cook invited me into her home, showed me photographs and patiently answered questions that she must have been asked hundreds of times before. She was grace personified. And all of the following Cook employees, former employees and/or people who had something to tell me about the company took time to meet with me or to talk with me or send me background information. Their memories and insights enliven this book, and I am indebted to them all: Brian Bates, Dexter Elkins, Dave Emhardt, Dr. Neal Fearnot, Steve Ferguson, Jerry French, Staffan Grigholm, Bob Harbstreit, Kem Hawkins, April Lavender, Phyllis McCullough, Rick Mellinger, Tom Porter, Geoff Reeves, Fred Roehmer, Dr. Al Rutner, Dan Sterner, Marlene Vass, Dr. Sidney Wallace and Jerry Williams.

Finally, I owe thanks to Dave McCarty from Cook's marketing communications team and especially to Jim Heckman, who unerringly guided me through the research. Jim spent hours talking with me about the company and helping me unravel various Gordian knots in its history. More than that he showed me around Bloomington, hosting me at Janko's Little Zagreb, driving me down to French Lick and West Baden and introducing me to the special culture of Indiana. From now on, whenever I think "Hoosier," I will always think of you, Jim.

The unique, visionary architecture of its new, state-of-the-art product development center defines Cook's MED Institute, which supports Cook Group companies in their development of new devices and conducts Cook's global clinical trials of new products.

Timeline

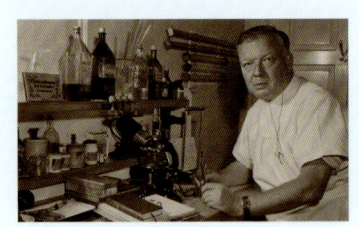

Werner Forssmann

Sven-Ivar Seldinger

Charles Dotter

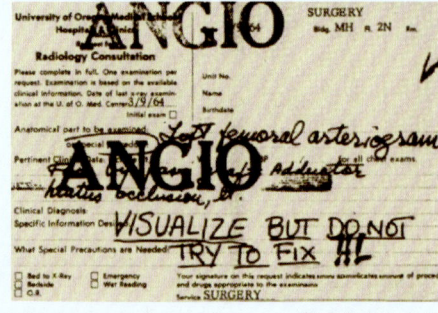

Angiogram request sent to Charles Dotter

1929 — **1957** — **1964** — **1965**

1929
Dr. Werner Forssmann risks his life to prove that coronary catheterization is possible.

1953
Dr. Sven-Ivar Seldinger introduces a simple technique for percutaneous catheter insertion.

Northwestern University graduate Bill Cook becomes a medic in the U.S. Army Medical Service Corps, where he is exposed to new tools that fuel his imagination about the future of medical technology.

1956
Bill Cook enters the medical technology industry with a job at American Hospital Supply and helps his college roommate, Brian Baldwin, land a job there, as well.

Forssmann, whose self-catheterization in 1929 was initially disdained by the medical community, is awarded the Nobel Prize in Physiology or Medicine.

1957
Bill Cook leaves American Hospital Supply to join Nelson Instrument Company. His boss, Lloyd Nelson, introduces him to Gayle Karch. Bill and Gayle are married in September.

Baldwin founds Manufacturing Process Laboratories (MPL) in Chicago to manufacture hypodermic needles. He invites Cook to become his partner, and by 1958 they are in business together.

1960
Bill Cook's cousin, Dr. Ivan "Van" Fucilla, introduces Cook to the Seldinger catheterization procedure and shows him tools for performing it.

1962
Bill and Gayle Cook's son, Carl, is born on August 19.

1963
Bill Cook resigns from MPL.

The Cooks move to Bloomington, Indiana. On June 24 they found Cook Incorporated to manufacture the tools for percutaneous catheterization. The first "factory" is the spare bedroom in the Cooks' apartment.

On August 29, Illinois Masonic Hospital becomes the first customer for Cook catheters and wire guides.

Bill Cook meets Miles Kanne and Ross Jennings, who later will play important roles in the company.

Bill Cook meets Dr. Charles Dotter. Cook and Dotter begin a long-term friendship and collaboration.

1964
On January 16 Dotter performs the first percutaneous transluminal angioplasty, demonstrating the value of catheterization for intervention.

In June Bill Cook hires his first production employee, Tom Osborne, who helps the young company rapidly grow by customizing catheterization equipment to meet physicians' unique needs.

Bill Cook hires Miles Kanne as the company's first full-time salesperson.

1965
Dan Sterner, a corporate attorney from Indianapolis and former fraternity brother of Bill Cook, is contracted to provide legal services.

Outgrowing the Cooks' apartment, Cook Incorporated moves to its second location—a former dentist's office at 300 South Swain Avenue in Bloomington.

Dr. Cesare Gianturco retires from his position as chief of radiology at the Carle Clinic in Champaign, Illinois, and joins Dr. Sidney Wallace on the staff of the M. D. Anderson Cancer Center in Houston. Gianturco will go on to collaborate with Cook on the development of many innovative medical devices.

1966
Cook Incorporated moves to its third location—a five-room house at 925 South Curry Pike in Bloomington.

Young lawyer Steve Ferguson begins to handle legal projects for Cook Incorporated, and accountant Phil Hathaway starts managing the company's books.

Early catalog

Bill Cook

Phyllis McCullough

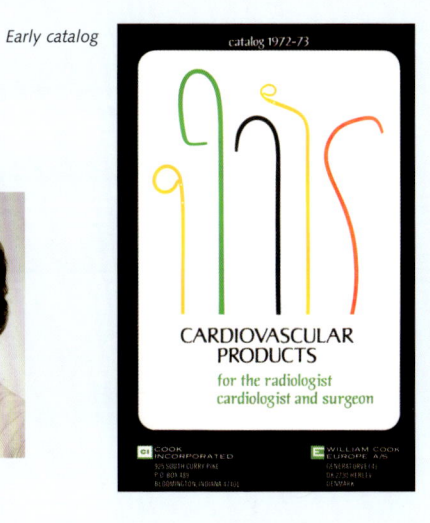

An issue of the Angio-Gram from December 1977.

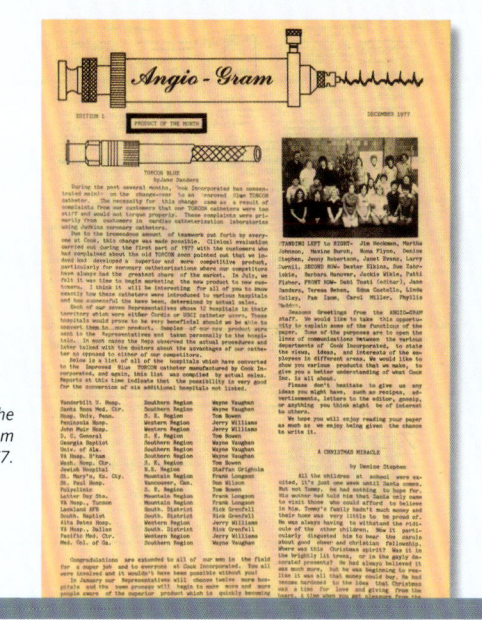

1967 *1971* *1974*

1967
Cook Incorporated employs 20 people.

1968
A new, 5,000-square-foot building is completed adjacent to the Curry Pike offices.

Technician Ross Jennings joins Cook Incorporated and becomes the company's first West Coast representative.

With the help of Canadian businessman Don Wilson, Bill Cook sets the stage for his company's advance into Europe, where catheterization has become well accepted.

1969
Cook Incorporated makes its initial foray outside North America with the founding of William Cook Europe ApS in Denmark.

Cook founds Cook Group Europe to coordinate its family of European sales organizations.

Bill Cook founds custom plastics manufacturer Sabin Corporation.

Dotter experimentally demonstrates the possibility of successful intraluminal stenting.

1971
Cook Incorporated employs 80 people.

Cook Incorporated founds Northern Financial & Guaranty Company, Ltd., to provide the company with self-insurance.

1972
Cook Incorporated is manufacturing 24 different categories of equipment, and with the workforce doubling to 160 people, the South Curry Pike plant enlarges for the third time in five years.

Phyllis McCullough joins Cook Incorporated as an executive secretary.

1973
Cook Incorporated is shipping enough products to enable 2,000 cardiovascular catheterizations to be performed per day.

Cook Canada is incorporated, allowing Cook Incorporated to sell its products directly in Canada without intermediary sales agents.

CFC Incorporated is founded to finance loans to Cook employees. It will eventually evolve into the company's real estate development and management company.

1974
Bill Cook undergoes coronary bypass surgery. While he's recovering in California, Van Fucilla introduces him to Dr. Al Rutner, who shows Cook that urologists can benefit from the kinds of tools being pioneered at Cook Incorporated.

Brian Baldwin leaves MPL and establishes a joint venture with Bill Cook to produce needles in Denmark.

1976
Dr. Leslie Geddes begins a long and successful collaboration with Cook Incorporated. Two years earlier he had been recruited from Baylor University to Purdue University to establish a biomedical engineering program and develop new medical technologies.

Bill and Gayle Cook take on their first historic preservation project by acquiring and renovating the James Cochran House in Bloomington. The Cooks—on their own and through CFC—will go on to restore many historic buildings throughout southern Indiana.

Cook pioneers the real beginning of therapeutic intervention with the introduction of embolization coils, percutaneous nephrostomy and biliary drainage.

1977
As a result of Bill Cook's introduction to Rutner, Vance Products is founded to develop products for the urological market.

The *Angio-Gram*, Cook Incorporated's employee newsletter, debuts.

Sabin Corporation opens a new building to house its rapidly growing operations.

1978
Cook Incorporated introduces the company's first employee incentive program.

Cook Incorporated purchases its first computer.

Dotter is nominated for a Nobel Prize in Medicine.

Timeline

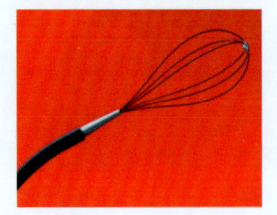

Stone Basket
1979

Kem Hawkins
1982

Gianturco-Roehm Bird's Nest Filter
1983

The Central Venous Pressure Monitoring Catheter

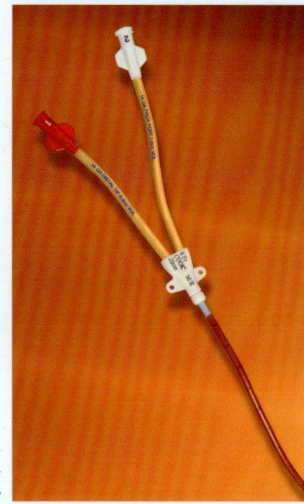

Cook acquires a G. D. Searle plant in Denmark and founds Asik to manufacture disposable syringes and needles.

1979
Cook Incorporated expands into Spain with a sales facility.

William A. Cook Australia Pty. Ltd. is founded in Melbourne, Australia, to manufacture and distribute medical products for customers in markets located around the Pacific Rim and Southeast Asia.

Cook purchases Baxa Corporation, which Baldwin and Ron Baxa had founded in 1975 to market inhalation drugs in pre-filled syringes.

1980
California Cook Incorporated is founded to sell Cook products directly in the burgeoning California market. The subsidiary replaces Stanco Medical, Cook's last unaffiliated distributor.

1981
Cook Pacemaker is founded in Vandergrift, Pennsylvania, absorbing the assets of Cook-acquired Arco Pacemaker Company, a manufacturer of nuclear-powered pacemakers. Its goal is to develop and produce a self-regulating pacemaker.

The first successful surgery on a human fetus is performed, using a pigtail catheter produced by Vance Products.

Vance Products becomes Cook Urological Incorporated. It begins an evolution into a manufacturer of equipment for urological, obstetric and gynecological uses.

Kem Hawkins accepts Bill's invitation to join Cook Incorporated.

1982
Cook (UK) Ltd. is founded.

Cook Imaging Corporation is founded to develop a new, non-ionic radiologic contrast medium.

K-Tube Corporation is founded. It will become the largest independent hypodermic needle tubing manufacturer in the United States.

1983
Medical Engineering and Development (MED) Institute, Incorporated is established in West Lafayette, Indiana, to work collaboratively with Cook Group companies to help identify and develop new medical product concepts.

Wilson-Cook Medical Incorporated is established in Winston-Salem, North Carolina, to provide innovative products for gastrointestinal endoscopy.

Cook's global expansion continues, with new subsidiaries in Germany and Italy.

1984
Cook's presence in Europe expands with new sales offices in Sweden and France.

1986
Cook Incorporated introduces BioGuard coating, which enables antibiotics to adhere to catheter surfaces to prevent infection.

Cook opens new subsidiaries in Belgium, Switzerland and Southeast Asia.

1987
Baxa Corporation is sold to Brian Baldwin.

The first balloon inflatable stainless steel stent is introduced.

Cook Aviation Incorporated is founded to provide aircraft refueling and a fixed base operation for general aviation at the Monroe County Airport in Indiana.

1988
Phyllis McCullough is named president, CEO and chairman of the board of Cook Incorporated.

The sales facility Cook Asia Ltd. is founded.

1989
The sales facility Cook Taiwan Ltd. is founded.

A new research and development facility is completed in Bloomington.

1990
The Charles Dotter Institute of Interventional Therapy is established at Oregon Health Sciences University—made possible by Cook Group.

TIMELINE 163

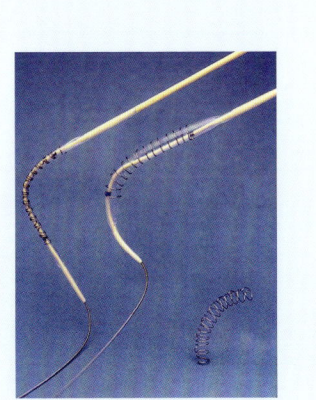

Gianturco-Roubin Coronary Stent

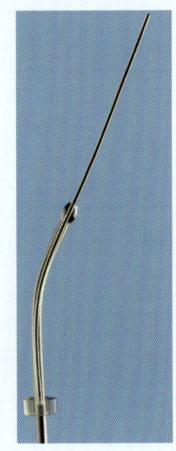

Sydney Embryo IVF Transfer Catheter

Cook Group world headquarters

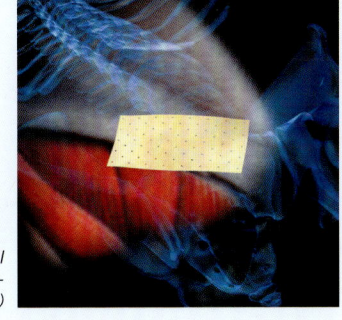

SIS (small intestinal submucosa)

1992 **1996** **1998** **2003**

The sales organizations Cook Asia (Malaysia) SDN BHD and Cook Denmark are founded.

1992
Cook introduces the first coronary stent approved by the FDA for use in the United States.

1993
Cook Incorporated is the first company to market coronary stents.

Cook Ireland Ltd. is established in Limerick, Ireland, to meet the needs of European clinicians in the fields of gastroenterology, urology, obstetrics and gynecology.

1995
Cook licenses from Purdue University the rights to produce and sell SIS, a collagen-based material that has the capability to duplicate almost any of the tissues it touches when placed on the body or in an organ.

Cook Biotech Incorporated is founded to develop and manufacture biomaterials from natural tissue sources—including SIS—for use in medical products.

1996
Cook Pacemaker changes its name to Cook Vascular Incorporated, reflecting the growing market in vascular devices.

CFC begins restoration of the historic West Baden Springs Hotel in southern Indiana, a project that will eventually embrace restoration of nearby French Lick Springs Hotel.

1997
A conglomerate of 42 companies, Cook Group is now the largest privately held medical device manufacturing group in the world, with about 1,300 employees. Cook has manufactured more than 140,000 different products and combinations of products for diagnosis and treatment of disease.

Cook Incorporated announces plans to build a $30 million, one million-square-foot company headquarters in Bloomington.

The FDA revises the way it approves new drugs and medical instruments, a process that has delayed development and introduction of many Cook products since the 1980s. Cook has taken an active role in providing input into legislative changes.

Cook launches Cook Pharmaceutical Services to serve pharmaceutical manufacturers and clinical researchers needing a turnkey operation specializing in formulation and filling, release and stability testing and clinical-to-commercial batch production services.

1998
Cook acquires Colorado-based Global Therapeutics to develop coronary stents that could be coated with the anti-restenosis drug paclitaxel, to which Cook has co-exclusive rights with Boston Scientific.

1999
Cook receives regulatory permission from the FDA to sell SIS-based products.

2001
Cook Imaging Corporation is sold to Baxter Healthcare.

Cook MyoSite is founded in Pittsburgh to develop technologies involving the use of autologous muscle-derived cells for treating urinary incontinence and other diseases.

Kem Hawkins is named president of Cook Group and Cook Incorporated. Phyllis McCullough remains chairman of the board.

2003
Cook Medical Incorporated is founded in Bloomington to offer a synchronized service for the efficient purchase and distribution of all Cook medical devices.

2004
Cook Group moves to its new headquarters at Park 48 in Bloomington.

Cook Pharmica LLC is founded to provide contract manufacturing services to the biopharmaceutical industry.

2005
Cook Biotech develops a line of products that can remodel native tissues using a biomaterial made from SIS.

Cook Medical Company Officers

Christine Anné
1990–Present

Jerry Arthur
1996–2008

Merry Lee Bain
1986–2005

Brian Baldwin
1979–1987

Brian L. Bates
1972–Present

Ronald Baxa
1979–1983

Mark W. Bleyer
1987–Present

Bill A. Bobbie
1982–Present

David Breedlove
2001–Present

Tamisha Clark
1998–Present

Thomas A. Connaughton
2003–Present

Carl A. Cook
1988–Present

Gayle T. Cook
1963–Present

William A. Cook
1963–Present

Stefaan Coomans
1986–Present

Andrew Cron
1987–Present

Peer Daamen
1986–2004

John DeFord
1990–2001

Connie Degen
2000–2008

Gene DeVane
1974–2000

Carl Dickie
1983–1999

Jim Dickinson
1981–1998

William Doherty
1994–Present

Scott Dougall
1987–Present

Marsha Dreyer
1984–2006

Scott E. Eells
1983–Present

Dexter Elkins
1977–Present

Neal E. Fearnot, Ph.D.
1983–Present

Stephen L. Ferguson
1983–Present

Frank Fisher
1986–Present

Charles W. Franz
1984–Present

Jerry French
1980–Present

Jim Gardener
1984–1986

James B. Gardner, M.D.
1998–Present

William S. Gibbons
1999–Present

Chuck Gifford
1982–1997

Bruce E. Gingles
1979–Present

Enrique Cluá Giró
1981–Present

Louis Goode
1993–Present

Tedd Green
2005–Present

Perry Guinn
2002–Present

Phil Hathaway
1974–1992

M. Kem Hawkins
1981–Present

James R. Heckman
1976–Present

Dave Heine
1984–1998

Ted Heise, Ph.D.
1997–Present

Art Hicks
1983–2001

Michael F. Hiles, Ph.D.
1995–Present

Don Hollinger
1973–2001

Joe Horn
1998–Present

COOK MEDICAL COMPANY OFFICERS

Ernest Hughes
1974–1980

John M. Hughes
1991–Present

Paul Hughes
1984–Present

Bob Irie
1979–1992

Connie Jackson
1978–Present

Ross Jennings
1968–1992

Paula A. Joyce
1993–Present

John R. Kamstra
1984–Present

Miles Kanne
1964–1992

Tom Kardos
1982–Present

Herb Karlinski
1978–1999

John Karpiel
1982–Present

Durwood Karr
1986–Present

Jennifer L. Kerr
1995–Present

Karl Kock
1982–1994

Linda Kortea
1979–2004

Kevin J. Kotowich
1991–2007

Gert Kristensen
1978–1982

Fred Larimore, Ph.D.
2006–2008

April Lavender
1976–Present

Bob Lendman
1982–2004

David Lessard
1991–Present

Robert Lyles
2003–Present

James MacNaughtan
1982–Present

Greg May
2002–Present

Phyllis E. McCullough
1972–Present

Terry McCune
1991–Present

Jeff McGough
1975–1988

Charles McIntosh, M.D.
2003–Present

Rick A. Mellinger
1981–Present

Lars Milling
1987–Present

Bob Mitchell
1988–2004

Ronald E. Mobley
1979–Present

Aimee Hawkins–Mungle
1991–Present

Thomas A. Osborne
1964–Present

Tom Palco
1982–Present

Umesh H. Patel
1995–Present

Daniel J. Peterson
1989–Present

William Powell
1973–1975

David J. Reed
1982–Present

Geoff Reeves
1978–1999

B. Thomas Roberts
1983–Present

Joe Roberts
1979–Present

Frederick Roehmer
1980–Present

Robert L. Santa
1991–Present

Carol M. Seaman
1991–Present

Scott J. Sewell
1987–Present

Victor Sheaffer
1981–2005

Christian Simonsgaard
1968–1981

Gregory J. Skerven
1990–Present

Barry A. Slowey
1996–Present

Francine Small
1984–Present

Richard A. Snapp
1988–Present

Gunnar Staffe
1978–1984

Don Stephens
1981–1991

Dan Sterner
1963–Present

Gus Taddeo
1987–Present

Barry Thomas
2001–Present

Jim Vance
1977–1981

Albert van Vliet
1986–Present

Dave Volz
1990–Present

William D. Voorhees III
1990–Present

Claes–Henric Waller
1984–Present

Matthew S. Waninger
1998–Present

Erik Wennergaard
1987–Present

Jackie Wikle
1977–1996

Kelly Wikle
1982–1988

Jerry Williams
1977–Present

Don Wilson
1968–2000

Joe Witkiewicz
1968–1979

Pete Yonkman
2001–Present

Cook Group Affiliate Company Officers

Mike Attebury
1989–Present

Richard J. Campbell
1993–Present

Everett Farley
1989–2005

James E. Furr
2000–Present

Donna Harbstreit
1988–2008

Nathan Harbstreit
1996–Present

Robert Harbstreit
1980–2003

Mark A. Harting
2000–Present

Rex Hinkle
1985–Present

Pete Hudson
1984–1992

Francie Hurst
1993–Present

Jim Mason
1984–2004

Jerry McCullough
1978–1986

Jim Murphy
1987–Present

Ian Patton
1989–2005

Michael Ranstead
1998–Present

Wayne Schuman
1984–1998

Ted Swaldo
1989–1998

Andy Tynan
1984–1991

Jeffrey A. Wright
1994–Present

Index

Bold listings indicate illustrations.

A

AAA Stent Grafts, **124,** 125
Adolph Coors Company, 121
Affiliated Hospital Products, 63
airway management products, 141
Akers, Brenda, 74, **74**
Allen Court, 128
American Heart Association, 56
American Hospital Supply, 13, 15
American Latex, 80
American Society of Anesthesiology convention, 65
American Urological Association, 80
anal fistula plug, 154, **154**
Angio-gram, the (newsletter), 72, **72,** 73–74, 80
angioplasty
   balloon, 50, 101
   coronary artery stent and, 114, 122
   diagnostic, 29
   Dotter, Charles, and/dottering procedure, 38, 39, 42, 61
   first, 37–38, 38, 39
   percutaneous transluminal (PTA), 33, 37, 38, **39,** 49
   percutaneous transluminal coronary (PTCA), 115
   polyethylene balloon, 101
   stents during, 106
   transluminal coronary, 106
   25th anniversary of, 104
Aortic Intervention business unit, 123
Aortogram Catheters, 47
Arco Pacemaker Company, 95
Arthur D. Young, 101
Arthur, Jerry, 107–10
Asia/Asian expansion, 89, 110, 117, 135, 139, 142
Asik/Asik A/S, 88, **88,** 106
assisted reproductive technologies (ART), 135, 147, 155
Auguste Viktoria Home, 9, 10, 11
Australia/Australian expansion, 68, 88, 89–91, 110, 111, 117, 123, 130, 135, 147
Austrian expansion, 57
autologous cell therapy, 144
Arterial Vascular Engineering, Inc. (AVE), 134, 136

B

Baldwin, Brian, 12–13, 15, **15,** 20, 40, 63, 88, 96, 98, 109
Baldwin & Cook ApS, 106
Bart Villa Apartments, 20, 31, 32, 34
Bates, Brian, 56–57, **56,** 62–63, 65, 85, 100, 111, 125
Baxa Corporation, 63, 88
Baxa Europe Aps, 106
Baxter International, 110
Baylor University, 66, 95
Behen, Dick, 80
Bethesda Naval Hospital, 115
Bill and Gayle Cook Chair in the Biological Sciences, 150
Bio-Guard AB Catheter, 132, **132**
Bleyer, Mark, 141, **141**
Bloom (magazine), 13
Bloomington Airport, 108
Bloomington Antique Mall, 128
Bloomington Courier Tribune, 50
Bloomington Herald-Times, 115, 116, 134
Bloomington Hospital, 82, 117, 121
Bloomington, Indiana, facilities, 20, 40, 117, 119, 121, 126, 134
Bloomington South High School, 95
Boger, Marylou Garrison, 57, **57**
Bohn Aluminum & Brass Corporation, 98
Bokkenheuser, Carl, 92, **92**
Boruff, Connie, 53, **53**
Boston Scientific, 93, 134, 139
Bowen, Tom, 56, **56,** 57, 62
Brass Theater, 150, 151, **151**
Breast Lesion Localization Needle, 100, **100,** 101
British Aircraft Corporation, 109
Bryant, Bear, 63
Bunch, Tyler, 156, **157**
Business in Bloomington, 70, 74, 100

Byrd, Charles, 94
Byrd Workstation Femoral Intravascular Retrieval Set, 94

C

California Cook Incorporated, 93
Canada/Canadian expansion, 49, 63, 88, 110, 117
Cardiovascular Specialties, 49, 63
Carle Clinic, 46, 58
Catheter Introducers, The (Geddes & Geddes), 11, **21,** 37
catheters/catheterization
   angiographic, 11, **21,** 61
   antibiotic-impregnated, 132, **132,** 133, **133,** 141
   balloon/balloon-tipped, 28, **28, 54,** 55, 74, **74**
   cardiac/cardiac output, 42, 155
   central venous, 111, 132, 141
   closed-end, 42
   customized, 47
   dilators, 106
   fallopian tube, 119
   Fucilla, Ivan "Van," and, 18
   intrauterine insemination, 119
   lead and, 67
   mandrils, 45
   needles, **64,** 65, **90,** 91, **91,** 95, 100, **100,** 113–14
   nephrostomy, 95
   nonsurgical, 106
   ostomy, 95
   percutaneous, 18, 19, **21,** 22, 26, 27, 28, **28,** 33, 34, 35, **35,** 37, 38, 46, 48, **48, 51,** 59, 79, 80, 95, 100, **100,** 101, 103, 106, 115, 136
   pigtail, 95, **118,** 119
   pioneers in, 103–6
   polyethylene, 67, 68, 101
   product development, 65
   prostatic aspiration biopsy, 95
   radiopaque, 91
   sheath sets, 91, 94, **94**
   shock-wave lithotripsy, 119
   stone extractors, 80, **80**
   subcutaneous pressure monitoring sets, 65
   Teflon, 22, 25, 26, 27, 29, 106

testing of, **86,** 87
torque control, 68
ureteral, 79, 80
urethral, **19,** 95
vascular, 9–11, **9, 19, 20**
wire guides, 22, 26, 27, 28, 29, 30, 31, 34, 35, **35,** 38, 42, 43, 45, **45,** 47, **64,** 65, 91, 131, 143, **143**
Cedar Farm, **126,** 127, **127,** 128
cell expansion process, 152, **152**
Central Venous Pressure Monitoring Catheter, 119, **119**
Cessna 210/Cessna 340, 108
CFC Inc., 126, 128
Chamness, Dale, 57, 80
Charles Dotter Research Institute of Interventional Therapy, 104
chemotherapy pump project, 113
Chiba Biopsy Needle, 100, **100,** 101
Chuter, Tim, 123
Clarke, Arthur C., **10,** 11
Clark, Edna Costello, 57, **57**
Class I/II/III products, 65, 116, 131, 156
Clay, Henry, 126
Cleveland Clinic, 66
CMS-1533-P, 132
Cochran House, 62, **62,** 126
Cochran, James, 126
Colonel William Jones house, 126
contrast media/dyes, 103, 106–7, 107, 143
Cook Athletic Stadium, 150
Cook Australia, 89, 91, 110, 111, 117, 147
Cook Aviation, 109
Cook Belgium NV/SA, 117
Cook, Bill
   Bloomington Hospital donation, 117, **117**
   catheterization start-up business, 18–20, 22, 30–34, 38, 40
   company philosophy and, 156
   computers and, 87
   Cook Urological Inc. visit, **78,** 79, **79**
   coronary problems, 63–66, 79, 82, 100
   disintegrators business idea, 20
   disposable needle product/company, 13, 15–18, 19, 20

   Dotter Institute, The, and, 104
   early life, 12, **12,** 13
   employee awards dinner and, 71, 72, 73, **73**
   employee incentive program and, 74
   employee meeting and, 68, 69, **76,** 77
   employment, 11, 13, 15, 16, **16,** 19, 20
   engagement/marriage, 16, **16,** 17
   first customer, 22, 26
   first trade show, 25–27, **25,** 62
   growth philosophy, 88
   as healthcare innovator, 155–56, **156**
   historic preservation by, 62, 126–29, **126**
   Jennings, Ross, and, 47, **47**
   lawsuit and, 63, 87, 96
   legacy, 150
   marketing and, 92
   military service, **11,** 13, 15
   move to Europe, 51
   needle manufacturing company started by, 63
   new products and, 155
   pacemaker business and, 95
   planes and, 12, 16, 40, **41,** 55, 108–9, **108**
   product development and, 65
   sale of company and, 144–47
   "snowing in Chicago" story and, 19–20
   YMCA and, 82–83, **82**
Cook Biotech Inc., 130, 131, 141–42, 147
Cook Canada Inc., 63, **63,** 110, 117
Cook, Carl, 19, 20, 22, 38, 51, 58, 82, **82,** 93, 95, 110, 144, **144**
Cook Critical Care, 111, 113, 141
Cook Deutschland GmBh, 106
Cook Endovascular, 134
Cook España, S.A., 89
Cook France S.A.R.L., 106
Cook, Gayle
   Bloomington Hospital and, 117, **117**
   Bloomington, Indiana, and, 18, 20, 34, 40
   company philosophy and, 156
   company start/ownership and, 22, 27, 156
   first customer and, 22, 26
   Fucilla, Van, and, 18, **18**
   as Gayle Karch, 16, **16,** 17
   Guide to Southern Indiana, A, 126

   historic preservation by, 62, 126–29, **126**
   kidney stone, 80
   legacy, 150
   move to Europe, 51
   positions held, 22, 33, 38, 40, 42, 92
Cook Group Europe ApS, 106, 110
Cook Hall, 150, **150**
Cook Imaging Corporation, 107, 134
Cook Incorporated/Cook Group Incorporated. *See also* specific businesses/products/technologies
   accountants, 101
   biotech investment by, 155
   Bloomington, Indiana, facilities, 152, **153**
   catalog, 22, **23,** 47, 50, **51,** 60, 63, 92, 136
   central venous catheter problem, 111–13
   company philosophy, 70, **70,** 156
   competition, 119
   computers and, 87
   corporate culture, 68–71, 152
   customization by, 31, 45, 47–49
   early years, 38–44
   employee awards dinner, 71–73, **72, 73,** 81, **148,** 149, **149**
   employee health clinic, 121
   employee incentive program, 74
   employee loans, 126
   employee meeting, 68, 69, **69,** 76, 77
   employee morale, 68–71, 74, **138,** 139
   employee picnic, 81, **81**
   expansion/growth, 34, 68, 88, 89–91, 106, 117–19, 131
   first customer, **26**
   founding, 20, 87–88
   gifts, 150, 151
   growth, 50–51, 88, 117–19, 121, 136
   headquarters, 134, **134,** 136, 152, 155
   Japan and, 142
   lawsuits/legal issues, 63, 87, 88, 96, 119, 122
   logo, 91, **91,** 122, **122,** 144
   management, 142, 147–52
   marketing, 62–63, 65, 92, 144
   national professional associations and, 60
   newsletter, 72, **72,** 73–74, 80
   new technologies, 119, **120,** 121

overtime mandate, 100
personnel advisor position, 68
planes, 108–9, **108–9**
pricing, 125
product development, 65, 98, 100–101
production department/display, 52, **52,** 57
production engineers, 100
productivity problem, 67–68, 69, 74
product line streamlining, 144
quality/quality control, 22, 33, 68, 71, 77, 85, 87, 98–100, 130, 136, **136,** 142
radiographic images and, **25**
real estate development/management company, 128
reference/training manual, 125, **125**
regulatory affairs/issues, 71, 74, 85–87, 107, 111, 113–17, 119, 132, 156
reorganization, 144, 147–52
research and development staff/facility, 53, **53,** 119
revenue/sales, 52, 57, 88, 91, 134, 155
sale of company, 144–47
sales force, 55–60, **56,** 62–63, 84–85, 111, **111,** 122, 144
self-insurance business, 61–62
selling/selling model, 40–42, 65, 88, 91
strategic business units (SBUs), 144, 147, 155
subsidiaries, 63, 106
Taiwan and, 110
tenth anniversary, 51, 52
Cook Ireland Ltd., 121
Cook Italia SRL, 106
Cook MyoSite, 144
Cook Pacemaker, 95, 130
Cook Pharmaceutical Solutions, 107–10, **107**
Cook Pharmica LLC, 152, 155
Cook Southeast Asia Pte. Ltd., 117
Cook Sweden AB, 106
Cook (Switzerland) AG, 117
Cook Taiwan Ltd., 117
Cook (UK) Limited, 96
Cook Urological Inc., 77, 79, 91, 93–95, 110–11, **110,** 117, 142, 146, 156
Cook Urological Switzerland Ltd., 117
Cook Vascular Incorporated, 94, 130, 142, 144

Cook-Z Stent/Z Stent, 59, 114, 115, **115,** 123
Cordis Corporation, 25, 30, 122
Cornell University, 28
Corporate Challenge event, 99, **99**
C. R. Bard, 91
Critical Care Division/medicine, 111, 113, 141, 155

D

Daily Herald-Telephone, 52
Data Solutions, 87
Deal, Stephen, 143
defibrillators, 66
Deming, W. Edwards, 68
Denmark/Denmark expansion, 49, 50, 51, 57, 84, 88, 100, 111, 123
Desilets-Hoffman Catheter Introducer Sheath Set, 42, 47
DeVane, Gene, 55, 56, **56,** 57, 60, 62, 98, 109, 142
DeWitt, Harry, 15
Dickie, Carl, 142
Dictaphone, 51
Doherty, Bill, 149, **149**
DomeTip technology, 143
Doppler probe, 130
Dotter Angioplasty Catheter Set, 42
Dotter, Charles, 26-27, 28, 29–30, 33, 37–38, **38,** 39, 40, 47, 49, 50, **50,** 52–53, 55, 58, 61, **61,** 79, 103, 106-7, 113, **113,** 114, 115
Dotter Dilation Set, 30
Dotter Interventional Institute, The, 28, 104, **105,** 150
Dotter technique, 19
Drewes, Dave, **140,** 141
Drum Corps International championship, 150

E

East, Russ, 68, 108
Echotip Double Lumen Aspiration Needles, **90,** 91
Echotip Soft-Pass Embryo Transfer Set, 135
Edwards, Pam, 139, **139**
Edwards, Irene, 33, **33**
Eells, Scott, 98–100, **98,** 147
El Camino Hospital, 19, 79

Eli Lilly and Company, 107, 110
Elkins, Dexter, 60, **60,** 98, 111–12
Ellett, Carol, 57, **57**
Ellettsville, Indiana, facility, 96, 117
Emmy award, 150, 151
Emory, 115
endoscopy business/products, 77, 110, 143, 155
Endovascular Today, 155
Ensco, 25, 57
EuroIntervention, 114
European Society of Human Reproduction and Embryology, 135
European Union, 50
Europe/European expansion, 49–50, 51, 57, 84, 88, 89, 96, 100, 106, 110, 121, 147
Evangelical Hospital, 92
Evolution Dilator Sheath, 94, **94**
Extraction Registry, 94

F

Fearnot, Neal, 66–67, 95, 119, 130, 154
Ferguson, Steve, 42, 63, 117, 130, **130,** 131, 134, 136, 147
filters business, 112
Fisher, Patty, 57, **57**
Forssmann, Werner Theodo Otto, 9–11, **9, 10,** 92
Fountain Square Mall, 128
Franz, Chuck, 142
French, Jerry, 122, **122**
French Lick Resort Casino, 128
French Lick Springs Resort, 128, **128**
Fucilla, Ivan "Van," 18, **18,** 19, 20, 79, 80, 150
Fucilla, Judy, 18, 19
Fusion products/Fusion Oasis Stent Introducer, 143

G

gastroenterology business/products, 75, **75,** 121
G. D. Searle & Company, 88
Geddes, Leslie A., 66–67, **66,** 95, 119, 154
General Electric Company, 33
German business/expansion, 57, 88
Gianturco, Cesare, 46, 47, 48, **48,** 50, 55, 58–59, **58,**

59, 101, **102**, 103, 106, 113, 114-116, 121, 122, 123, 125,
Gianturco Duodenal Intubation Set, 47
Gianturco-Roehm Bird's Nest Vena Cava Filter, 59, **59**, 101, **102**, 103
Gianturco-Roubin Flex-Stent Coronary Stent, 59, **59**, 114–16, 121–25, **121**
Gianturco-Wallace Chemotherapy Pulser, 59, **59**
Gibbons, Bill, 142
Gifford, Chuck, 107
Gillette, 121
Gingles, Bruce, 89
Global Therapeutics, 139
Goode, Louis, 142
Good Laboratory Practice testing, 156
Good Manufacturing Practices (GMP), 71, 85, 152
Goodyear Tire & Rubber Company, 121
Graham Plaza, 128
Grant Street Inn, 128
Great Britain, expansion to, 88
Greater Bloomington Chamber of Commerce, 52
Grenfell, Rick, 56, **56**, 85, 109
Grigholm, Staffan, 56, **56**, 57, 62
GR-II Coronary Stent, 134–36, 139, 147
Grüentzig, Andreas, 55, 103–6, **106**, 114, 115, 121
Guerbet LLC, 110
Guidant Corporation, 134–36, 147
Günther, Rolf, 112
Günther Tulip Vena Cava Filter, 112, **112**
gynecology business/products, 77, 119, 121, 155

H

Harbstreit, Bob, 108, 109
Harbstreit, Nathan, 109
Hartung, Richard, 44
Harty, Patrick, 92, **92**
Hathaway, Phil, 42, 62, 101, 117
Hawkins, Kem, 60, **60**, 93, **93**, 98, 100, 111, 113, 130, 142, 147-52, **149**
Health Care Hero Award, 66
Heckman, Jim, 73, 92, 117
Heflin, Howell, 115
Heine, Dave, 142

Hendrickson, Donna, 43, **43**
high-speed syringe-filling/vial production businesses, 110
Hinant, Mike, 50
Historic Landmarks Foundation of Indiana, 128
History of Dotter Interventional Institute: Fifteen Years of Education, Research and Patient Care 1990-2005 (Greene and Linton), 104
Hjørring DK, 106
Hollinger, Don, **86**, 87, 89, 142
HOOSIERFEST, 99, **99**
Horn, Joe, 139
Hudson, Pete, 62
Hughes, Ernest ("Ernie"), 89
Hughes Medical, 89
Hughes, Mike, 125, 130

I

Illinois Central railroad depot, 128
Illinois Masonic Hospital, 22, 26, **26**
Indianapolis Business Journal, 66
Indianapolis Star, 115, 141
Indiana University, 16, 40, 82, 89, 98, 101, 150
Indiana University Law School, 42
Indiana University Medical Center, 30, 37, 46
Indiana University School of Medicine, 150
Indiana University School of Music, 150
Internal Revenue Service (IRS), 62
International Harvester, 13
interventional radiology, 155
Ireland/Irish expansion, 49
Irie, Bob, 88, 93, 95, 101, 111, 117

J

Jackson, Angel, 156, **157**
James Cochran House, 62, **62**
Jennings, Ross, 30, **36**, 37, 44, **44**, 45, 46-47, **47**, 50, **50**, 51, 52, 56, 57, 85, 117, 142
J. Gardener & Associates, 106
John Deere, 121
Johnloz, Dave, 82
Johnson & Johnson (J&J), 122, 125, 131, 134

J-Tipped Wire Guide, 42
Judkins, Melvin, 103, **103**
Judson, Walter, 30, 37

K

Kahn, Henry, 57, 62
Kamstra, John, 101
Kanne, Miles, 25-26, 30, 33-34, 40, 42, **42**, 43, **43**, 44, **44**, 51, 56, 57, 60, **60**, 61, 65, 67, 68, 77, 80, 85, 98, 117, 122
Karolinska Institute, 21
Keller, Fred, 28, 104
Kelly, Linda, 57, **57**
Kessler, David, 116
Kirts, Beth Ann, 53, **53**
Knight, Bobby, 98, 101
Korean War, 11, 13
K-Tube Corporation, 63, 96, **96**
Kyvsgaard, Erik, 49

L

Lao, Melody, 152, **152**
Lavender, April, 85–87, **85**, 116
Lendman, Bob, 142
Liberator Locking Stylet, 94
Life (magazine), **29**, 37
Lincoln, Abraham, 126
Logic Coronary Stent, 139
Longson, Frank, 25–26, 56, **56**, 57–60, 60, **60**, 62, 65, **65**, 85
Los Angeles County Hospital, 47
Lymphangiographic Catheter Set, 47

M

Maglinte Enteroclysis Catheter Set, 75, **75**
Malecot catheters, 95
Malibu Wellness, 83
Manufacturing Process Laboratories (MPL), **14**, 15–18, 19, 20, 22, 63, 87, 88
Martin Aircraft, 13
Mayo Clinic, 46, 58, 115

McCarty, Dave, 136, 137
McCough, Jeff, 122, **122**
McCullough, Jerry, 87
McCullough, Phyllis, 52, **52**, 60, 61, 67-71, 74, 87, 98, **98**, 99, **99**, 100, 101, 109, 111, 113, 115, 116, 117, 134, 142, 144, 147, 155, **155**
McDonald's, 22, 26, 126
McGough, Jeff, 91, 111, 117
McGruder, Cleo, 57, **57**
McLean-Ring Enteral Feeding Tube Set, 75, **75**
McNeely Stone Company, 96
Medicaid, 132
Medical Device Act of 1976, 71, 85, 101, 114
Medical Device Manufacturers, 131
Medical Device Reporting, 111
Medical Engineering and Development (MED) Institute Inc., 95, 156, 158, **158**
Medicare, 132
Mellinger, Rick, 111, 155, **155**
Memorial Stadium, 150
Methodist Hospital/Clarian Health Partners, 130
Miami Vascular Institute, 150
Microdata Reality computer, 87
Microsoft, 136, 137
Microvasive, 93
MINC Benchtop Incubator, 135
Mobley, Ron, 142
Monroe County Airport, 109
Monroe County YMCA, 82, 83, **83**, 150
Monroe Guaranty Insurance Company, 62, **62**, 126
Muffin Corporation, 88
Multi-Link Coronary Stent, 134, 147
Myers Spring Company, 43

N

National Sunday Magazine, **10**, 11
NCircle Kidney Stone Extractor, 146, **146**
needle manufacturing company, 63
Needle's Eye Snare, 94
needle tubing company, 96, **96**
Nelson Instrument Company, 11, 12, 15, 16
Nelson, Lloyd, 16
Newton, Hans, 45

Nike, 136, 137
Nixon, Richard M., 101
Nobel Prize, **10**, 11, 28, 92
Noble Roman's Pizza, 88
Northern Financial & Guaranty Company, Ltd., 62
Northwestern University, 11, 12, 150

O

Oasis/Oasis Wound Dressing, 141, 142, **142**
obstetrics business/products, 77, 119, 121, 155
Occluding Spring Emboli, 59
Ohio River, 128
OMNI Breakthrough Channel technology, 143
O'Neill International, 57
O'Neill, Oscar, 57
Oregon Health Sciences University, 104
Orlandi, Enrico, 92, **92**
Orr, Robert, 52
Osborne, Dick, 31
Osborne, Tom, 31, **31**, 32-33, 34, 38, 42, 43-44, 47, 59, 72, 73, **73**, 79, 87, 128
Oxilan, 107, **107**, 110

P

pacemakers/pacemaker leads, 66, 94, 119, 130, 142
Pacific Rim, 89, 91, 110
Paclitaxel, 139, 147
Palmaz, Julio, 122
Palmaz-Schatz Coronary Stent, 122, 134
Palmer House Hotel, 25
Park 48 facility, 136
Parmenter, Matthew, 141
Parodi, Juan, 123
Parrish, Frank, 53, **53**
Parseghian, Ara, 63
Perfecta Electrosurgical Dissection Sheath, 94
Peripheral Intervention business unit, 112
Peterson, Dan, 155, **155**
Pizzo, Angelo, 13
Pohost, Gerry, 115
Polyethylene Balloon Angioplasty Catheters, 101
Polystan, 49, 51, 63

Poplars Research and Conference Center, 52
Porter, Tom, 83
Prince, Jean, 57, **57**
Pritchett, Richard and Charles, 126–28
Purdue Research Foundation, 95, 130
Purdue University, 66-67, 95, 119, 131, 150
PVA Foam Embolizaton Particle, 144, **144**

R

Radiological Society of North America (RSNA), 25, 27, **27**, 30, 57, 58, 92, **92**
RCA (Radio Corporation of America), 33
Reeves, Geoff, 89–91, **89**
Reinke, Dean, 83
Rink, Larry, 82
Rodby, DK, 106
Roehmer, Fred, 122, **122**
Rosch, Jösef, 104, **104**
Rose-Hulman Institute of Technology, 150, 151
Roubin, Gary, 114–16, 121
Royal Perth Hospital, 91
Rutner, Al, 79, **79**, 80
Rutner, Phyllis, 79, **79**

S

Sabin Corporation, 46, 84, **84**, 89, 141, 142
Safe T-J Wire Guides, 30
Schrader, Bill, 88
Sears, Roebuck & Company, 88
Seldinger, Sven-Ivar, 11, 12, 18, 20, 21, 25
Seldinger technique, **20**, 28, 38, 65
Sensor Model Kelvin 500, 119
Shaffer, David J., 115
Shure Brothers, 13
Simonsgaard, Chris, 49
Singapore and, 110
Singer Corporation, 98
small intestinal submucosa (SIS), 66, 119, 130, 131, **131**, 141–42, **142**, 144, 147, 154
Snapp, Rick, 87, **87**
Society of Cardiovascular & Interventional Radiology, 150

Sones, Mason, 103
South Curry Pike location, 44, 46, 47, 50, 51, 71, 80, 84, 155
South Swain Avenue location, 40, **40**, 43
Spectrum Catheter, 132, 141
Spectrum Glide Catheter, 132
Spectrum PICC Catheter, 133, **133**
Spencer Evening World, 77
Spencer, Indiana, facility, 77, 84, 95, 110, 156
Stanco Medical, 56, 93
Stanford University, 47, 115
Star of Indiana Drum and Bugle Corps, 150, 151, **151**
Star of Indiana Mini Grand Prix, 99, **99**
Steirteghem, Van, 135
stents/stent technology
    for artery narrowing, 147, **147**
    balloon/ballon catheters and, 101, 123
    coronary, 59, 106, 114–16, 121–25, **121**, 125, 134–36, 139, 147
    Dotter, Charles, and, 50, 106, 115
    drug-coated, 139, 147
    drug-eluting, 95
    endovascular, 91
    flex, **114**, 115
    Gianturco, Cesare, and, 59, 106, 114–16, 121, 122, 123, 125
    intraluminal, 50
    research, 119
    stent-graft, 123, **124**, 125
Sterner, Dan, 34, 42, 49–50
Strother, Bill, 111
St. Vincent Hospital, 115
Sugar Bowl football game, 63
Sunday Herald-Times, 88, 111
Supra-G Coronary Stent, 139
Surgisis Biodesign Anal Fistula Plug, 154
Swiatek, Jeff, 141
Switzerland expansion, 57
Sydney IVF, 135
Sydney IVF Embryo Transfer Catheter, 135, **135**

T

Taxol, 139
Terwiske, Matt, 156, **157**
Theory Z management, 68
Timmermans, Hans, 53, **53**
Tony award, 150, 151
Torcon Blue Catheters, 67, 73
trade-show booth, 62, 144, **145**
Tulane Stadium, 63
Tulip Vena Cava Filter, 112, **112**
TurboFlo PICC Catheter, 141

U

University of Alabama, 63, 104, 115-16
University of Berlin, 9, 58
University of California, 45, 47
University of Michigan, 115
University of Minnesota, 58
University of Naples, 58
University of Notre Dame, 63
University of Oregon Medical School, 28
University of Pennsylvania, 150
University of Pittsburgh, 144
University of Rome, 58
University of Texas, 48, 122
University of Texas M.D. Anderson Cancer Center, 46, **46**, 58, 59
University of Utah, 85
urology business/products, 77, 79, 91, 93–95, 110–11, 117, 121, 142, 146, **146**, 155, 156
U.S. Congress, 114, 117, 131, 132, 136
U.S. Environmental Protection Agency (EPA), 67, 106
U.S. Food and Drug Administration (FDA), 65, 71, 74, 85, 87, 98, 101, 106, 107, 111, 113-17, 122, 123, 125, 131, 134, 136, 156
U.S. Navy, 20
U.S. Olympic basketball team, 101
U.S. Senate, 131

V

Vance, Jim, 80, 84, 93
Vance Products Incorporated, 84, 93
Van-Tec, 93
vascular business/products, 130–31, 142, 155
Vaughan, Wayne, 56, **56**, 57, 60, **60**, 62
V-Flex Coronary Stent, 139

W

Wallace, Sidney, 46, **46**, 48, 50, **50**
Wall, Chuck, 96, **97**
Watts, Kay, 68
Weeks, Craig, 92, **92**, 109
Werth, Brian, 116, 117, 134, 152
West Baden Springs Hotel and Spa, 73, 128, **128, 129**, 149
Western Angiographic and Interventional Society, 104
Westinghouse, 33
Wikle, Jackie, 71, **71**, 117
William A. and Gayle K. Cook Hall, 150
William A. Cook Australia Pty. Ltd., 89
William and Gayle Cook Music Library, 150
William Cook Europe, 49, **49**, 51, 110, 147
Williams, Jerry, 56, **56**, 85, 89, 109
Wills-Oglesby Percutaneous Gastrostomy Set, 75, **75**
Wilson-Cook Medical Inc., 110, **110**, 125, 130, 142, 144, 147
Wilson, Don, 49, **49**, 63, 67, **67**, 110, 142
Witkiewicz, Joseph ("Joe"), 46, 89
Women's Health business unit, 135
World War II, 20
Wrightsman, Randy, 156, **157**

Y

Young Men's Christian Association (YMCA), 82–83, 99

Z

Zenith Abdominal Aortic Aneurysm Stent, 123, **123**
Zilver Stent, 147, **147**
Z Stent/Cook-Z Stent, 59, 114, 115, **115**, 123